THE WEB AS PUBLISHING MEDIUM

CW01501189

Just as desktop publishing profoundly changed the lives of typesetters and publishers more than a decade ago, the World Wide Web is causing a stir among those who have always thought exclusively in terms of print publishing. What started out in 1993 as a way for geeks and academics to share information over the Internet has become so important as a publishing medium that some periodicals exist only on the Web—nowhere in print. Corporations often demand that marketing campaigns and corporate presences include a splashy Web component. Small and large businesses use the Web to sell a vast array of products and services. Even governments, non-profit organizations and individuals already do at least part of their publishing on the Web.

What a difference five years makes!

Like desktop publishing did in its day, the Web has spawned a new breed of publisher, who may never have been involved in laying galleys to paper, or even using desktop publishing tools. These new publishers have been quick to see the Web's promise but aren't necessarily equipped with the experience or software to produce professional Web content. Today, organizations with serious Web publishing needs have turned to experienced print publishers—people who can design, write, edit and produce top-flight publications, whatever the medium.

More than most people, print-based publishing professionals have had to respond to the sea change brought about by the Web. Whether their end-product is a Web-based magazine, a multimedia corporate billboard or a product catalog, people who are used to laying out pages in QuarkXPress and sending their work to an imagesetter have had to trade the jargon and workflow of the print world for the new frontier of Internet publishing.

✔ Tip

- For many new *webtop* publishers with a background in print publishing, the challenge is three-fold: learning the basics of Internet publishing and how to bring documents to the Web; finding tools with the sophistication and features they've come to expect from desktop publishing applications; and establishing a workflow and information management system for complex Web projects.

THE WEB AS PUBLISHING MEDIUM

VISUAL QUICKSTART GUIDE

GoLive CyberStudio 3.1

FOR MACINTOSH

Shelly Brisbin

 Peachpit Press

Visual QuickStart Guide
GoLive CyberStudio 3.1 for Macintosh
Shelly Brisbin

Peachpit Press
1249 Eighth Street
Berkeley, CA 94710
(510) 524-2178
(510) 524-2221 (fax)
(800) 283-9444
Find us on the World Wide Web at: http://www.peachpit.com

Peachpit Press is a division of Addison Wesley Longman

Cover design: The Visual Group
Editor: Corbin Collins
Production: Maureen Forys
In-house Production: Mimi Heft

ISBN: 0-201-35374-1

0 9 8 7 6 5 4 3 2

Printed and bound in the United States of America

♻ Printed on recycled paper

For my parents,
Emma and Windel Brisbin

Acknowledgements

Thanks to Corbin Collins for his calm presence and steady supply of patience. Thanks also to Mimi Heft and the rest of the crew at Peachpit Press.

Thanks to Maureen Forys for her spiffy and speedy layout services.

Thanks to agent extraordinare, Claire Horne, who walked me through this process with patience and skill. I think she's done this before, too.

Thanks to Oren Ziv, Greg Rewis and GoLive Systems for their support and encouragement.

Thanks to Mike Cogliandro for the use of his NanciNet artwork.

Warm fuzzy thanks to Frank Feuerbacher, the kindest person I have ever known. Without his support and love, writing a book would still be a dream. I think I'll keep him.

About the author

Shelly Brisbin has written about technology for more than ten years. Currently a freelance writer based in Austin, Texas, Brisbin writes a weekly Internet column for the CitySearch/Austin Web site and contributes features and reviews to national computer magazines. Before taking up the freelance life, Brisbin served as Networking Editor for *MacUser* magazine, leading the publication's connectivity and Internet coverage. Brisbin has written for *MacWorld*, *MacWeek*, *NetProfessional*, *The Net*, *SunWorld* and others, and has contributed to four computer books. Brisbin has also worked as a system administrator and consultant. In her free time, she runs a music-related Web site and mailing list.

TABLE OF CONTENTS

INTRODUCTION

Welcome to *GoLive CyberStudio 3.1 for Macintosh: Visual QuickStart Guide*. This book is intended to help you get the most from CyberStudio and to acquaint you with webtop publishing.

Even if you've used Web authoring tools before, you'll probably find that CyberStudio is a new experience: a Web authoring tool with a comprehensive approach to page design and site management that isn't available elsewhere.

But I'm not here to sell CyberStudio to you. You probably own a copy or are considering making it a part of your publishing arsenal. Whatever the case, my goal is to give you the information you'll need to make the most of the software and to provide for you a convenient reference as you learn how to work with it.

Chapters 1, 2 and 3 of this book introduce you to Web publishing, and to the ways in which it is similar and different from traditional publishing. You'll also learn how GoLive CyberStudio fits into the Web revolution and what you'll need to know to get started. There's a tour of the CyberStudio interface and a glimpse at its most important tools and features.

Chapters 4 through 14 get down to the nuts and bolts of Web page assembly, layout and design with CyberStudio. I start with the most basic element of any Web page—text— and move through all of the layout tools and HTML editing features you have at your disposal with CyberStudio.

Finally, Chapters 15 through 17 introduce CyberStudio's extensive Web site management tools, moving Web publishing beyond merely linking a bunch of pages. You'll learn how to create and manage an effective site, and how to publish it on the World Wide Web.

World Wide Web basics

What is it about the Web that is so compelling for publishers and just about everyone else who's seen it? First of all, the Web brings page layout, text formatting and images to computer users, regardless of platform or operating system. Unlike most software applications and computer document formats, users need only fire up a browser to view Web pages. Publishers can design these Web pages without concern for the types of machines on the other end.

HTML

This platform-independence is possible because of HTML (HyperText Markup Language), the language that turns text files into Web pages. Once a document is encoded in HTML and uploaded to a Web server, anyone on the Internet can view it. That notion was amazing in 1993 when the Web was born, and it's still pretty heady stuff today.

An HTML page is simply a plain old ASCII text file that can contain pointers to images, audio, video and other multimedia objects. Using HTML, Web authors can also format text as bold, italic, different levels of heads, and so on, although on a much more limited basis than in print publishing.

Another fundamental element of HTML is its ability to embed links to other HTML pages, which can be anywhere on the Web. This *hypertext* element of the language is its very essence, because it allows people to navigate the Web as if it were all one huge publication. HTML links created the concept of Web *surfing*, making it seem possible to catch a wave and end up anywhere in the world with just a click.

Tags

HTML accomplishes all this with *tags*. Tags are commands embedded in an HTML document. Tags surround text elements and links. Web browser software, such as Netscape Navigator and Microsoft Internet Explorer, reads each file's tags and interprets them according HTML standards set by the World Wide Web Consortium (W3C).

Tags are enclosed by the < and > symbols, which together are called *angle brackets*. **Figure 1-1** shows a very basic HTML page with tags included.

HTML tags come in several varieties. Some tags specify parts of the Web page (headers and body, for example). Formatting tags provide instructions for formatting text. Link tags include pointers to other Web pages or locations within the same page. Still another type of tag makes it possible to display images and play audio and video files in a Web page by pointing to the media file and specifying how it should look (size, border, and so on) in the page.

In short, it's the structure provided by HTML tags combined with words and images that make up a Web page.

Putting your page on the Web

HTML wouldn't impress anyone if the Web didn't make distributing content so easy and inexpensive. When you've completed an HTML page, putting it on the Web is as simple as uploading the file (and any image or multimedia files associated with the page) to a Web server.

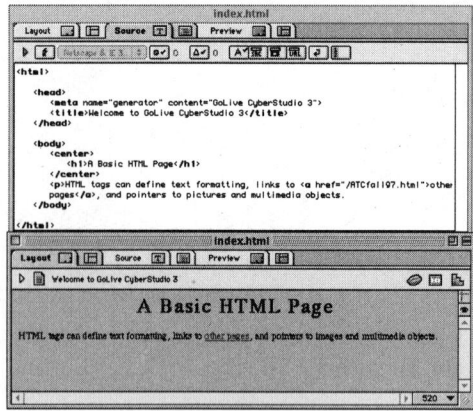

Figure 1-1: A basic HTML document (top) and the Web page it creates (bottom).

Many large organizations operate their own Web servers, which are continuously connected to the Internet. Individuals and small organizations usually rent hard disk space from an Internet Service Provider (ISP), which runs its own Web server, and update their HTML files over the Net as needed.

With the files in place, the Web server owner gives the publisher a URL (Universal Resource Locator) for the new Web page. A URL is the Web address visitors use to locate your page on the Internet. URLs look like this:

http://www.peachpit.com

Once you have your site up and publicize your Web address, anyone on the Internet can look at your page by typing the URL into a Web browser.

Now you're on the Web.

Pages and sites

One more important concept to keep in mind as you wrap your brain around HTML and how it structures Web pages is this: most Web pages are plural, grouped together as a Web site. Like other kinds of publications, Web sites combine a variety of content under one banner. Most sites have a home page (like magazines have a cover) which often doubles as a table of contents (TOC). The TOC leads to other pages within the site, and each page has its own text elements and pointers to graphics that appear on the page—not to mention links that point to other sites on the Web.

In this book, I concentrate not only on the ways in which CyberStudio can help you design spiffy Web pages but also on the process of creating a complete Web site.

Publishers migrate to the Web

After the Web shed its initial geeky status, publishers and would-be publishers began to take notice and dipped tentative toes into the unknown waters of electronic publishing.

Many were tentative not just because the medium was new but because the software available to create HTML pages was scarce or rudimentary. HTML is relatively intuitive, as formatting schemes go, but typing angle brackets with one eye on a Web page and the other eye on a tag reference in the HTML document is no way for publishers to work, especially after they've been using using high-quality desktop publishing tools such as QuarkXPress and PageMaker for nearly a decade.

Web authoring applications

It was a giant step forward when HTML-unaware word processors gave way to text editors with built-in macros that let you apply HTML tags by clicking a button, and an even greater leap forward when the first WYSIWYG (What You See Is What You Get) Web authoring software reached the market. Finally, publishers could create Web pages the way they created other kinds of documents: by selecting text, applying formatting and creating a layout, complete with images and other graphical elements.

WYSIWYG tools such as GoLive CyberStudio make it possible to apply HTML tags without having to type them. Simply select some text and choose a tag from a menu or toolbar (Heading and Bold are some formatting examples—see **Figure 1-2**), and the tag's

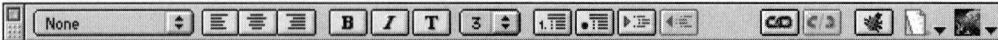

Figure 1-2: HTML tags are hiden behind the friendly GoLive CyberStudio toolbar.

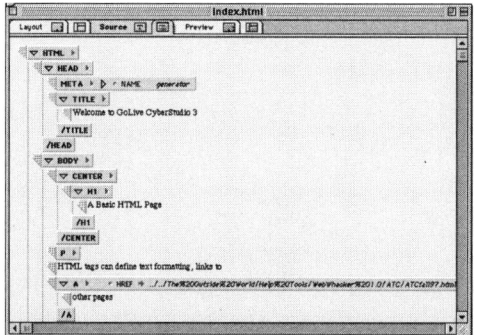

Figure 1-3: Behind the WYSIWYG interface is a good, old-fashioned HTML editor.

style—but not the tag itself—is displayed on the page. To reassure those who actually like to work with raw HTML that there's actually something under the pretty interface, CyberStudio also provides an optional view of the page that displays the HTML tags (see **Figure 1-3**).

Basic Web-authoring applications like Adobe PageMill, Claris Home Page, and my personal low-end favorite, Symantec Visual Page, make it easy to get a page on the Web, but professional publishers often find them lacking because they don't include layout tools or text and image manipulation features like traditional desktop publishing tools.

The demand to integrate multimedia and Java with Web pages further pushes the envelope for publishers. Rather than simply adapting familiar design and production concepts to the Web, publishers must add to their knowledge and to their production arsenal if their Web sites are to be the best they can be. Since publishers don't usually want to become Java programmers, they need tools that allow them to work with multimedia in as straightforward a manner as they work with text and traditional images.

Today Web-authoring tools have progressed beyond basic page creation into the realm of real webtop publishing. GoLive CyberStudio is one of those tools, built from the ground up to support publishers who are used to a wide array of layout and design features.

The latest innovation for Web authors, grown accustomed to HTML and site-wide management, is HTML 4.0, the current version of the rules that govern the way Web pages are created and displayed. With HTML 4.0 innovations like Cascading Style Sheets and Dynamic HTML (DHTML), Web authoring has taken another step closer to print publishing. Style sheets allow precise, conditional text formatting and positioning, whereas DHTML gives you access to animation and, well, dynamic content.

As useful and powerful as style sheets and DHTML are, they require knowledge of a whole new set of tags and an understanding of how to write or connect scripts to standard HTML elements. Again, CyberStudio simplifies the process of using HTML 4.0 tools by putting a graphical interface on top, allowing you to create spiffy animation and to precisely position text without touching the code needed to create them.

Web sites are work

Web pages are usually linked to a number of other pages within a Web site, and to images and multimedia files. A Web site quickly becomes more than a collection of text and image files—it becomes a full-blown project, with an overall design concept to work with, lots of files and file types and—probably—multiple contributors and great expectations for style and substance.

✔ Tips

- The most basic way to turn a collection of Web pages into a Web site is to plan it that way from the beginning. Starting with a good grasp of your own goals for the site, and a design that allows you to achieve them, you should be able to plan how content will be divided between the pages that make up your site, and how those pages will be linked together.

- You'll also want to gather all the elements of your site (HTML files, images, multimedia) in a single location. That will help you plan the site, but it will also be invaluable as you create links and relationships between elements.

- If your site design includes a lot of movement from page to page, and/or you want to keep visitors from getting lost, you might want to create templates for all of

WEB SITES ARE WORK

your component Web pages. They might simply include your company's logo or a consistent navigation scheme (links and design elements) that allows people to move easily from any page in the site to any other page with a single click. Besides providing an intuitive sameness that makes navigating your site easier for visitors, a templated approach also makes creating pages much simpler and faster.

■ After you have the site up and running, you'll quickly find that that's just the beginning. You'll be making periodic changes—Web sites have to stay fresh. Along with the passage of time, these changes will occasionally introduce errors (most commonly "broken" links—links that don't work) into your site, as files are moved in and out and around (see **Figure 1-4**). You will want to create a strategy for controlling these changes, and for double-checking the site to make sure nothing has gone wrong.

Are you getting the idea that publishing Web pages and managing Web sites is a big job, and that you'll need some help to do it well?

That's where GoLive CyberStudio comes in. Built with publishers in mind, CyberStudio gives you the creative tools to build attractive, professional-looking Web pages and the organizational structure you'll need to manage a growing and changing Web site.

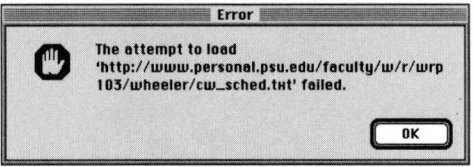

Figure 1-4: This message greeted visitors to a site which was up and running but whose links had begun to break when the pages were moved from one Web server to another.

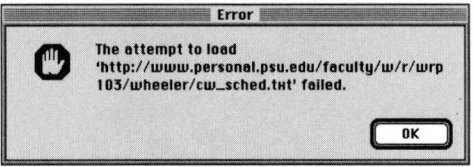
The attempt to load 'http://www.personal.psu.edu/faculty/w/r/wrp103/wheeler/cw_sched.txt' failed.

OK

LEARNING
YOUR WAY AROUND

CyberStudio 3.1 brings the power of traditional desktop publishing tools to the task of creating Web pages. Like most Web-authoring software, CyberStudio hides the HTML code associated with Web pages behind an interface. More importantly, CyberStudio provides professional Web page designers the sophisticated features and tight element control of a desktop publishing application.

Like most desktop publishing applications, CyberStudio features are stored within a number of palettes, tools and windows. You'll also find a number of views that allow you to look at and work with your Web pages in different ways. In this chapter, I'll give you a quick tour of CyberStudio, touching on the following:

- Using Views to display Web pages.

- Formatting text with the Toolbar.

- Adding content with palette tools.

- Configuring objects with the Inspector.

- Adding color with the Color Palette.

- Managing sites with the site management tools.

- Setting up Preferences.

- Referring to the Web Database.

Page Views

Views allow you to work with the same Web page in six different ways. CyberStudio's page Views are:

- Layout.
- Frames.
- Source.
- Outline.
- Preview.
- Frames Preview.

The Layout View

In the Layout View, CyberStudio functions like a frame-oriented desktop publishing application, giving you a WYSIWYG view of your Web pages. You will probably spend most of your time working in the Layout View.

When you launch CyberStudio and create a new page, or open an existing one, it appears in the Layout view by default. Displaying the page in a different view is as simple as clicking on the corresponding tab at the top of the main window (see **Figure 2-1**).

The Frames View

Use the Frames View to examine and work on frames-based Web pages. Frames-based pages are actually composites of two or more HTML pages. The Frames View shows frames, and icons for each file that makes up the frameset.

The Source View

The Source View displays the raw HTML code that makes up your page. If you know HTML you can use the Source View to check or edit the contents of your page. **Figure 2-2** shows the Source View.

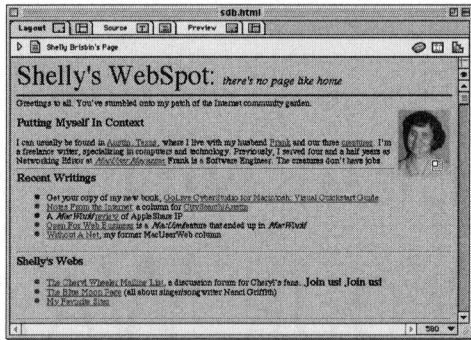

Figure 2-1: You can edit text, add and move objects and create links in the Layout View.

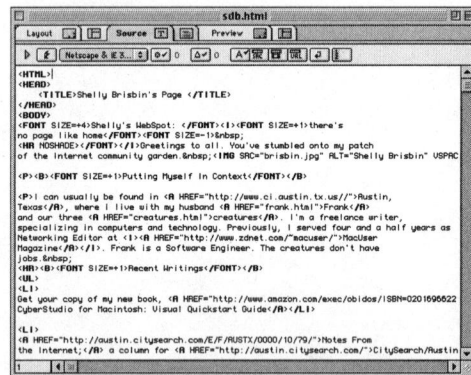

Figure 2-2: The Source View shows the HTML code for my home page, the same page displayed in Figure 2-1.

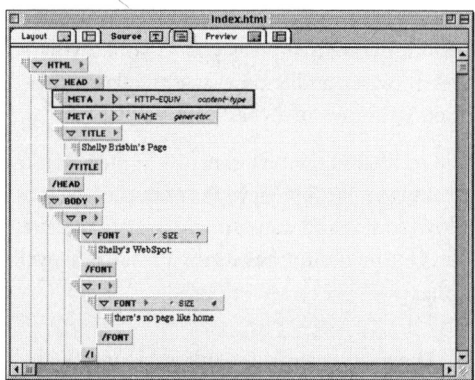

Figure 2-3: Here's my home page in Outline View. You can see more of the page by collapsing the headings.

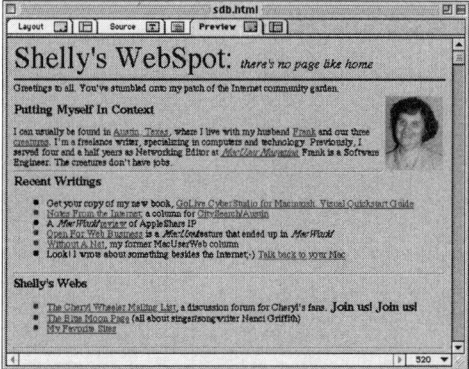

Figure 2-4: Preview your Web page to see how it will look in a Web browser.

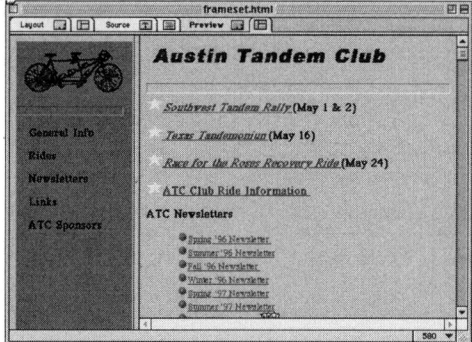

Figure 2-5: Preview all of the frames that make up a frames-based page.

The Outline View

In Outline View, CyberStudio displays the HTML tags behind your Web page within a hierarchical structure. Use this view as a reminder of your page's organization and to place new elements at the correct hierarchical location (**Figure 2-3**).

The Preview View

In the Preview view, you can see how the layout and links you've created will look and act when viewed from a Web browser. In many cases, the preview will look very much like the Layout view. It certainly does in **Figure 2-4**.

The Frames Preview

The Frames Preview puts the frames that make up a frames-based Web page all together and displays them as they will look from a Web browser (**Figure 2-5**).

PAGE VIEWS

The toolbar

Just like most word processing applications, CyberStudio's screen is topped by a toolbar. Also as in most word processors, the toolbar is primarily used to format text. You can choose a style (head, body text, preformatted, and so on) and apply font size, indent and more. You can create or break HTML links and create lists in several formats. **Figure 2-6** shows the toolbar.

To use the toolbar:

1. Go to the Layout View.

2. Type some text.

3. Select the text.

4. Choose an alignment or formatting item from the toolbar. Your text changes accordingly.

You'll find a few other items on the toolbar, including one that takes you to your favorite Web browser, and another that toggles between open windows in CyberStudio.

The toolbar is context-sensitive: when you're working in the Site View, for example, the tools allow you to add content and update the site. The Outline Editor has its own toolbar as well.

✔ Tip

■ The toolbar includes an item that will switch you to a Web browser, so that you can see how your Web page will look to a visitor using that browser (**Figure 2-7**). To compare the look of your page in several browsers, use CyberStudio's Preferences command to add as many Web browsers as you like to the toolbar menu.

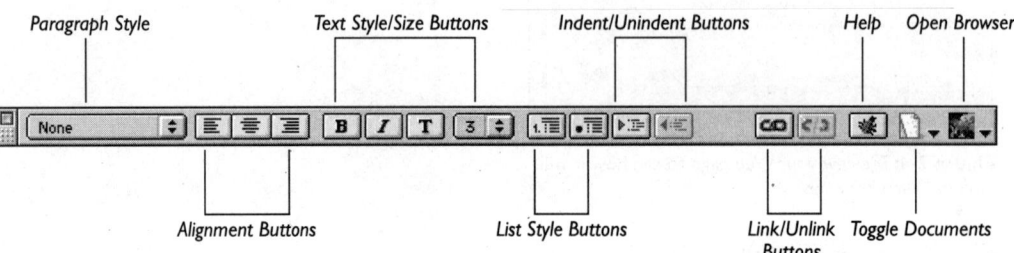

Figure 2-6: The toolbar works like the formatting toolbar found in most word-processing applications.

Figure 2-7: The toolbar's Browser pull-down menu.

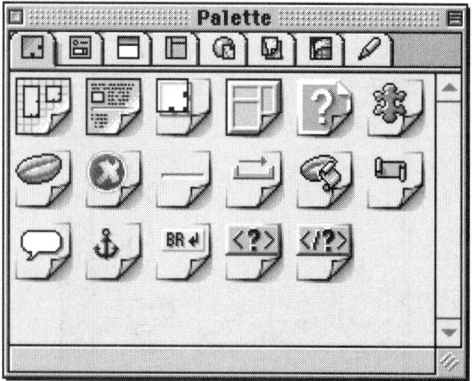

Figure 2-8: The basic tag tab includes 17 tools to add basic HTML elements to your layout.

Figure 2-9: You can position any palette tool, like this image tag, by dragging it onto your Web page.

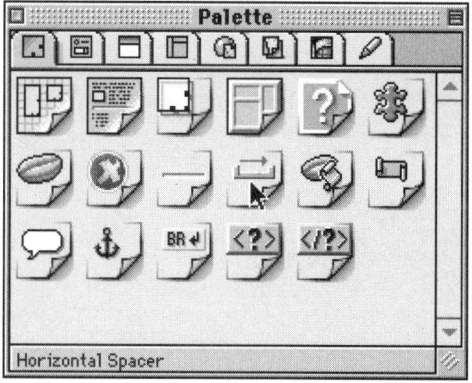

Figure 2-10: With your cursor over a palette tool, CyberStudio displays the item's name at the lower left of the window.

The palette

Most of the tools you will use to add items to your Web pages can be found in the palette window. The palette is actually composed of eight separate sets of tools, which are accessible from tabs at the top of the palette. Similar palette tools are grouped together under the tabs. You'll learn more about each of the palette tools in chapters 5 through 11.

The eight palette tabs are:

- The basic tag tab.
- The forms tag tab.
- The header tag tab.
- The frames tag tab.
- The site tag tab.
- The extra tab.
- The cyberobjects tab.
- The custom tab.

Figure 2-8 shows the palette's basic tags tab; it's displayed by default when you launch CyberStudio.

To use a palette tool, drag and drop it onto the document window or double-click it. You use palette tools to add text, layout grids, images, lines, Java applets and more. **Figure 2-9** shows an image tag being dragged from the palette to an empty document window.

✔ Tips

- Palette tabs are not labeled, but palette tools are, sort of. Place your cursor over a palette tool and notice that its name appears in the lower border of the window (see **Figure 2-10**).

■ Depending on the size of your computer screen, the palette may overlap your document window, making it hard to get a complete view of your work. You can resize the palette to get it out of the way, while keeping it available onscreen. Just use your mouse to grab the resizing box at the bottom right corner of the palette. Drag the box downward and to the left. The palette tags will fill the narrower window. Now move the palette to the right, leaving plenty of room for the main Web page window (see **Figure 2-11**).

■ You can move the palette window (and other CyberStudio tool windows, for that matter) completely out of your way by dragging the window all the way to the right of your screen. CyberStudio replaces the window with a small tab, visible at the edge of your monitor. Drag the tab back onscreen to bring back the palette window.

Figure 2-11: Narrowing the Palette window rearranges the tools within the window.

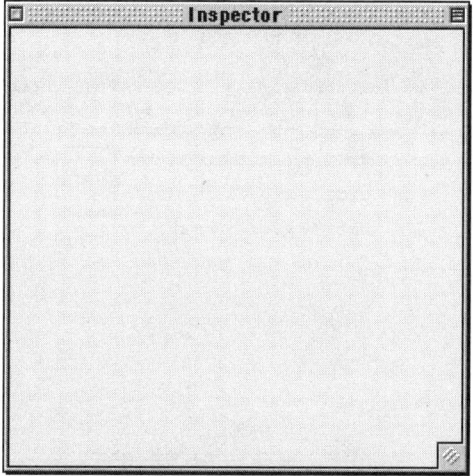

Figure 2-12: An empty Inspector window.

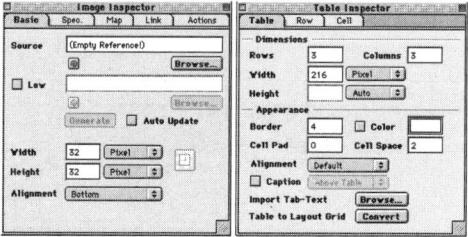

Figure 2-13: Clicking on a placeholder in the document window causes the Inspector window to change, allowing you to configure an image (left) or a table (right).

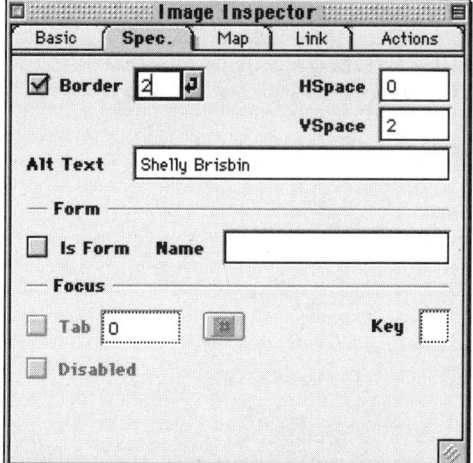

Figure 2-14: Click on the Special tab within the Image Inspector to create spacing and a border for your image.

The Inspector

The palette and the context-sensitive Inspector window work together to give you control over the look of your Web pages. Once you have placed an item (text, image, spacer, applet or other object) on your Web page, you can fine-tune its appearance from within the Inspector window. The Inspector window is empty (**Figure 2-12**) until you select an object within a Web page, and its appearance changes depending upon the object you choose.

To use the Inspector:

1. Drag a tool from the palette into the main window, or click on an object already in the Web page window.

2. Notice that the Inspector window is no longer empty, but contains buttons and checkboxes (**Figure 2-13**). (If you don't see the Inspector window, choose Inspector from the Windows menu.)

3. Click on another object on your Web page, and notice that the Inspector window changes again to display the options for that type of object.

As **Figure 2-13** shows, some Inspector windows have more than one set of preferences. Click on one of the tabs in the Image Inspector to view more options. **Figure 2-14** shows Special preferences for my mug shot.

✔ Tip

■ If you need to change an object's preference after you've laid out a page, just click on the object, and the Inspector window returns.

THE INSPECTOR

The Color Palette

As its name implies, the Color Palette allows you to add color to elements of your Web pages. You can color text, background, links and just about any other object CyberStudio can create. Once you've chosen a color you like, you can drag and drop it onto Web page objects to change their color.

The Color Palette window appears when you choose it from the Windows menu.

Just like the palette, the Color Palette contains tabs that organize its tools and color choices. (See **Figure 2-15**). Four tabs represent the color types found in image manipulation applications like Photoshop. The Apple Color palette tab displays colors the same way the Macintosh does, and the two Web color tabs allow you to choose colors that are supported by most Web browsers, on all computer platforms.

The eight Color Palette tabs are:

- The RGB tab.
- The CMYK tab.
- The Grayscale tab.
- The Indexed Color tab.
- The Apple Color palette tab.
- The Real Web Colors tab.
- The Web Named Colors tab.
- The Site Colors tab.

To add color to text:

1. With a document open in the main window, and the Color Palette showing, choose a color from one of the Color Palette tabs by clicking on it.

2. Click on the Color Palette's Preview pane and drag onto text on your page. The text changes color (**Figure 2-16**).

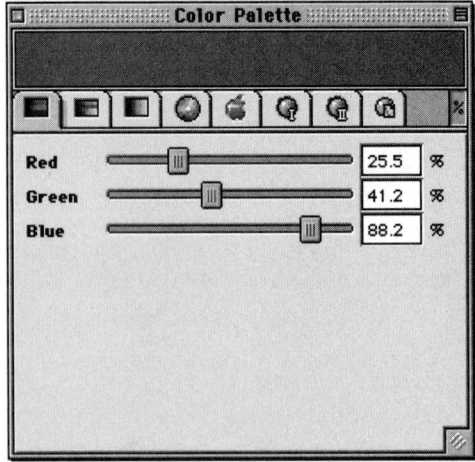

Figure 2-15: The Color Palette lets you add color to text, backgrounds or other objects. You can choose from seven color palettes and create your own colors combinations.

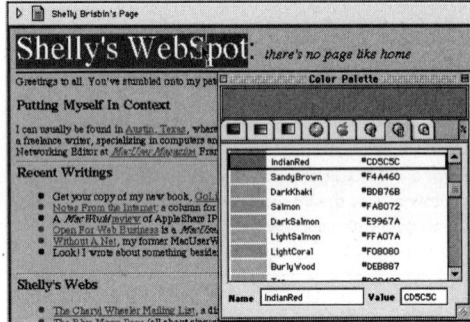

Figure 2-16: Drag your chosen color from the Color Palette's Preview pane to color Web page text.

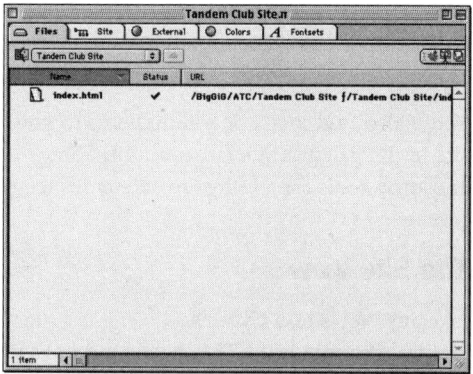

Figure 2-17: When you create a new site, you'll see a new site window with preferences for your site.

Site management tools

CyberStudio both creates Web pages and manages complete Web sites. By gathering elements of your Web site, you can make global changes to the site, organize HTML and media files, and verify that all of your links work. You can also use site management tools to view a map of your entire site, especially the Site window.

The Site window

To use the Site window, the primary view of your Web site, you'll need to create or open an existing site.

To create a new site:

1. Choose New Site from the File menu.

2. Name your site when the dialog box appears and place the site file in a folder that is convenient. You'll be adding your Web site's files to this folder.

CyberStudio creates a site file, a home page file (called index.html), and a folder hierarchy where you will add the components of your site. The Site window (**Figure 2-17**) appears.

Like the Palette window, the Site window includes a number of tabs. But unlike the palette, the Site window stores elements of your Web site rather than the tools you use to build it. You can drag files into the Site window to add them to your site or you can create pages from scratch with CyberStudio.

Behind each Site window tab are different elements of your Web site. You can view each by clicking on a tab at the top of the Site window. Until you add files and resources to your Web site, the Site tabs are empty.

The Site window tabs are:

■ The Files tab.

■ The Site tab.

continued on next page...

continued from previous page...

- The External tab.

- The Colors tab.

- The Fontsets tab.

Each Site window tab shows a different view of your site. The Files tab displays your site's component files. Other tabs display remote URLs and saved colors and fonts. **Figure 2-18** shows a site with the Files tab selected. Some files are properly linked, but others need attention.

The Site toolbar

When you create or open a site file, the CyberStudio toolbar (**Figure 2-19**) displays a selection of tools that are specific to site

management. You can add and remove files, create new folders, and view your site in different ways.

You'll also find tools for adding items to your site in the palette's Site tab. You'll find drag-and-drop tools for adding new elements to the site.

The Site View

Like any Web site, a CyberStudio site is a hierarchical grouping of HTML pages and links to other Web sites. The Site View is designed to make it easier for you to visualize and work with your site in these terms. You can even use the Site View to organize your site before you design its individual pages.

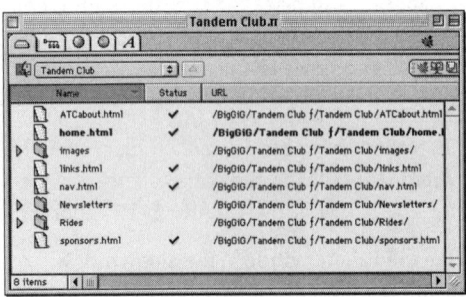

Figure 2-18: Files are displayed in the Site Widow:Files tab. You can also see the entire local directory path to each file.

Figure 2-20: The Site View Controller appears in the Inspector window when you click the Site tab in the Site window.

Figure 2-19: The Site Toolbar gives you access to a number of tools you'll need to display and maintain your site.

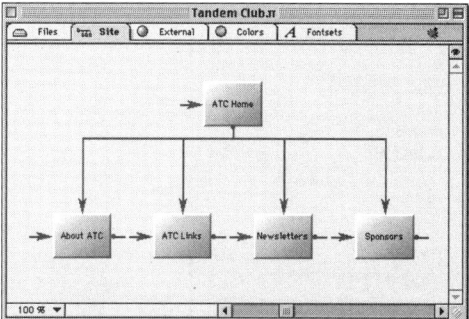

Figure 2-21: When you choose Link Hierarchy in the Site View Controller window, the Site view changes to display a tree representing your site's files.

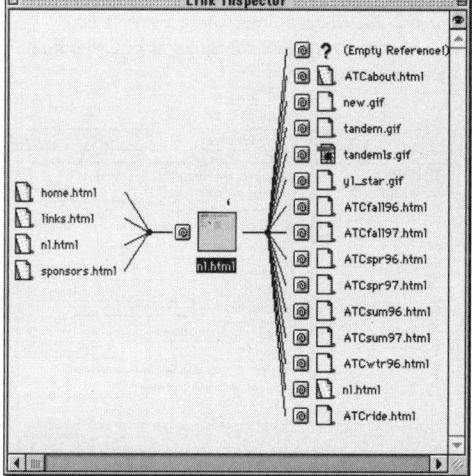

Figure 2-22: The Link View shows a single page with pointers to all the links that appear on that page (both local and remote items).

To view a site in the Site View:

1. Open a CyberStudio site file.

2. In the Site window, click the Site tab.

3. If it isn't already visible, choose Inspector from the Windows menu, to display the Site View Controller (**Figure 2-20**), an inspector window that lets you set site-wide preferences.

4. Click the Link Hierarchy button. The display in the Site window changes to display a hierarchical view of your site (**Figure 2-21**).

You can work with files while using the Site View. Clicking once on a file displays its reference Inspector window and highlights the file's relationship to others in the site (**Figure 2-22**).

✔ Tip

- Double-clicking a file in the Site View opens it.

The Link View

Whereas the Site View provides an overhead view of the pages that make up your Web site, the Link View digs one step deeper by displaying links associated with each page.

To display pages in the Link View:

1. In the Site View, click on a page.

2. Click the Link View button on the Site Toolbar, to display the Link View window.

   The page's icon and name appear near the center of the Link View. The parent page appears on the left. All items linked from the page appear on the right.

Preferences

Like most software applications, CyberStudio includes controls that allow you to set global parameters. You can choose default fonts, set parameters for CyberStudio files and sites, and much more.

You can reach the Preferences window by choosing Preferences from the Edit menu (**Figure 2-23**).

The Preferences window actually contains several panels of preferences (**Figure 2-24**). The parameters you can set in the Preferences window fall into the following categories:

- General.

- Modules.

- Fonts.

- Encodings.

- Site.

- Browsers.

- Find

- Spell Checking.

- Plugins.

- Network.

- Source.

- JavaScript.

✔ Tip

- In most cases, you won't need to alter CyberStudio's preferences. It's a good idea, though, to take a look at each option so you'll know what changes you can make.

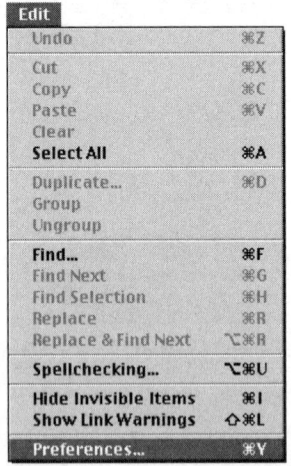

Figure 2-23: Choose Preferences from the Edit menu to reach a window containing all of CyberStudio's global preferences.

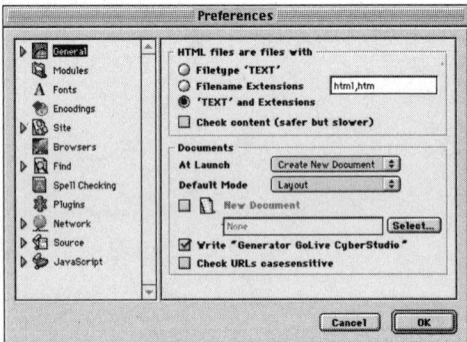

Figure 2-24: To view a set of preferences, click on the labeled icon on the left side of the window.

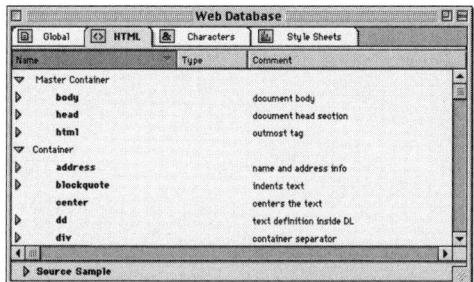

Figure 2-25: You can use the Web Tag Database as a reference when looking at your own HTML code. You can also add new tags to the database as they are published by HTML standards creators like Netscape, Microsoft and the World Wide Web Consortium (W3).

The Web Tag Database

Although CyberStudio's graphical interface means you don't have to know HTML to create a Web site, CyberStudio has included a handy database of HTML commands and special characters. It's available from the Windows menu and includes listings of tags that make up several HTML standards.

You can't use the tags directly in CyberStudio documents, but you can use the database as a reference when creating or editing your pages. **Figure 2-25** shows the database.

YOUR
FIRST WEB PAGES

You've had a look at the world into which CyberStudio emerged and a walking tour of the important features of CyberStudio. Now it's time to dive right in and make some Web pages. In this chapter, I give a more practical face to the tools introduced in Chapter 2 but keep things fairly simple, leaving the exploration of the full power of CyberStudio for subsequent chapters.

In this chapter I cover:

■ Setting CyberStudio preferences.

■ Setting up a Web page.

■ Setting up a site.

Setting preferences

You could just start typing the text into the document window to create your Web page. If you've used a word processor, you can probably figure out how to create bold text, enlarge it or center it. But things will go more smoothly if you take the time to set up your CyberStudio environment before you create your masterpiece.

CyberStudio's extensive collection of preferences covers everything from controlling page and HTML display to determining how media files are handled. The General Preferences window includes most of the tools I'll cover in this chapter; the rest are specific to topics I'll cover later on.

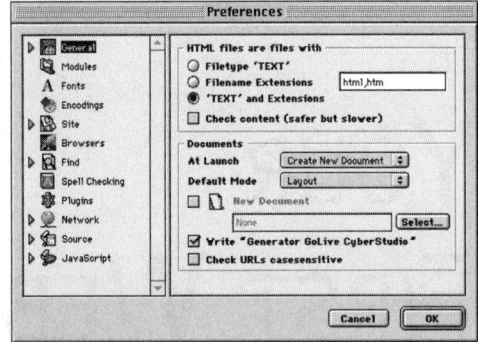

Figure 3-1: When you open the Preferences window, CyberStudio displays the General Preferences with these default settings.

To open the Preferences window:

Choose Preferences from the Edit menu. The General Preferences item is already selected. General Preferences appear by default, looking like **Figure 3-1**.

To set page preferences:

1. To tell CyberStudio that all plain text files should be considered HTML files, leave the "Filetype Text" button checked.

2. To use a filename extension, such as .html or .htm, choose the appropriate button. The 'Text and Extensions" button identifies both kinds of files as HTML. Filename Extensions is the best choice, because only files with the .htm or .html extension are recognized as HTML files by Web servers.

3. Click the "Check content" box to have CyberStudio verify the HTML within files when they're opened. The option slows down the process of opening files, but ensures that files are properly named.

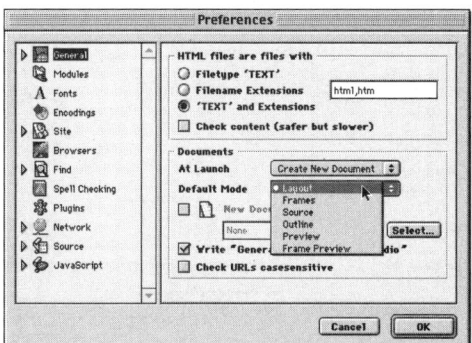

Figure 3-2: You can change the default page view from Layout to one of CyberStudio's other editing environments.

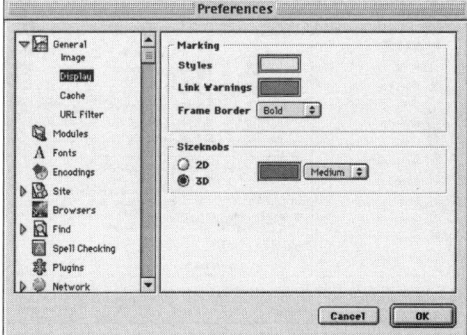

Figure 3-3: General Display preferences include the option to change the color of warnings you receive about bad links within your CyberStudio documents.

4. To change the items CyberStudio displays when you open the application, use the popup menus under the Documents label. You can choose to display a new document, an Open dialog box, or nothing at all. With the Default Mode menu, pick a default editor. **Figure 3-2** shows your choices.

To view other general preferences:

1. Click the triangle next to the General item, on the left side of the Preferences window. Four subcategories of preferences appear.

2. Click Display to reveal preference sub-categories (**Figure 3-3**).

To adjust CyberStudio's cache:

1. Click on the Cache item under the General Preferences label.

2. Click Cache Enable checkbox to reserve disk space for a CyberStudio cache that will buffer your pages as you work.

3. Adjust the Maximum Size of the cache if you wish. The amount of cache you reserve will be lost to you for file storage.

To control URLs and file mapping:

1. Click on the URL Handling item under the General Preferences label.

2. Click Check URLs casesensitive if you want to control the case of URLs within your site.

3. Leave Auto-add "mailto:" to addresses checked if you want the mailto: portion of an e-mail addresses URL to be added when you type the address in an Inspector field.

4. Click the File Mapping item under the General Preferences label.

5. Leaving the "Enable file open in other applications" item checked allows you to launch files with other applications from within the Site window. You can edit the list of file types and applications below to choose applications to use.

6. Choose Internet Config from the File Mapping popup. The list now displays the file mapping settings you've set (or the defaults) in Internet Config.

7. You can change file mapping by selecting Custom from the popup, and choosing a new application to open the file.

To add or remove a module:

1. Click on the Modules item in the Preferences window. The result looks like **Figure 3-4**.

Like the Mac OS, CyberStudio lets you enable and disable certain tools, to customize your working environment. Like Mac OS extensions or control panels, CyberStudio modules can be turned off and on to save memory or desktop real estate. By default, most of CyberStudio's modules are enabled. The major exception is WebObjects, which is turned off when you first install the software.

2. Scroll through the Modules folder until you locate the WebObjects item.

3. Click the checkbox to enable WebObjects. A warning symbol appears below the list of modules.

4. Click the Show Item Information triangle, to reveal details about this module (**Figure 3-5**).

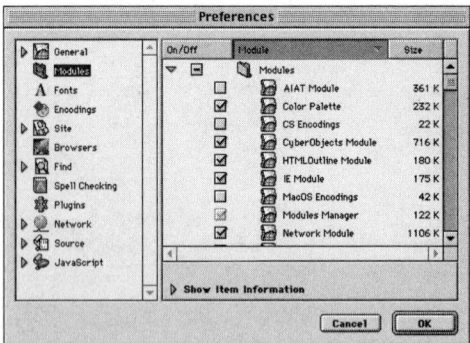

Figure 3-4: Add or remove modules just as you would system extensions, under the Modules Preferences.

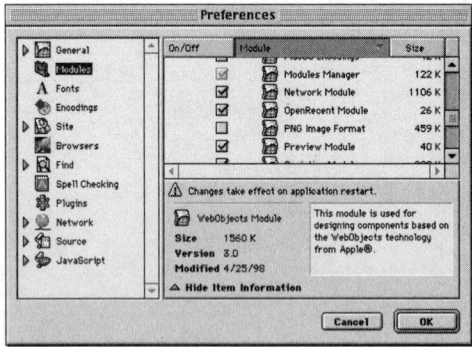

Figure 3-5: You can add functionality to CyberStudio by enabling new modules, or you can save memory and space on your desktop by disabling them.

5. Click OK to close the Preferences dialog box.

6. Quit CyberStudio and open it again, so that you can see the effect of adding the WebObjects module.

7. If it isn't already onscreen, open the palette. Notice that there are now nine tabs, not eight. The new tab contains tools that support Apple's advanced WebObjects development technology. If you don't intend to use WebObjects, disable the module in the Preferences window to save system memory.

✔ Tip

■ You can get information about any CyberStudio module by clicking on its name in the Modules window and opening the Item Information triangle.

Setting up your first page

It's a good idea to define a few basic parameters and settings for your Web page before you begin adding text and graphics.

To give your page a title:

1. Open a new CyberStudio document.

2. Click anywhere within the title "Welcome to GoLive CyberStudio." You'll find it at the top of the document window, to the right of the Page icon. See **Figure 3-6**.

   When you click, notice that the entire title is selected and that there's a box around it. Type a name for your page. Typing that will overwrite the original title.

   The title you type is the text that will identify your Web page when it is added to a Web browser's bookmark list. The title should clearly indicate what your Web page is all about in clear, concise terms.

To name your HTML page:

1. Choose Save from the File menu.

2. Give the file a name that conforms to the HTML standard; e.g. **index.html**.

3. In the Save dialog, create a new folder for your home page and the other documents you'll add to your site.

4. Click Save.

✔ Tip

- Naming your Web page file in any other format than *name*.html or *name*.htm will prevent you from using it with your Web site. The HTML standard expects pages to include the .html or .htm suffix. That's part of the secret to displaying Web pages on a variety of different computer platforms. Windows and UNIX machines also expect to see filenames with no spaces or slashes (/). Even though you're working

Figure 3-6: Replace the default page title with one of your own.

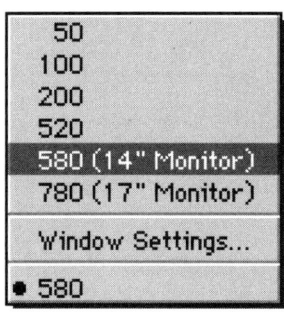

Figure 3-7: Choose a window size from the Page Size popup menu.

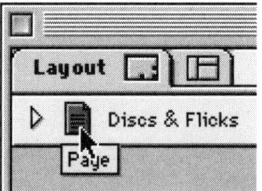

Figure 3-8: Clicking the Page icon brings up the Page Inspector.

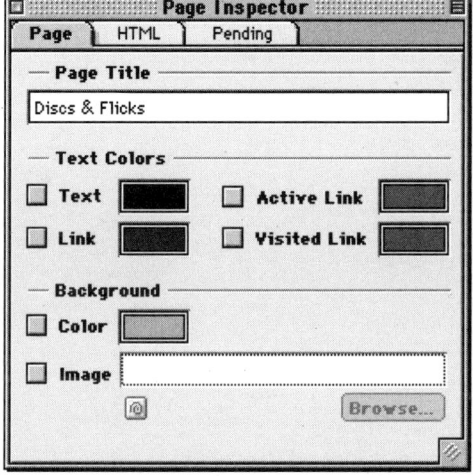

Figure 3-9: You can change text, link and background colors with the Page Inspector.

on a Mac, your files will most likely be displayed on other computers whose file-name rules are stricter.

To choose a default page size:

1. Click and hold the Page Size popup menu in the bottom right corner of the main window. **Figure 3-7** shows the popup menu.

2. Choose an appropriate size for your page— the window size that site visitors will see when they browse it. CyberStudio includes sizes that support 14-inch and 17-inch monitors, and some smaller page sizes as well. The 580-pixel choice (14-inch monitor) is probably the safest choice, since most current computer monitors are at least 14 inches. CyberStudio resizes the main window.

✔ Tips

- Be careful to set a single page size for all of the pages in your site, so that your site's elements display consistently to your visitors.

- Experienced Mac users may be tempted in fiddle with the main window size in order to get more space or manage onscreen windows. Don't do it! Using the Macintosh size box (rather than the menu) to resize the window will not only alter your view of the page but will also affect your visitors' view.

To create page colors:

1. Click on the Page icon in the title bar of the main window. It's shown in **Figure 3-8**.

2. Note that the Inspector window now displays Page settings. If the Inspector window isn't visible, choose Inspector from the Windows menu. The Page Inspector is shown in **Figure 3-9**.

3. To change the color of text, links or background, click on the color box to the right of the item you want to change. CyberStudio brings up the Color Palette window.

4. Select a color and click in the Preview pane at the top of the Color Palette.

5. Drag from the pane to the color field that you want to change in the Page Inspector. The box changes color, and the checkbox is now selected (**Figure 3-10**).

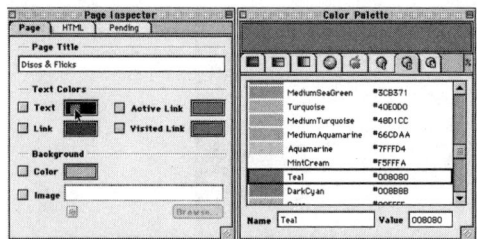

Figure 3-10: Drag a color from the Color Palette to the Page Inspector to change the page's background color.

✔ Tips

■ Don't feel as if you have to change link colors just because you can. Using unusual colors can actually be confusing for visitors to your site, because most sites and Web browsers use a standard set of link colors, and Web surfers are used to getting consistent visual cues as they browse.

■ If you decide to use custom colors for text, links or background, use the Preview or a Web browser to check colors you've chosen.

To add a background image:

1. In the Page Inspector window, click the Image checkbox.

2. When the Browse button lights up, click on it.

3. Locate an image you want to use as a background for your Web page and click Select. You'll see the image in the main window, and visitors to your Web page will see the image behind all of the page's other elements.

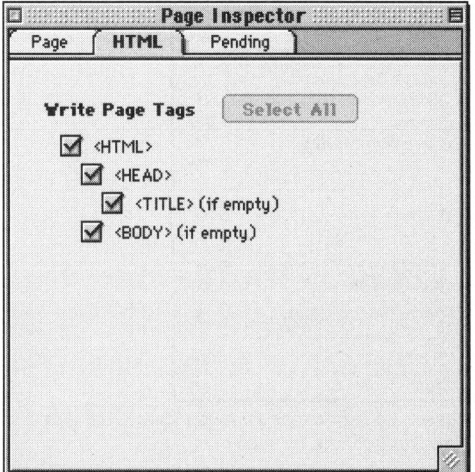

Figure 3-11: Change standing HTML elements in the Page Inspector's HTML tab.

To specify standing HTML elements:

1. In the Page Inspector, click the HTML tab (see **Figure 3-11**).

2. By default, CyberStudio creates an HTML page framework on each new page you create. You don't see the framework unless you choose the Outline or Source View, but it's there just the same. You can remove these defaults by unchecking one or more of the boxes under the HTML tab.

   I recommend that you leave them all checked unless you have a specific reason to remove them.

Setting up a site

Until this point, we've been working with individual Web pages. In many cases, you'll start with a single page or two and then add new items as your needs grow. CyberStudio supports that way of doing things, but the real power of the software is its ability to create and maintain groups of Web pages and other elements that make up a complete Web site.

When I talk about a CyberStudio site, I mean a group of elements (HTML files, images and other files) that form a Web site are managed as a unit and are saved under the umbrella of a single *site file*. The CyberStudio site file contains pointers to all of the elements of the site. It does not contain the HTML pages and other files themselves; it simply keeps them organized.

In this section, I introduce you to CyberStudio's site management tools by showing you how to set up a simple site. For a more in-depth look at sites, see Chapter 15.

You can create CyberStudio Web sites from scratch or you can import files belonging to an existing Web site into a new CyberStudio site file. Because we've already created a Web page, albeit an empty one, in this section, we'll import that file into a CyberStudio site.

To create a new site:

1. With CyberStudio open, choose New Site from the File menu (**Figure 3-12**).

2. Create an empty folder on your hard disk to store your new site or have CyberStudio create a folder by leaving the Create Folder button checked.

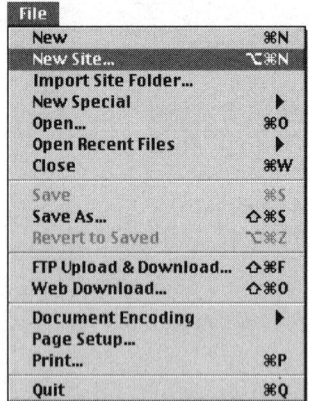

Figure 3-12: To create a CyberStudio site, choose New Site from the File menu.

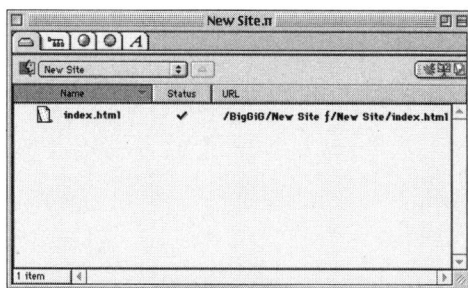

Figure 3-13: When you create a new site, CyberStudio starts you off with a home page, index.html.

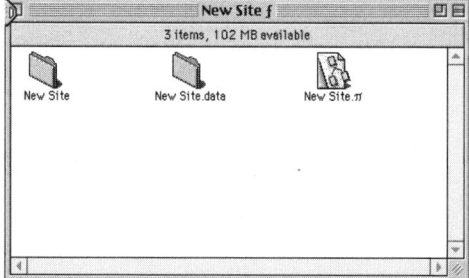

Figure 3-14: Your new site includes a site file and two folders that will contain the site's pages and media files.

3. Name your site.

4. Click Save. The Site window appears (**Figure 3-13**). It contains a single item, a page called index.html. The page name is bold, because index.html is the home page for your new site.

With a new site created, the next task is to get your home page up and running. You can either work directly with the home page CyberStudio has created for you (setting it up just as you did in the first section of this chapter) or you can replace the site's default home page with one you've already worked on.

To change your site's home page:

1. Quit CyberStudio.

2. In the Finder, locate and open the new site folder you created just now. Notice that there are two folders and a file within the new Site Folder (**Figure 3-14**). The New Site.π file is the actual CyberStudio site file, while the folders hold (or will hold) elements of your Web site.

3. Open the New Site Folder. Notices that the file index.html is stored here.

4. Locate the index.html file you created earlier in this chapter, and drag it into the open New Site Folder.

5. When asked if you want to replace the existing index.html file, click OK.

6. Open your site by double-clicking on the New Site.π icon. As before, index.html appears in the Site window. If you open it, by double-clicking, you'll see that the file has the title and attributes you gave it earlier.

SETTING UP A SITE

To add other items to your project:

1. In the Finder, locate an image (GIF or JPEG file) on your hard disk.

2. Copy or move the file into the folder where your project file and Web pages are stored.

   This step is not critical to the process of adding graphics files, although it is easier to manage projects if all files are stored in the same folder.

3. Return to GoLive CyberStudio and click on the Project window.

4. Click the Media tab.

5. Drag your image file onto the Project window.

WORKING WITH TEXT

CyberStudio's text handling features are a familiar combination of word processing and desktop publishing tools. You can use the tools to create text in CyberStudio or import it from elsewhere. From there, you can edit, search, spell check and manipulate text and text blocks to polish your Web pages.

In this chapter, I cover:

- Adding text to Web pages.
- Formatting text.
- Spellchecking.
- Find & Replace.

Entering text

You can add text to a CyberStudio document in several ways. You also have a choice of views in which to add your text. In most cases, you will use the Layout view, either typing directly into the main window or using CyberStudio's Layout Grid and text frames to place text blocks into a layout. You can also use other views to add or edit text—more on that later in this chapter.

As do most word-processing and desktop publishing applications, CyberStudio obeys accepted conventions for text entry. You can use the cursor keys, delete key and other keys to move around the main Web page window as you type text, and text will wrap from line to line as you type. You can cut and paste text or use drag and drop to move text around. As we'll see later in this chapter, you can also format text much as you do in other applications.

Using CyberStudio text frames and layout grids, you can precisely position text on your Web pages and later move the frames around as you perfect your layout.

To type text directly into a document:

1. Open a new or existing CyberStudio document. Make sure that the main window is visible.

2. Type some text in the main window.

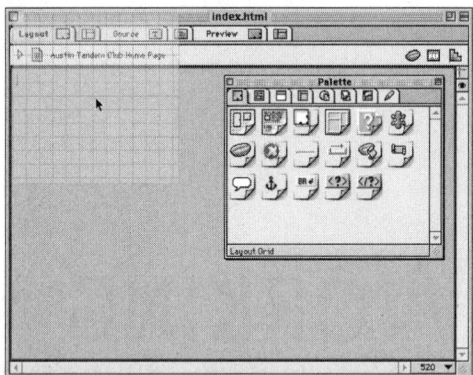

Figure 4-1: When you drag the Layout Grid icon from the palette onto the main Web page window, CyberStudio creates a default layout grid.

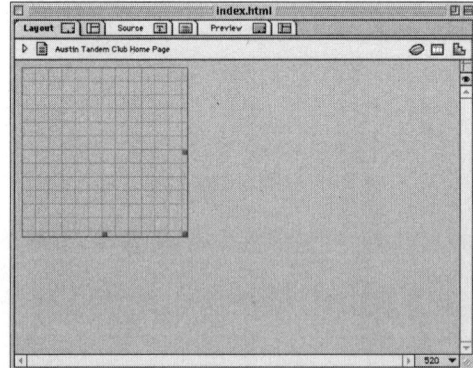

Figure 4-2: To resize a layout grid, you must first click on the border of the grid to display its handles. If you don't see the handles when you click, move the cursor (without holding down the mouse button) over the border of the grid until the hand cursor appears. Then click to display handles.

ENTERING TEXT

Figure 4-3: When you drag the Text Layout Box from the palette, CyberStudio creates a small text box in the main window.

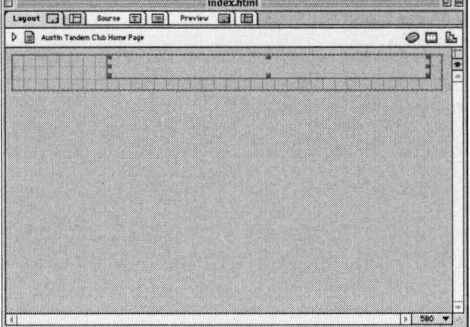

Figure 4-4: If you expand your text frame before typing, it's easier to manipulate the frame and edit the text when you're done.

To add text frames to a layout:

1. Open a new or existing CyberStudio document.

2. Drag the Layout Grid tool from the palette onto the document window. (see **Figure 4-1**).

3. Use the mouse to grab the handle at the bottom right-hand corner of the grid you've created and drag the handle to the right, so that the layout grid becomes a horizontal rectangle (see **Figure 4-2**).

4. Drag the Layout Text Box tool from the palette onto the layout grid. (see **Figure 4-3**). Like the grid, the text frame has highlighted handles for resizing the frame. You'll also notice that the mouse pointer is positioned within your new frame.

5. Grab the handle at the bottom right-hand corner of the text frame you've created and drag to the right, so that you'll be able to see what you're about to type. (see **Figure 4-4**).

6. Click within the text frame and type some text.

7. Click on the text block, but not on the text itself. Now you can drag the block to any position within the layout grid. Dragging to any position is useful for creating photo captions or positioning floating text elements.

ENTERING TEXT

✔ Tips

- If you type or paste text into a text frame without enlarging the frame first, CyberStudio expands the frame vertically as text is entered. You can resize the frame after you enter text, but it's easier to resize the frame first.

- You can make the text block as large or small as you like and type or paste an unlimited amount of text.

- When you click on the text frame, you may notice that the frame is selected but that the handles aren't visible. Without pressing the mouse button, move your pointer over the text frame until it displays a hand icon (when the pointer is on the border of the frame). When you click, you'll see the handles and can move or resize the window.

- If your page layout calls for a number of free-floating text elements, it's a good idea to create each element in a separate text frame so that you can move them independently of one another as you revise your layout.

- When you click on the text frame, so that the handles are visible, the Inspector window changes. **Figure 4-5** shows the Text Box inspector window. Here, you can choose a background color for your text box. To change the color of the text, you need to select the text and use the toolbar or menus. I have more to say on that subject later in this chapter.

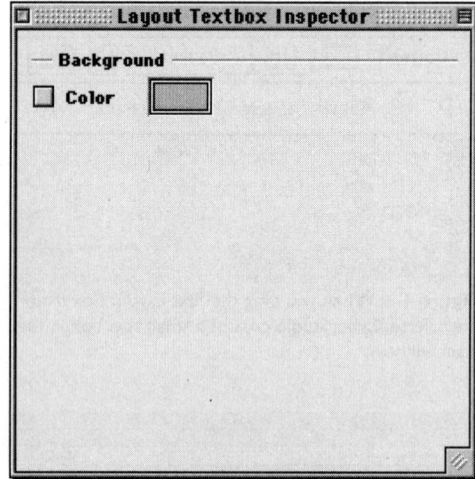

Figure 4-5: The Text Inspector gives you control of your text's background color.

Formatting text

Although CyberStudio uses HTML codes to mark text for the Web, you don't need to know HTML to add formatting. Like a word processor, CyberStudio uses familiar formatting tools. They are available from the Style and Format menus. Some of them appear on the toolbar, above the main window.

CyberStudio's four text formatting tool types are:

- Paragraph styles.

- Text alignment.

- Text styles.

- Lists.

The most often used formatting commands are on the toolbar for easy access (**Figure 4-6**). In fact, most of the toolbar is devoted to text formatting. The toolbar is roughly divided into the four types of formatting tools just listed. The toolbar consists mainly of text-formatting tools.

"Paragraph" styles

What CyberStudio calls paragraph styles are mostly heading styles. HTML provides for six levels of headings that you can use to call attention to and organize text on your Web pages. Like headlines and subheads in print publishing, HTML headings are larger and bolder than standard Web page text. Heading 1 is the largest. Heading 6, the smallest. Headings are bold.

You can add headings in CyberStudio via the toolbar or the Format menu.

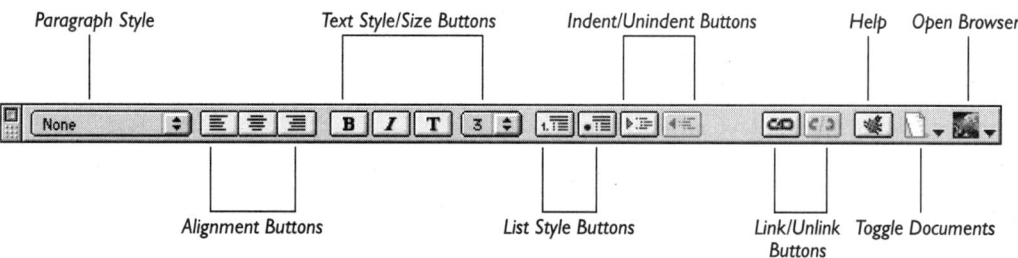

Figure 4-6: The toolbar includes formatting and navigation tools.

To create a heading:

1. Select some text or type some new text in an open CyberStudio window. This text will be the main heading of your Web page.

2. From the toolbar, choose Heading 1 (see **Figure 4-7**) by clicking on the Heading menu and dragging your cursor down to highlight Heading 1. Release the mouse button. The text is now larger and bold.

More paragraph styles

You'll find two items on the Paragraph Styles menu that do not create headings. The two styles are Address and Preformatted.

The Address style displays text as address information. This format usually identifies the owner/copyright holder/author of your Web page that is traditionally located at the bottom of a Web page (**Figure 4-8**).

Text that is preformatted does not include the HTML tags that give Web page text its typeset look. Instead, using the preformatted style displays the text exactly as it looks when you type or paste it in. Many Web browsers display preformatted (unformatted, actually) text in the Courier typeface, as does CyberStudio (**Figure 4-9**). Preformatted text is most often used to display code or ASCII text, differentiating it from the rest of the page, and to preserve already written text exactly as it appears.

Text alignment

You can align text to the left, center or right margins with the toolbar. To align text, select it and choose the Left, Center or Right icon from the toolbar. In **Figure 4-10**, the text is centered within its text frame.

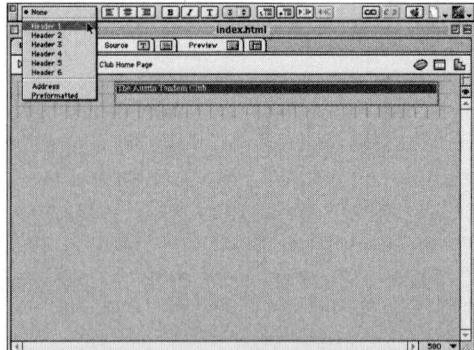

Figure 4-7: Add a heading by choosing it from the toolbar.

Figure 4-8: The Address format italicizes text.

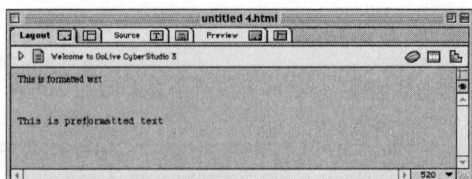

Figure 4-9: Formatted versus preformatted text.

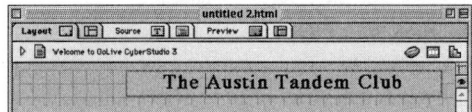

Figure 4-10: This heading text has been aligned to the center of its text frame. Note that it is not centered on the page.

FORMATTING TEXT

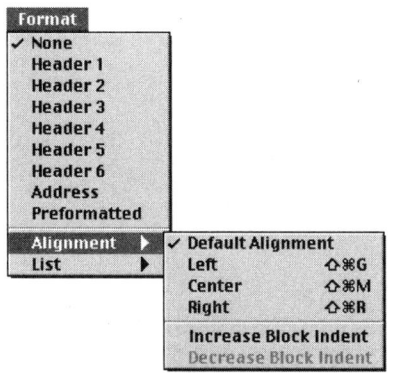

Figure 4-11: You can use the Format menu's Alignment submenu to change alignment and text indentation.

✔ Tip

- When you align text by centering it, the text may not be centered on your page. Check to see that the text frame and layout grid extend to the edge of your page to be sure that your text is centered. If you want to center text over a column or over a portion of the Web page, first center the text frame.

Using the Format menu's Alignment submenu, as shown in **Figure 4-11**, you can change alignment and increase or decrease the indentation of text blocks. That's useful if you're including an outline or some other hierarchical text element in your layout.

Text styles

You can change the appearance of Web page text with text style tools. A few are available from the toolbar. All of them reside on the Style menu.

CyberStudio supports the two kinds of text formatting recognized by the HTML language. They are:

- *Physical styles* such as bold and italic that always look the same, regardless of their position in your document or the browser being used to view the page.

- *Structural styles*, including strong and emphasis, which may vary in appearance with the context of your document or the browser being used.

Like the style commands in a word processor, the toolbar items let you add physical styles, including bold, italic and teletype. You can also increase the size of text—not by fixed point sizes as you would in a word-processing application, but according to the HTML conventions for relative font sizing.

CyberStudio supports a number of other physical styles. They are:

- Underline.

- Strikeout.

- Superscript.

- Subscript.

- Blink.

✔ Tip

- You can't display the blink tag in either the Layout or Preview Views. If you want to use it to make Web page text flash, you'll need to use a browser to view it.

The structural styles supported by CyberStudio appear on the Structure submenu of the Style menu. They are shown in **Figure 4-12**.

Fonts

HTML fonts come in sizes from 1 to 7. The default for Web page body text is 3. Each size is relative to the default size for a particular text element. If you use the font size menu or toolbar items, you are overriding the standard size for the text you're styling. For example, selecting a heading, which is already larger than body text, and increasing the font size from 3 to 5 will make the heading bigger still. Performing the same change on a body text paragraph does not increase your paragraph to heading size but simply adds two points to your body text (see **Figure 4-13**).

If you're familiar with desktop publishing tools, or even word-processing applications, you'll notice that CyberStudio does not include a font menu, with different typefaces for you to choose from. That's because HTML, in order to remain a platform-independent language, does not directly support typefaces. The Microsoft Internet Explorer Web browser, however, does make provision for typefaces, so Web page viewers who have certain fonts

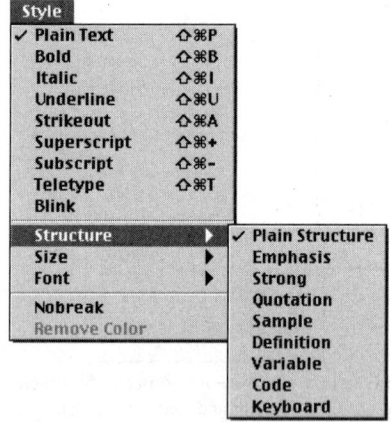

Figure 4-12: The Structure submenu of the Format menu lists CyberStudio's structural text styles.

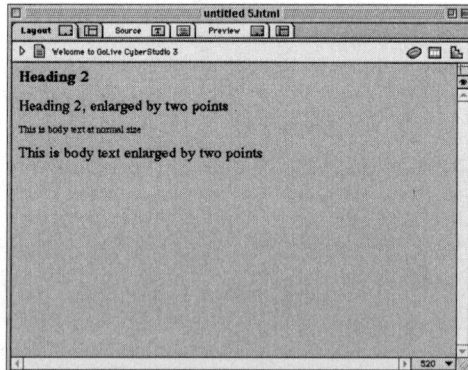

Figure 4-13: The two enlarged lines of text both have font sizes of 5, two points larger than normal, but not identical to one another.

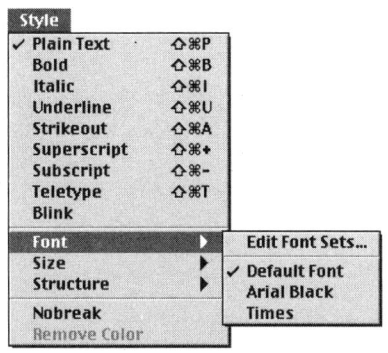

Figure 4-14: Choose Edit Font Sets from the Fonts submenu of the Style menu.

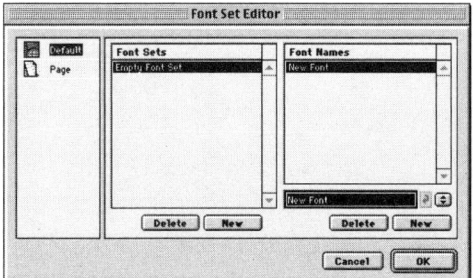

Figure 4-15: The Font Sets window displays all the fonts currently installed in your system.

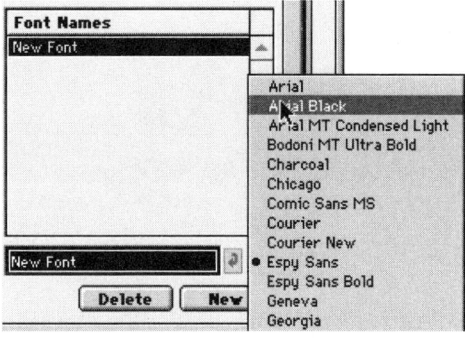

Figure 4-16: Choose a font to add to your font set.

installed can view them in the Explorer browser. To take advantage of this capability, CyberStudio includes font sets, which allow you to specify typefaces within your HTML documents.

CyberStudio allows you to store and use fonts globally, making them available for all documents you work on, or as page font sets, that work with and are saved with individual pages or sites. All of the fonts, whether global, page-specific or site-specific, are available from the Font submenu of the Style menu.

Font Sets

Not every computer or Web browser uses the same fonts. As a Web author, you run the risk of creating content that doesn't look as you intended within a given browser. Font sets allow you to provide options for the browser by creating a first, second and perhaps even a third choice. If, for example, you create a font set that includes Ariel, Helvetica and Geneva, then use Ariel to produce a page, users who don't have Ariel installed can view the text in Helvetica or Geneva, depending on the fonts supported by their system or Web browser.

To edit a font set:

1. Choose Edit Font Sets from the Font submenu of the Style menu (**Figure 4-14**).

2. If it isn't already highlighted, click on the Default icon in the left pane of the window. Default fonts are those that Cyber-Studio makes available regardless of the document or site you have open.

3. Click New in the middle pane of the Font Sets editor. A new, unnamed font set appears (**Figure 4-15**).

4. Choose a font from the popup menu (**Figure 4-16**). The fonts on this menu are those currently installed in your Macintosh System Folder.

5. To add another font, click New under Font Names and choose another font from the menu.

6. To create a second font set, click New in the Font Sets pane, and repeat steps 3-5.

7. When you've finished adding fonts, click OK to close the Font Sets window.

To use a font:

1. Select some text in a document window.

2. Choose a font from the Font submenu of the Style menu.

To create page font sets:

1. To create a font set that is specific to the Web page you're working on, open the page and choose Edit Font Sets from the Font menu.

2. In the Font Sets Editor, click Page.

3. Create the font set and save the page, as described in the previous section. When you open this page in the future, the font sets you have applied will appear on the Font submenu, along with the Default fonts.

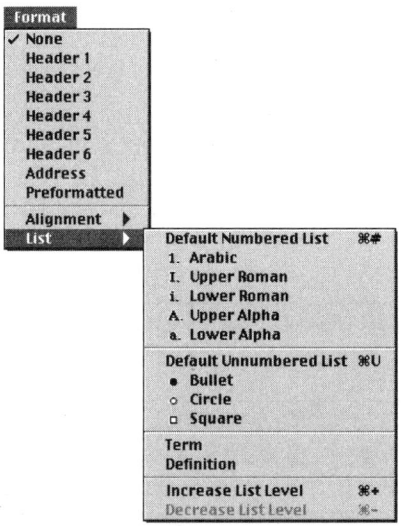

Figure 4-17: You can choose from a number of list types in CyberStudio.

Figure 4-18: To see how this Upper Roman list would look to a Web page visitor, you need to look at it in CyberStudio's Preview mode.

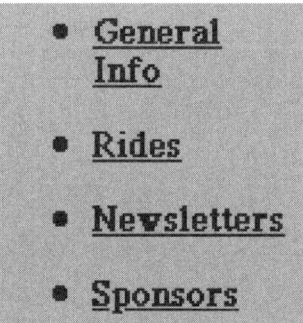

Figure 4-19: One of several bulleted list formats.

Lists

Lists are an easy way to organize content on your Web page. Whether you need to create a numbered list of instructions, an outline or a bulleted list of links, HTML and CyberStudio provide a list format to cover it.

To create a list:

1. Type the items for your list in a text frame or directly into the document window. After typing each item, press Return.

2. Select the items in the list.

3. Choose a list format from the Lists submenu of the Format menu. It looks like **Figure 4-17**. The Upper Roman (uppercase roman numerals) style is shown in **Figure 4-18**.

4. With the text selected, choose a different list format and notice how the appearance of the text changes. **Figure 4-19** shows a bulleted list.

The toolbar includes two list-making options and one tool each for increasing and decreasing the indentation of your list.

✔ Tip

■ To add a greater indent to your list or to move it back one level, use the Increase List Level and Decrease List Level commands on the Lists submenu.

Spellchecking

CyberStudio's built-in spelling checker can
locate spelling errors in a single page or
throughout your site. You can use one of several English language dictionaries and add
your own words to a Personal Dictionary.

To check spelling:

1. Open a CyberStudio document and
   make sure that you're working in the
   Layout view.

2. Choose Spellchecking from the Edit menu.
   The Spellchecking window appears. It looks
   like **Figure 4-20**.

3. Click Check.

   The spellchecker locates words that it does
   not recognize, whether they're misspelled
   or simply not included in the dictionary.

4. If you would like to use a dictionary other
   than the default US English dictionary,
   choose it from the Language popup menu.

5. To correct a spelling mistake, click on one
   of the suggestions offered and click the
   Replace button. If you don't see a sugges-
   tion that you like, type a new spelling in
   the blank provided.

   You can also tell the spellchecker to
   simply skip a word that it doesn't know.
   Skip All passes over all occurrences of
   the word.

6. If the spellchecker has pointed out a word
   that should be added to your personal
   dictionary, click the Learn button. This is
   shown in **Figure 4-21**.

7. Your check is completed when the Spellchecking window displays No Errors. Click
   the Close box to close the Spellchecking
   window.

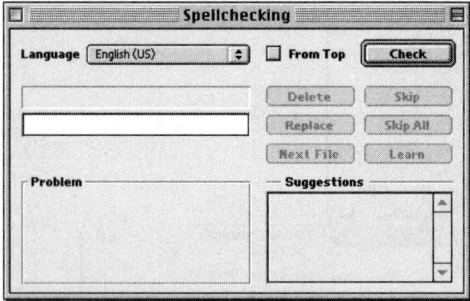

Figure 4-20: The spellchecker offers suggested
spellings when it detects a word it doesn't recognize.

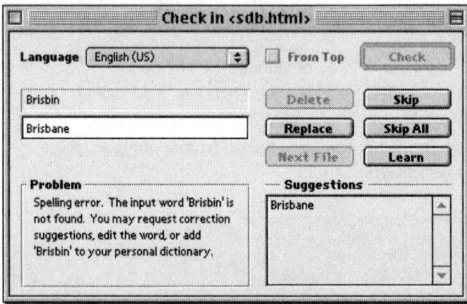

Figure 4-21: Click Learn to add an unknown word
(like your own last name) to a personal dictionary.

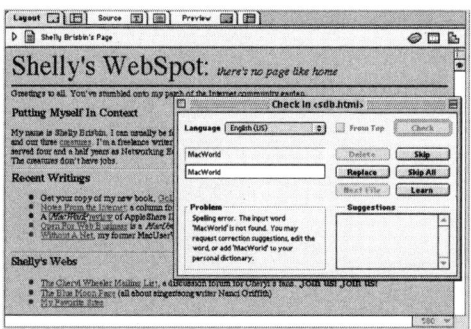

Figure 4-22: Can't find the questioned word in your document? Try moving the Spellchecking window.

Figure 4-23: Click Next File to continue checking files on your site.

✔ **Tip**

- While you have the Spellchecking window open, CyberStudio highlights the questionable word in your document. You may need to move the Spellchecking window in order to see the highlighting. That's what I did in **Figure 4-22**.

The spellchecker checks all text in a single document, whether it appears in one or more text frames or is simply typed into the main window. If you're working in the Source or Outline View, the spellchecker ignores the HTML code that surrounds your text when performing its check.

To spellcheck an entire site:

1. Open a CyberStudio site file, so that the Site window is visible.

2. Choose Spellchecking from the Edit menu.

3. As before, the Spellchecking window appears, and begins to check the first document in your site, when you click the Check button.

4. When you've finished checking the first file in the site, click Next File to move on to another document, and so on until all of the files in your site have been checked. See **Figure 4-23**.

   When you click Skip All, or Learn, your instructions are carried throughout the current checking session, including all of the files in your site.

SPELLCHECKING

Find & Replace

You can search one document or a whole site with CyberStudio's Find & Replace feature. As the name implies, this feature allows you to search text (including Web page content and HTML code) for characters, words or phrases. Find & Replace works in the Layout, Source and Outline Views.

You can search one document or a whole site with CyberStudio's Find & Replace feature. As the name implies, this feature allows you to search text (including Web page content and HTML code) for characters, words or phrases. Find & Replace works in the Layout, Source, and Outline Views.

CyberStudio performs three types of Find & Replace functions. They are:

- Local Find & Replace.
- Global Find & Replace.
- Find File.

Both local and global options include the ability to simply search for text and the ability to replace a string of text with something you specify.

Local Find & Replace

Local Find & Replace lets you search for and replace taxi in a single document. You can use this feature while working within a site, or by simply searching a single open file.

To find text locally:

1. Open a CyberStudio document and make sure that you are in the Layout, Source or Outline View.

2. Choose Find from the Edit menu.

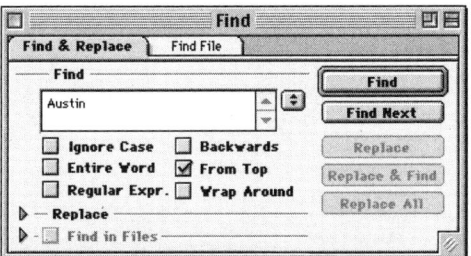

Figure 4-24: You can enter a word, a phrase, or a string of characters into the Find field. Choose whether to consider the word's case and press Find.

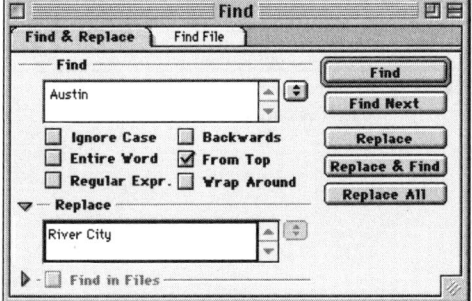

Figure 4-25: The Find & Replace dialog looks like this when the Replace triangle is open.

3. Type a word that can be found within the document you are searching. **Figure 4-24** shows the Find window, ready to search.

4. Click Find.

5. When CyberStudio finds an instance of the word you've searched for, it is highlighted in the main window. You can click Find Next to look for another instance of the word.

To find & replace text locally:

1. If it's not still visible, open the Find dialog box from the Edit menu.

2. Type some characters to search for.

3. If it is not already visible, open the Replace field by clicking on the triangle near the bottom of the dialog box. **Figure 4-25** shows the fully open dialog.

4. Type some text to replace the characters you're going to find.

5. Click Find. Notice that you have the option to replace the text or to automatically find and replace all occurrences within your document. If you would rather make the decision to replace text on a case by case basis, simply click Replace and then Find to locate another occurrence of your text.

Global Find & Replace

Using global find and replace, you can expand your search for characters, words, phrases, or HTML tags to multiple files within your site. You can even search multiple sites.

To find text globally:

1. Open a site by double-clicking on the Site file.

2. With the Site window visible, choose Find (or type Command-F) from the Edit menu.

FIND & REPLACE

3. In the Find window, click the triangle next to the Find in Files label.

4. Click Add Files in the newly revealed pane to add files and/or sites to be searched. A dialog box appears.

5. Navigate to the folder containing the files you want to add.

6. Add files by clicking the Add button. If you want to search all files within your site, open the site's folder and click Add All. The files you add appear in the lower portion of the dialog box.

7. When you have added all of the files you want to search, click done. The Find and Replace window now displays the files you've added to the search. The result looks like **Figure 4-26**.

8. If you want to search for an HTML tag or to see your search results within the Source view, click the Source Mode checkbox.

9. Begin your search by clicking Find. When it locates the search string, CyberStudio opens the file containing the first reference and highlights the text in question.

10. Click Find Next to locate more occurrences of the text.

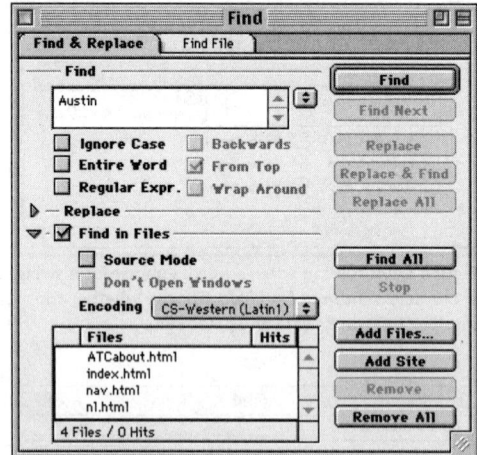

Figure 4-26: Search your site, or any group of files with the Find in Files option.

✔ Tips

■ You can search for and replace text globally by opening the Replace pane (click the triangle next to the Replace label) and entering text as described in the Local Search section of this chapter.

■ You can drag files directly from the Site window to the Find in Files box.

Figure 4-27: Find files by choosing a name or URL to search for.

Finding Files

In addition to locating text within files, you can use Find & Replace to locate files themselves.

To find a file:

1. With a CyberStudio site open, launch the Find & Replace window from the Edit menu.

2. Click the Find File tab to display its window.

3. Type all of part of a filename in your site. If you want to search for a file according to its URL, click the "whose" popup menu to choose URL. Otherwise, leave the Name item selected.

4. Choose from the next popup, depending on whether you want to find the file's complete name or a portion of the name. My search appears in **Figure 4-27**.

5. Click Find. CyberStudio highlights the files that match your search in the Site window.

6. To find another file with the name or URL you selected, click Find Next.

7. When you're finished locating files, close the Find & Replace window.

FIND & REPLACE

LAYING OUT WEB PAGES

5

In many ways, this is the most important chapter in the entire book. Here I explain how you can use GoLive CyberStudio to construct Web pages and add the elements that almost every Web page has in common: text, graphics and spacing devices. I'll start with a layout grid and work my way through adding items to the page, fine-tuning each one.

In this chapter, I cover:

- Working with layout grids.

- Using images.

- Using lines and spacers.

- Using line breaks.

- Using tables.

- Using marquees.

- Using multiple objects.

- Using the favorites tab.

Layout grids

CyberStudio's layout grid is among the application's most unique and useful features. Using the grid, you can precisely place text frames, images, lines, spacers, tables and plugins on a Web page, using gridlines for visual and physical layout guidance.

Layout grids can also obviate the need for traditional HTML trickery, such as using tables or frames to create multi-column pages. From a designer's point of view, a CyberStudio layout grid acts just like a traditional publishing application's grid. Underneath the visual grid, though, CyberStudio actually generates HTML tables. It uses tables to display free-standing elements or multiple columns on a Web page. Finally, because the grid itself is customizable, you can choose settings and spacing that matches the page you're working on.

I introduced the layout grid in Chapter 4. In this chapter, I make fuller use of grids and customize them for different applications.

To create a layout grid:

1. Open a new GoLive CyberStudio document. By default, the main window displays the Layout View.

2. Drag the Layout Grid tool (**Figure 5-1**) from the palette onto the main window. A square layout grid appears (**Figure 5-2**).

3. Click on the grid to display the Layout Grid Inspector (**Figure 5-3**). In the Layout Grid Inspector window, you can resize the entire grid, set a color for the grid, and align it to either side of the screen.

4. With the Layout Grid Inspector visible, click in the Horizontal field under the Grid label. Type **12**, replacing the default value of 16.

5. Press Tab. The Vertical field is now selected. Notice how the horizontal lines on the layout grid have changed, bringing them closer together.

Figure 5-1: The Layout Grid tool.

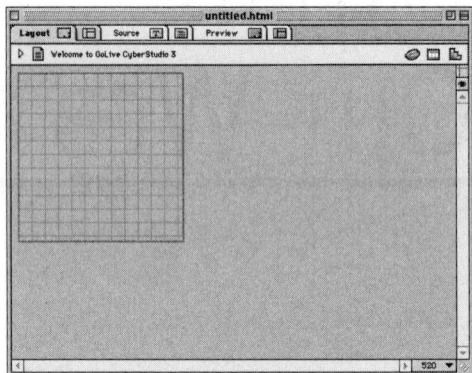

Figure 5-2: Here is a brand new layout grid.

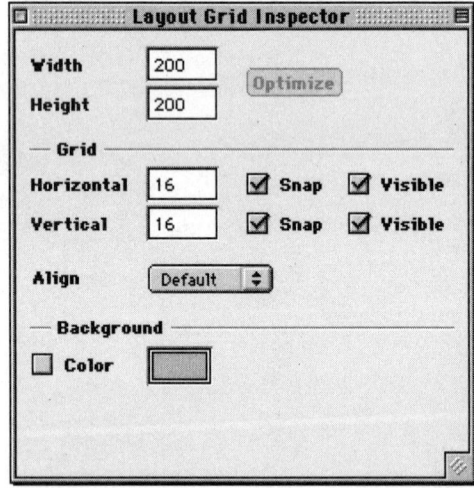

Figure 5-3: The Layout Grid Inspector appears when you click on a layout grid.

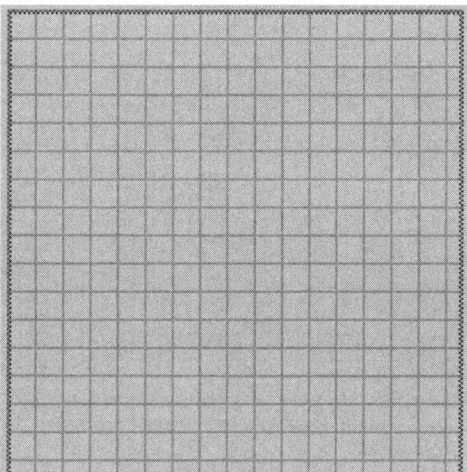

Figure 5-4: The grid on the left displays the default 16x16 grid. The one on the right is 12x12 pixels.

6. Type **12** in the Vertical field, and press Tab. You can compare the original grid with the new one in **Figure 5-4**.

Closer grid spacing can be useful if you want to place a number of objects close together on a page. Likewise, adding space between grid-lines gives you more space between objects on the page.

✔ Tips

- By default, the horizontal and vertical Snap checkboxes are selected in the Layout Grid Inspector. With Snap turned on, objects you drag onto a layout grid snap to the gridlines.

- Turning off the Visible checkbox hides the grid from view but doesn't prevent it from snapping objects into place. Hiding the grid can make previewing pages in the Layout View a bit easier.

Positioning a layout grid

You can use a single layout grid for an entire Web page, or you can divide the page into multiple grids. A single grid forms a consistent background for the entire document and is usually a good choice if you don't want to create a modular Web page. If your page is modular with distinct sections that might be moved or copied to other pages, a grid for each section is the best choice. In the following example, I create two grids to accommodate a modular layout.

To position a layout grid:

1. Click on the border of the grid to select it. You'll know where to click on the grid by your cursor's behavior. Without pressing the mouse button, drag the cursor over the grid until the pointer changes from an I-beam insertion point to an arrow.

2. Click on the border to display the grid's handles.

3. Drag the handle at the bottom right-hand corner of the grid downward and to the right until the grid extends to the bottom and right edge of the window. The result, along with the Layout Grid Inspector, appears in **Figure 5-5**.

4. From the Page Size popup menu at the bottom right-hand corner of the document window, choose 580 (14' Monitor). This will enlarge your main window a bit.

5. Select the layout grid, and drag the bottom right handle of the grid to the edge of the window.

6. Save your work. We will be using this layout in the next section.

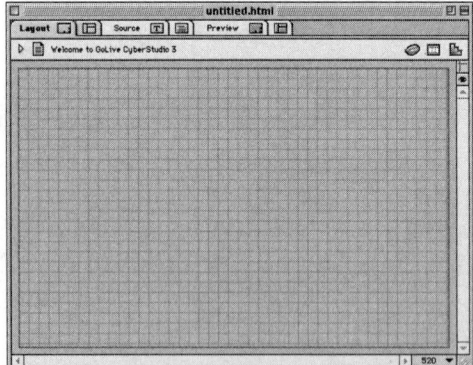

Figure 5-5: When you resize gridlines on a layout grid, it looks like this. The Inspector's size fields change accordingly.

✔ Tip

■ As you resize the grid, the horizontal and vertical measurements in the Layout Grid Inspector change. You can use the Inspector to precisely resize your grid if you prefer.

Beginning your layout

All of the text, images, lines, buttons and other objects that appear on your Web pages are created by adding objects (or pointers to objects) to a Web page, built in CyberStudio. In most cases, your Web site will consist of several pages that are tied together by hyperlinks. Because navigation is such an important part of creating a successful Web site, many designers start their sites by developing a modular, templated approach that helps users find their way around. Even if your site will not include a navigation bar, table of contents frame, or other common navigation element, chances are that some element of each page in your site will be designed according to a template.

Of course, it's best to put the template together before you launch into layout. In this section, I introduce you to some of CyberStudio's layout tools while building a template.

✔ Tip

- Chapter 3 includes a detailed discussion of how to prepare new pages for layout and how to tell CyberStudio which file will be the home page for your site. It's a good idea to review this material and make sure that you've set the appropriate preferences before you plunge into laying out your pages.

Many Web sites use a navigation bar, table of contents or other standing element to unify all the pages within a site. You can easily design individual pages around these standing elements by adding layout grids to your Web pages, using them as placeholders. Even better, you can save the entire grid under the palette's Custom tab and add the grid, along with its contents, to each page where you want the standing element to appear.

✔ Tips

- Adding a placeholder layout grid over an existing one is much easier than creating several grids that sit next to one another on the page. Grids *can* be placed next to one another, but problems with alignment make it tough to keep several grids in place. A small grid that overlaps the main grid will stay just where you put it, however.

- But don't get carried away. I recommend one main grid and the minimum number of others that you need to create a modular page.

To create a placeholder or standing element:

1. Open the document you created earlier in this chapter, or create one like it now. Make sure that you fill the document window with a layout grid.

2. Drag the Layout Grid tool from the palette onto the main window. The grid will snap to the top left-hand corner of the underlying grid.

3. Drag the lower right handle of the new grid down and to the left a bit, so that it looks like **Figure 5-6**. This will be your Web site's table of contents.

4. With the new grid selected, click on the Layout Grid Inspector window.

5. Change the gridline settings, if you like.

6. Click on the Color box in the lower part of the Inspector window. **Figure 5-7** points to it.

7. When the Color Palette window appears, choose a color for your layout grid and drag it onto the Layout Grid Inspector's Color field. (For details on using the Color Picker to choose colors, see Chapter 13). The newly colorful grid is displayed in **Figure 5-8**.

8. Save your work.

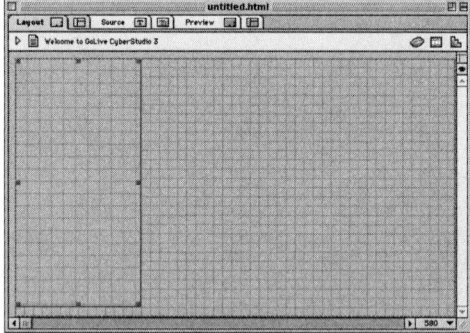

Figure 5-6: The new grid will hold a table of contents for the Web site. It should be wide enough to display a logo or other graphic and a few words of text per line. The spaces between gridlines differ between the two grids because I haven't yet configured the new grid.

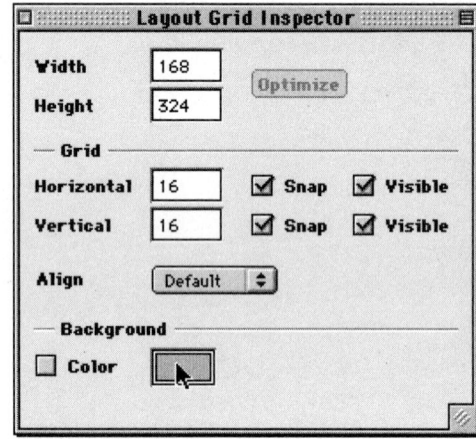

Figure 5-7: Use this field to choose a color for your layout grid.

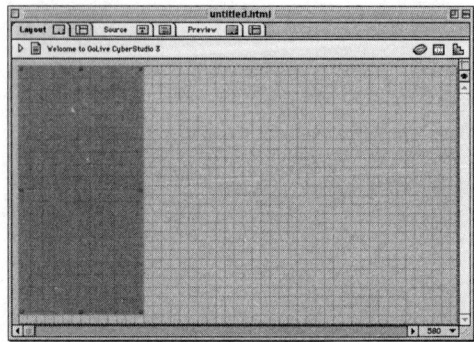

Figure 5-8: The new, colorful grid contrasts with the rest of the layout. And we've changed the gridline spacing to match the main grid's.

LAYOUT GRIDS

Figure 5-9: The Image tool, from the palette.

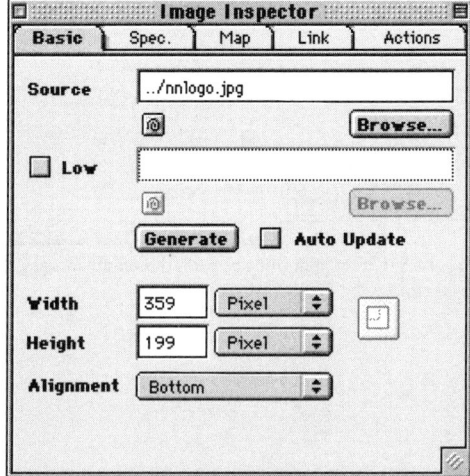

Figure 5-10: The Image Inspector.

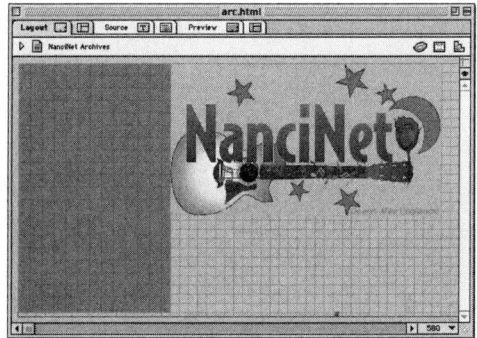

Figure 5-11: This JPEG image I imported is much bigger than I want it to be.

Images

Unlike the text elements you create in Cyber-Studio and format as parts of a Web page, images on a Web page are separate files, stored along with your HTML files on a Web server. When you add an image to your page, Cyber-Studio creates a pointer from the HTML page to the image. CyberStudio, like most Web browsers, displays these files inline—directly on the page. Using CyberStudio tools, you can manipulate the image's size and its alignment to other objects on the page.

The two most common image types on the Web are GIF (Graphics Interchange Format) and JPEG (Joint Photographic Expert Group). GIF and JPEG account for most of the still images on the Web. All browsers support both formats. Other file formats, such as QuickTime and PDF (Portable Document Format) are viewed with Web browser plugins. We'll discuss them fully in Chapter 9.

To add an image to a Web page:

1. Open a new or existing CyberStudio document. Be sure that the Layout View is visible.

2. Drag the Image tool (**Figure 5-9**) from the palette onto the document window. An icon with a question mark appears in the main window, and the Inspector window displays the Image Inspector. It looks like **Figure 5-10**.

3. In the Inspector window, click the Browse button.

   Using the dialog box that appears, locate a GIF or JPEG image file that you would like to add to the Web page. Click Open. The image appears in the CyberStudio window at full size, as shown in **Figure 5-11**.

✔ Tip

- Even though I want to place the logo on our table of contents, I dropped it on the main grid to preserve the smaller grid. When you add an image to a grid that is smaller than the image, the grid expands. In this case, I'll resize the image before I place it on the small grid, avoiding an unwanted expansion of the small grid.

To add an image with Point & Shoot:

1. If you have created a CyberStudio site, open it and then open the Web page where you want to add an image.

2. Drag the Image tool from the palette to the main window.

3. In the Image Inspector, click the Point & Shoot icon and drag the resulting line to the Site window's Media tab.

4. Choose an image by dragging the line over its icon (**Figure 5-12**). When you release the mouse button, the image appears in the main window.

✔ Tip

- Alternatively, you can drag an image file from the Site window directly into the main window to place the image.

Resizing an image

The Image Inspector provides three ways of measuring an image. You can set image width and height by typing numbers in the corresponding fields. Image sizes can be measured by:

- pixel—the image's size in pixels.

- percent—the image's size as a percentage of the size of the document window.

- image—automatically sets the width or height measurement to that of the original image.

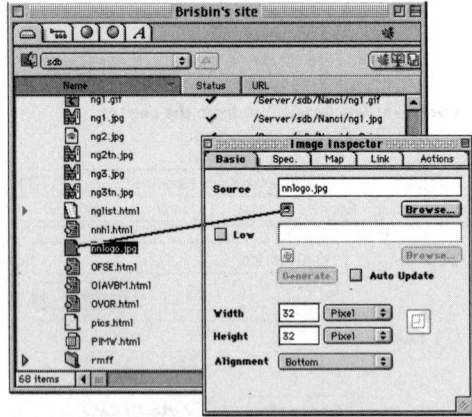

Figure 5-12: Point and shoot from the empty Image Inspector to the Project window.

IMAGES

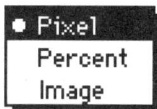

Figure 5-13: You can use the Width or Height popup menu to change the measurement method.

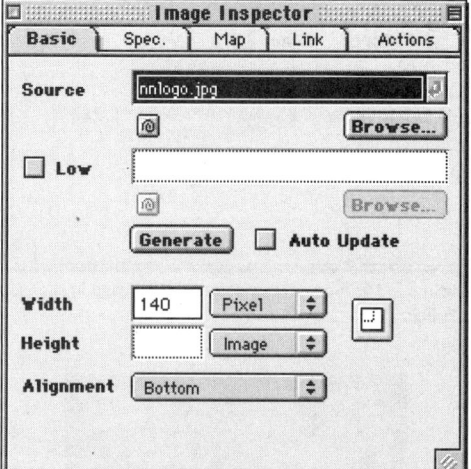

Figure 5-14: Use the Image Inspector's Height and Width boxes to resize an image.

Figure 5-15: Here is our image, which will serve as a logo for the table of contents.

- If you've chosen to use visible and/or snapping gridlines, it's easy to choose the proper position for the image. In our example, it is centered within the table of contents grid (**Figure 5-15**).

Pixel is the default measuring system. To use the percent or image option, make the appropriate choice from the Width or Height popup menu (**Figure 5-13**).

To resize an image:

1. Click on the image to be resized. The Image Inspector displays parameters including the current height and width of the image.

2. To resize the image proportionally, change the unit of measure in the Height popup menu to Image.

3. Type a number of pixels in the Width box, with the Pixel option still selected, as shown in **Figure 5-14**. The image resizes proportionally.

4. To return the image to its original size, click the Size button next to the Height and Width fields in the Image Inspector.

5. If necessary, drag the image you have resized into it proper location on the layout grid.

✔ Tip

- The best way to ensure that your image is the proper size is to set its width and height in the graphics program you used to create it. Besides saving you a step in CyberStudio, inserting a correctly sized image means that the file your Web site visitors download when they view your page is as small as possible. Images resized in CyberStudio maintain their original file size.

- It's easy to move from CyberStudio to an image-editing program. If, say, you add an image to your Web page, and realize that it needs a tweak, just double-click the image. If you have configured File Mapping preferences in the Preferences window (see Chapter 3), the image you click will open in an appropriate graphics program.

IMAGES

Adding alternative text

Some Web browsers, such as Lynx, do not support images. In addition, visually impaired users often have difficulty navigating Web pages with images included, especially if they use screen reading software to speak the contents of Web pages. To get around this problem, you can add alternative (Alt.) text to an image reference—just a word or two. Text-only Web browsers display these alternative tags where the image would otherwise be.

To add alternative text to an image:

1. Click on the image, making the Image Inspector visible.

2. Click the Special tab at the top of the window. The result looks like **Figure 5-16**.

3. Type a one or two word description of the image in the Alt. field.

To add a border:

1. Click on an image.

2. Click the Special tab at the top of the Inspector window.

3. Click on the border checkbox. The image now has a default border of three pixels. You can see he result in **Figure 5-17**. You can choose a border that matches your image. If you uncheck the Border checkbox, the border disappears.

✔ Tip

■ If you choose not to use a layout grid to construct your Web page, you can use the HSpace and VSpace fields of the Image Inspector to add space (in pixels) between an image and text. If you do use a layout grid, you can use gridlines to properly position images relative to text.

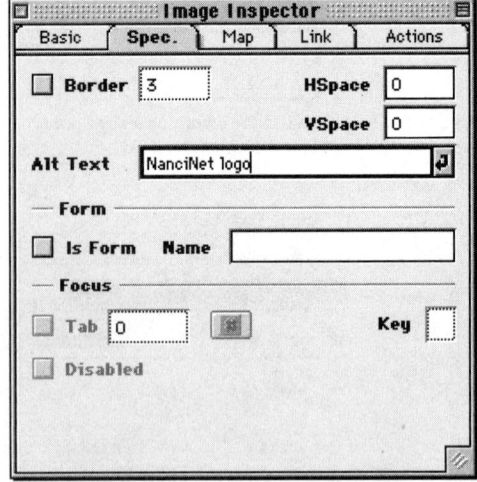

Figure 5-16: Type a description of the image in the Alt. field.

Figure 5-17: With a three-pixel border, an image looks like this.

Figure 5-18: An image placeholder inside a text frame looks like this.

Aligning images

In HTML parlance, aligning an image means aligning it to adjacent text. It's not necessary to align an image to text unless you want the text and image to move together. In other words, if you want text to wrap around an image or to maintain a certain position relative to the image, you need to use the alignment tools. With a layout grid, you need to insert the image into the text frame. Image alignment also works (and is almost essential) if you're designing pages without a layout grid.

You can align images vertically or horizontally, in one of several ways. It's simple enough to apply an alignment to an image, but it's trickier to know just which alignment to choose because many of the choices have similar properties.

To align an image to adjacent text:

1. Drag the text frame tool from the palette onto your layout grid. If you aren't using a grid, begin with step 2.

2. Drag the Image tool from the palette into the text frame. The result looks like **Figure 5-18**.

3. If you're not using a layout grid, just place the image anywhere on the page.

4. With the image icon selected, choose Browse from the Image Inspector window, or use Point & Shoot if you're working within a project.

5. Locate a GIF or JPEG image and click Open. The image appears on the page.

6. Resize the image if necessary.

7. Select the text frame by clicking on the border of the frame.

IMAGES

8. Enlarge the frame a bit by dragging one of the handles to the right.

9. Type some text into the frame; a sentence should do. If you're not using a text frame, type directly into the document window, right next to the image.

10. Click on the image to select it.

11. In the Inspector window, choose an alignment from the Alignment popup menu (shown in **Figure 5-19**).

Using an image as a link

Like hyperlinked text, images can be used to connect one Web page to another with just a click.

To link from an image:

1. Click on an image you want to link.

2. Choose the Link tab in the Inspector window. It looks like **Figure 5-20**.

3. Type a URL if you want the image to link to a remote Web site, or click Browse and locate the appropriate HTML file if you want to link to a location within your site. When the link is complete, you see a border around the image, indicating the link. The border is only visible in the Layout View.

You can give your site's visitors something to look at while large images load by adding a low-resolution version of the image to your site. This image is displayed while the high-quality graphic is downloaded to the user's computer.

To add a low-resolution image:

1. Under the Image Inspector's Basic tab, click the Generate button. CyberStudio creates a low-resolution version of the image you're working with. The file name appears in the Low field.

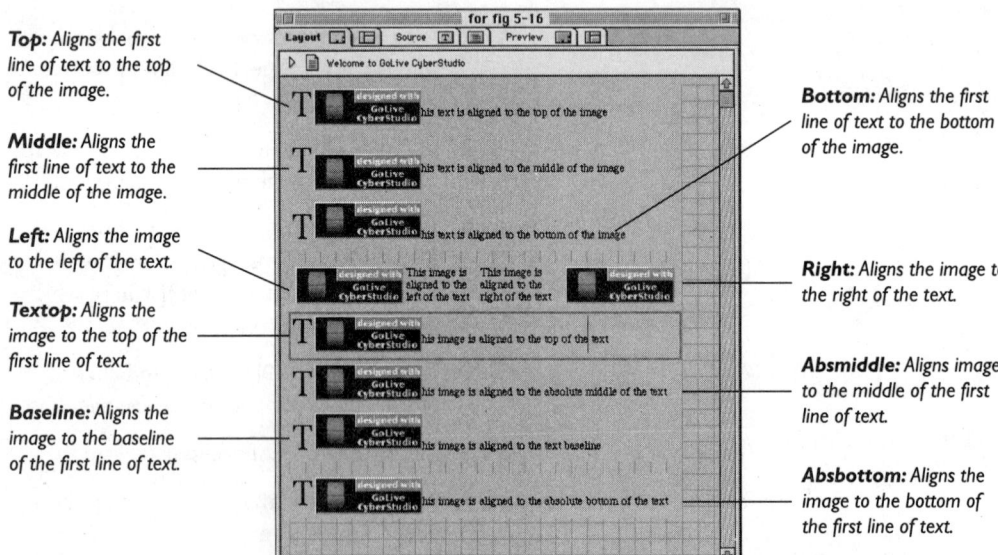

Top: Aligns the first line of text to the top of the image.

Middle: Aligns the first line of text to the middle of the image.

Left: Aligns the image to the left of the text.

Textop: Aligns the image to the top of the first line of text.

Baseline: Aligns the image to the baseline of the first line of text.

Bottom: Aligns the first line of text to the bottom of the image.

Right: Aligns the image to the right of the text.

Absmiddle: Aligns image to the middle of the first line of text.

Absbottom: Aligns the image to the bottom of the first line of text.

Figure 5-19: To align images and text, you must either insert the image into a text frame within a layout grid or work without a layout grid. The illustration shows a text frame with an image aligned to a line of text. The frame is intentionally narrow to show how different alignment affect text wrap and vertical alignment. Here are the options for aligning images to text blocks.

IMAGES

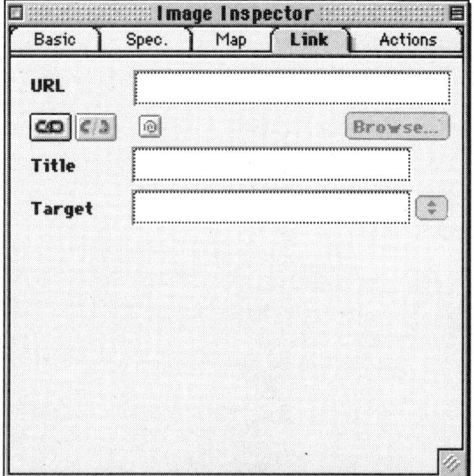

Figure 5-20: The Link tab of the Image Inspector allows you to link or unlink images to Web pages or sites.

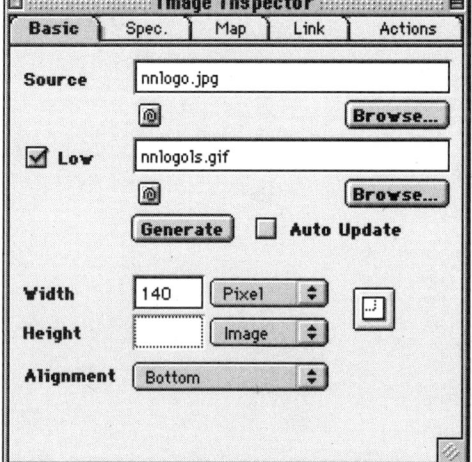

Figure 5-21: Choose a low-resolution image placeholder with the Image Inspector.

2. If you would rather create your own low-res image, use Adobe Photoshop, GraphicConverter or an image manipulation program of your choice to save a low-res version of your original image. Be sure to save the new image as a GIF or JPEG file.

3. Give the low-resolution image a name similar to that of the original (e.g. imagel.gif) and store it in the same folder as the original.

4. In CyberStudio, click on a high-quality image that you have already placed.

5. Under the Basic tab of the Image Inspector window, click the Low checkbox.

6. Click the Browse button next to the checkbox. (See **Figure 5-21**.)

7. Find the low-resolution image you created earlier and click Open.

Setting image preferences

Most of the image-related options you can set in the Preferences window refer to the way images should be dealt with when you import them into a CyberStudio site.

1. Choose Preferences from the Edit menu.

2. Open the General Preferences item by clicking on the triangle next to it.

3. Click Image to view Image Preferences.

4. To choose the default file format Cyber-Studio supports, click Ask User if you want to decide individually, or choose a format from the popup menu, if you want to specify a format. If you choose the GIF format, click the Interlaced checkbox to cause imported GIF images to be transparent.

5. Under the Low Source label, choose how you will handle the generation and storage of low-resolution versions of images.

IMAGES

Clickable image maps

We've seen that you can use an image not only as decoration for your site, but as a link to another location on the Web. Actually, you can include several links within a single image. That arrangement is called a *clickable image map*, and the locations your site's visitors will click on are called hot spots. Some site designers use image maps to add *hot spots* to logos or other large graphics to Web pages. A picture of a car, for example, might include hot spots on the tires, doors and hood, indicating that the user can get more information about these parts of the car by clicking on the appropriate hot spot.

You can invoke image maps in two ways. The first way is from the Web server, using a CGI (Common Gateway Interface) application to support the image map. The second, simpler way is to create *client-side* image maps, which are configured entirely within your Web pages. When you use a client-side image map, neither you as the page designer nor a user clicking on an image map needs to have any interaction with the Web server beyond the usual downloading HTML files and images. Client-side maps, as you can imagine, are easier to work with. GoLive CyberStudio allows you to create client-side maps.

There are two steps to creating a client-side image map; setting up the map and linking hot spots.

To set up a clickable image map:

1. Choose an image with which you will create an image map. The image you choose should be large enough to accommodate several hot spots and should include distinct sections that lend themselves to the image map treatment.

2. Add the image to a CyberStudio document.

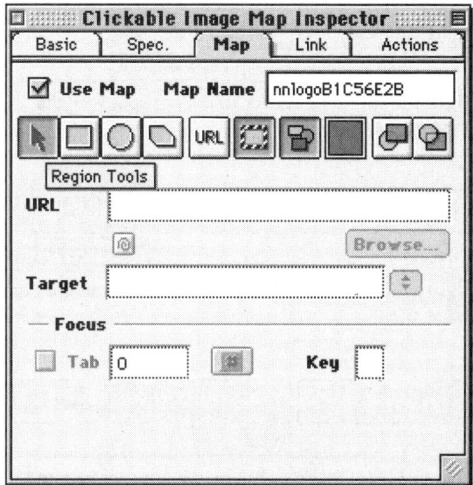

Figure 5-22: The Image Inspector's Map tab looks like this when the Map tools are activated.

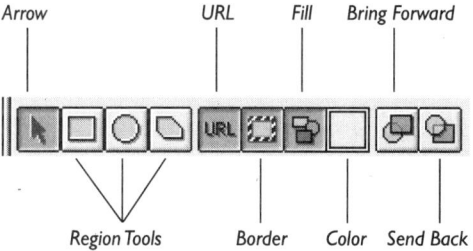

Figure 5-23: The Map toolbar includes the tools illustrated here.

Figure 5-24: Handles on the edges of each hot spot allow you to resize the spot as needed.

3. Using the tools we've described in this chapter, make any necessary changes to the image.

4. Click on the image.

5. In the Inspector window, choose the Map tab.

6. Click the Use Map checkbox to activate the Map tools. The result looks like **Figure 5-22**.

7. Type a name for the image map in the Name field.

   The Image Map toolbar contains the tools you need to create and modify image map hot spots. Refer to **Figure 5-23** for an illustration of all of the available tools.

8. Choose one of the three region tools (rectangle, circle or polygon) that best matches the hot spot shape you want to create.

9. Draw the hot spot on your image. Handles appear at the sides and corners, (**Figure 5-24**) so that you can adjust the size of the hot spot if you need to.

10. With the hot spot selected, type a URL for it in the Inspector window's URL field or click the Browse button and choose a local filet to link to.

11. Repeat steps 8-10 for each hot spot you want to create.

Once you have created hot spots, you can add borders or fill patterns, making it easier for users to see the hot spot. Of course, these patterns work best when preserving the appearance of the underlying image is not a major concern.

To enhance the display of hot spots:

1. With a hot spot selected, click on the Border icon of the Image Inspector Map tab. A border appears around the hot spot, as shown in **Figure 5-25**.

2. Click on the Map tab's Color icon to add color to the hot spot (**Figure 5-26**).

   To use a different color, click the Select Color icon. The Color Picker will appear, allowing you to choose a new color and drag it onto the Color icon.

3. To display a URL on the hot spot, click the URL icon (**Figure 5-27**).

4. To remove a border, color or URL, click the appropriate Map tab icon to toggle it off. You can use any combination of border, color and URL with your image map.

You can use the Arrow icon to resize or move hot spots and the Bring Forward or Send to Back items to work with hot spots that overlap one another.

Figure 5-25: Add a border to the hot spot with the Border tool.

Figure 5-26: Change the hot spot's color with the Color tool.

Figure 5-27: Display a URL on the hot spot with the URL tool.

CLICKABLE IMAGE MAPS

Figure 5-28: Add a hollow (left) or solid (right) line with the appropriate palette tool.

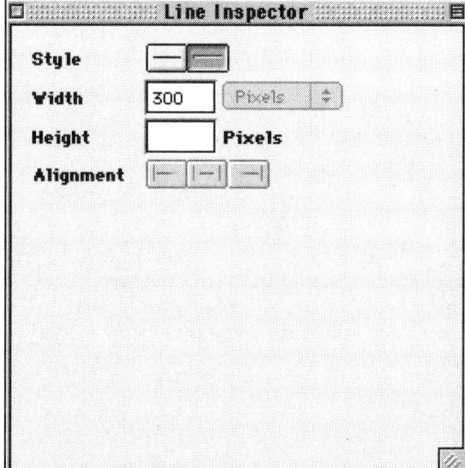

Figure 5-29: You configure lines with the Line Inspector.

Lines

You can use lines to divide your Web page into sections, or simply to give the text and graphics elements a little breathing room. Like most page elements, lines work best when you use a layout grid to position them, although you can work without a grid.

You can vary the appearance of lines by thickness and color.

To insert a horizontal line:

1. With a CyberStudio document open to the Layout View, drag the Line tool from the palette to the document window. **Figure 5-28** shows the tool.

2. When you add a horizontal line, the Inspector window displays the Line Inspector (**Figure 5-29**). By default the Hollow Line icon is highlighted.

✔ Tips

- You can shorten or lengthen a line by dragging one of its handles or by changing the value in the Line Inspector's Width field.

- When using layout grids, you can fit a line within a grid or text frame by dragging the line tool into the desired grid or frame. The line will snap to the width of the grid or frame.

- Even if you're not using grids, you can create lines that drop easily into place. To create a line next to an image, for example, place the image first and drag the line tool into place next to the image. The line is drawn to fill the available space.

LINES

To configure a line:

1. Click on a line you've created to select it. The Line Inspector appears.

2. To change the line from hollow to solid, click the Style button in the Line Inspector that matches your choice.

3. Note the measurement (it's in pixels) in the Width field and type a new one to shorten or lengthen the line.

4. In the Height field, type a number (in pixels) to change the thickness of the line.

5. If you are not using a layout grid, and want to measure the line in pixels or as a percentage of the width of the document window, choose one of the alignment buttons (**Figure 5-30**). The line will be aligned to the left, center or right side of the document window.

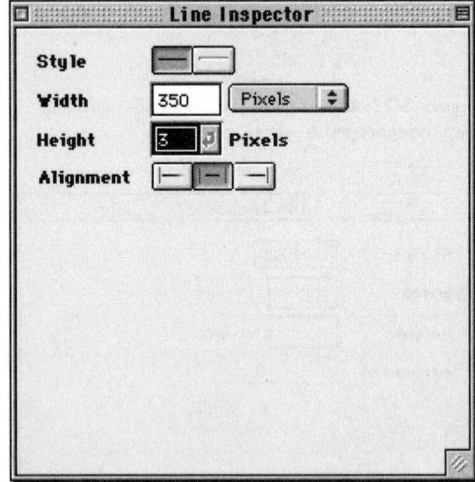

Figure 5-30: The left, center and right alignment buttons align lines to the document window and are only visible when the line is not on a layout grid.

LINES

Spacers

Spacers create room between elements on the page, making it easier to combine text and objects or to create desired text effects. Unlike alignment tags, which position items relative to other items, spacers enforce absolute boundaries. Spacers are especially useful when you work without a layout grid. Most of what they do can be accomplished by positioning objects on grids.

✔ Tip

- Spacers can be very helpful when you design pages specifically to be viewed with version 3.0 or later of Netscape Navigator, because Navigator can interpret spacer tags. Internet Explorer and other browsers, however, do not work as well with spacers. If absolute positioning of text or objects is important to your layout, consider the tools available with Cascading Style Sheets discussed in Chapter 11.

CyberStudio can create three types of spacers; horizontal, vertical and block spacers.

- *Horizontal spacers* are most useful in formatting lines of text. Insert one at the beginning or end of a line to precisely control line breaks or the width of an area of white space.

- *Vertical spacers* can work like line breaks to divide text blocks, or they can be used to correctly position images relative to the text above or below them.

- *Block spacers* are two-dimensional, meaning that you can create a square or rectangle to separate items on your page. Use a block spacer to create indents (when you're not using a layout grid or when you want to position text without using list tags to create indents).

To insert a horizontal spacer:

1. With a document open to the Layout View, drag the Horizontal Spacer tool (**Figure 5-31**) from the palette to the document window.

2. Position the spacer between words in a paragraph or headline. The text moves to accommodate the spacer (**Figure 5-32**).

3. Click on the spacer to select it. The Inspector window changes to display the Spacer Inspector (**Figure 5-33**).

4. Lengthen the spacer by typing a number (in pixels) in the Width field of the Inspector window or by dragging one of the spacer's handles.

To insert a vertical spacer:

1. With a document open to the Layout View, drag the Spacer tool from the palette to the document window.

2. Click the Vertical radio button.

3. Position the spacer between two lines of text that you want to separate. By default, the vertical spacer is 12 pixels in height (**Figure 5-34**).

4. Click on the spacer to select it. The Spacer Inspector is displayed. This time the Vertical button is selected, and the Height field is editable (**Figure 5-35**).

5. Resize the spacer by typing a number (in pixels) in the Height field of the Inspector or by dragging the spacer's handle.

Figure 5-31: The Spacer tool.

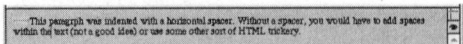

Figure 5-32: A horizontal spacer can create a paragraph indent.

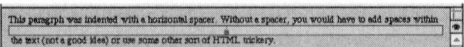

Figure 5-34: A vertical spacer creates space between text blocks.

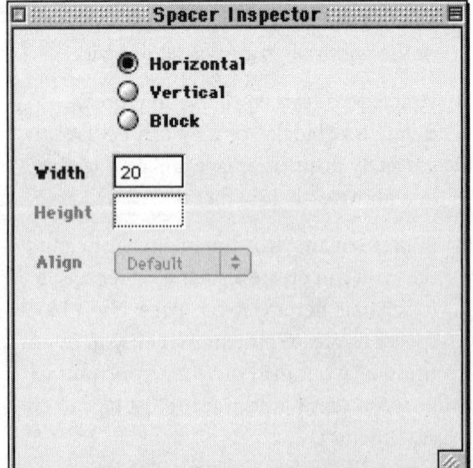

Figure 5-33: The Spacer Inspector includes tools for lengthening a spacer or changing its orientation.

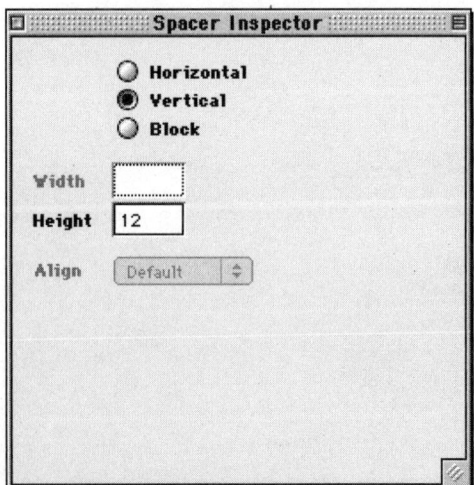

Figure 5-35: The Spacer Inspector allows you to change the spacer's height.

SPACERS

Spacer Inspector
Horizontal
Vertical
Block
Width
12
Height
24
Align
Default

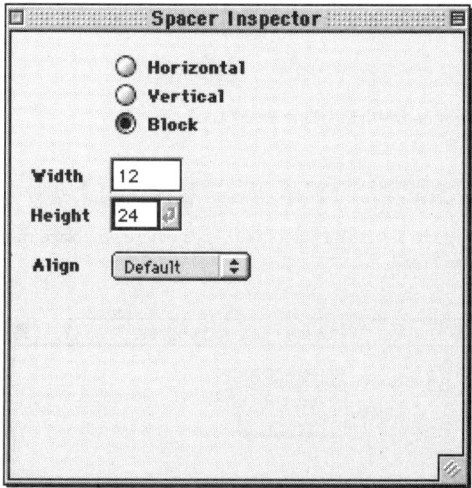

Figure 5-36: Choosing the Block Spacer button lights up the other fields in the Spacer Inspector.

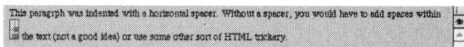

Figure 5-37: Block spacers are two-dimensional, whereas horizontal and vertical spacers are one-dimensional.

This paragrph was indented
within the text (not a good idea)

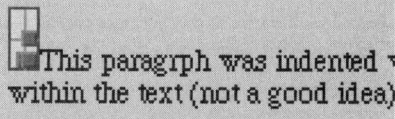

Figure 5-38: The block spacer creates horizontal and vertical space to the left of the text block. But the spacer isn't yet aligned properly.

To insert a block spacer:

1. With the vertical spacer you've just created selected, click the Block button in the Spacer Inspector. The Width, Height and Alignment fields are now editable (**Figure 5-36**), and the vertical spacer has changed to a small block (**Figure 5-37**).
2. Move the spacer to the beginning of the text block. The result appears in **Figure 5-38**.
3. Change the spacer's dimensions by using the Width and Height fields or by dragging the spacer's handles.
4. Align the block spacer to the left edge of the text by choosing Left from the Alignment menu. The rules for aligning block spacers are the same as those for aligning images. For a full description of alignment options, read the Images section of this chapter.

   The block spacer now indents the entire paragraph shown in **Figure 5-39**.

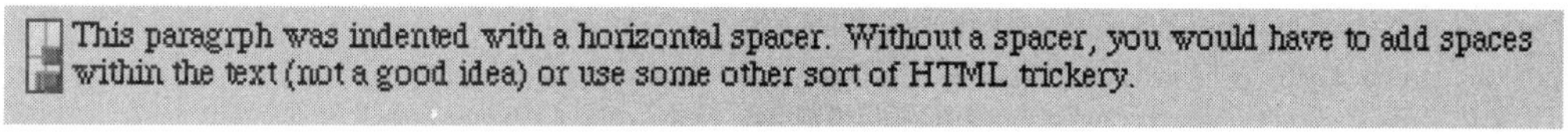

This paragrph was indented with a horizontal spacer. Without a spacer, you would have to add spaces within the text (not a good idea) or use some other sort of HTML trickery.

Figure 5-39: Aligning a block spacer to the left indents a full paragraph.

Line breaks

Because Web users' screens come in different sizes, and because Web browsers display pages in a variety of ways, lines of text do not always break where you want them to and certainly do not break in the same place every time. Manually inserting a line break forces the text to behave predictably.

To create a line break:

1. With a document open to the Layout View, drag the Line Break tool from the palette (**Figure 5-40**) into a paragraph containing several lines of text. The line now ends at the point where you insert the line break (**Figure 5-41**).

2. Click on the line break to select it.

3. In the Line Break Inspector window, check the Clear checkbox to have line breaks occur below an image (**Figure 5-42**).

The All, Left and Right options have the following effects:

■ *All*—text breaks below a left- or right-aligned image.

■ *Left*—text breaks below a left-aligned image.

■ *Right*—text breaks below a right-aligned image.

If you don't click the Clear box, line breaks will occur exactly where you place the line break item.

✔ Tip

■ You don't need the palette tool to insert a line break. You can create a line break at the insertion point by pressing Shift-Return.

Figure 5-40: The Line Break tool.

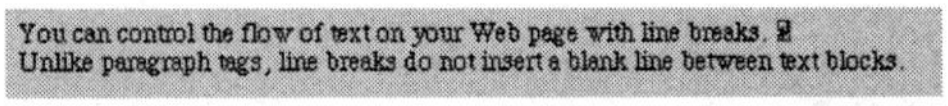

You can control the flow of text on your Web page with line breaks. ¶
Unlike paragraph tags, line breaks do not insert a blank line between text blocks.

Figure 5-41: The line of text ends where you place the line break.

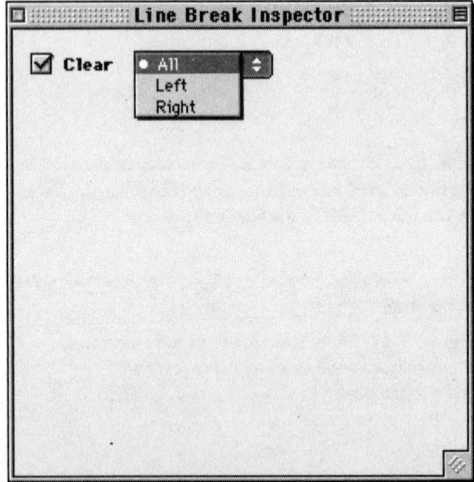

Figure 5-42: Choosing Clear within the Line Break Inspector reveals the break options.

Figure 5-43: The Table tool.

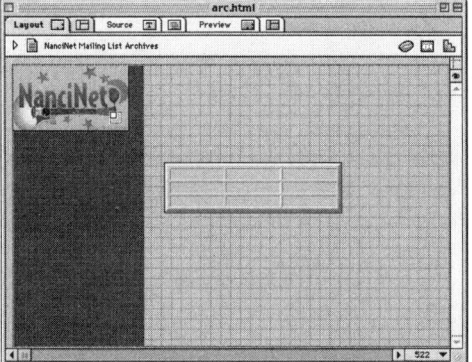

Figure 5-44: Dragging the Table tool onto the document window creates a three-by-three table.

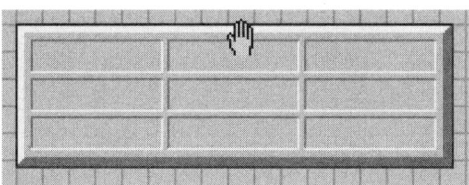

Figure 5-45: Move your mouse to one of the table's borders to select or move the table.

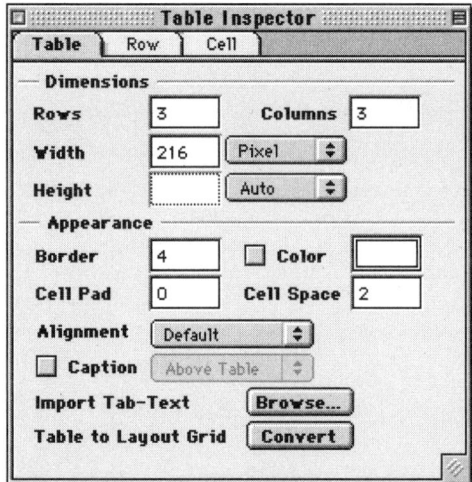

Figure 5-46: The Table Inspector.

Tables

Tables are a versatile HTML feature that you can use to create grid-like page elements such as spreadsheets, calendars or other items that use columns and rows. In many HTML editing applications, tables are also an important design tool, because they allow you to "fake" multi-column layouts in HTML. GoLive CyberStudio employs this fakery but hides it under every layout grid. In fact, if you look at the HTML source for any page with a layout grid, you'll find table tags.

The CyberStudio documentation goes so far as to suggest that you can use the layout grid instead of tables. You can use grids to create columns, or simulate frames, but conventional HTML table-making allows you to create and manage a large number of columns and rows simultaneously.

To create a table:

1. With a document open, drag the Table tool (**Figure 5-43**) from the palette to the document window. You can drag the table tool directly into the window or onto a layout grid. A three-by-three cell table appears in the document window (**Figure 5-44**).

2. Select the table. When you drag the Table tool onto the document window, the resulting table is selected, displaying the Table Inspector. If you deselected the table after you created it, place your cursor on the top, left or right border of the table—the cursor will change into a two-headed arrow on the right border, or into a hand (**Figure 5-45**) on the top or left border. Click the border to view the Table Inspector (**Figure 5-46**).

3. Type **4** in the Rows field.

4. Press Tab. The table expands downward to add new rows.

5. Type **5** in the Columns field.

6. Press Tab. The table expands to the right, adding two columns (**Figure 5-47**).

✔ Tips

■ If adding rows and columns has changed the table's position relative to other items on the page, you can relocate the table. Do this by moving your cursor to the left or top border of the table. When the cursor changes to a hand, click and drag the border to move the table to the desired location.

■ Clicking on the top or left border is also the quickest way to delete an entire table. Click and then press the Delete key.

Resizing tables

You can resize table cells, rows and columns, and even the table itself by dragging table gridlines or by typing values into the appropriate fields in the Table Inspector.

✔ Tip

■ If you plan to add rows and columns to a table, it's a good idea to do so *before* resizing the table, because placing new cells will expand the table.

To resize a table horizontally:

1. Move the cursor to the right edge of the table. The cursor changes to a dark blue, two-sided arrow. (**Figure 5-48**)

2. Drag the border to the left to shrink the table horizontally. All of the cells decrease in size proportionally.

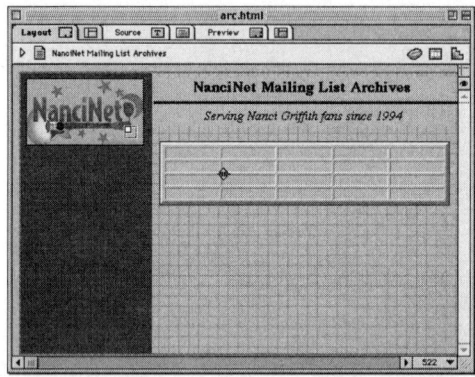

Figure 5-47: Adding rows and column enlarges the table.

Figure 5-48: The dark, two-sided arrow indicates that you are dragging the border of the table.

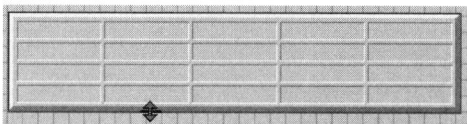

Figure 5-49: The dark blue, two-headed arrow indicates that you are dragging the border of the table.

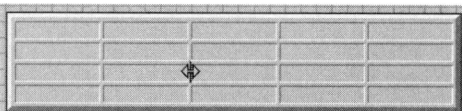

Figure 5-50: With the Option key held down, the cursor changes to a two-sided arrow and allows you to drag cell borders right or left.

Figure 5-51: Placing your cursor on a cell's border and holding down the Option key displays the light blue, two-headed resizing cursor.

Figure 5-52: A marquee appears in the table cell when you select it.

To resize a table vertically:

1. Move the cursor to the lower border of the table and hold down the Option key. The cursor changes to a dark, two-headed arrow (**Figure 5-49**).

2. With the Option key held down, drag the border downward to expand the table vertically. The cells increase in size proportionally.

✔ Tips

■ You can also resize the table using the Inspector. With the table selected, be sure that the Table tab is visible and type values (in pixels) in the Width and Height fields.

■ By default, the Inspector displays the width of a table in pixels. The first time you drag the table's border to resize the table vertically, the Inspector's Height measurement changes from Auto to Pixel and allows you to edit the table height from the Inspector.

■ When the table's height is measured in pixels, you need not hold down the Option key in order to change its dimensions. As you've seen, using the Option key the first time you resize the table resets the measurement scheme to pixels.

To resize a column:

1. Place your cursor on the right border of an interior cell of the table. Hold down the Option key. The cursor changes to a two-sided arrow (**Figure 5-50**).

2. Drag the border to the left to shrink the table cell and its column. Unlike resizing the table, resizing columns does not affect adjacent columns, although it does narrow the table as a whole.

TABLES

To resize a row:

1. Place the cursor on the lower border of a cell within the table. Hold down the Option key. The cursor changes to a two-headed arrow (**Figure 5-51** on previous page).

2. Drag the border downward to expand the row. Unlike resizing the table, resizing a row does not affect adjacent rows.

To customize a cell:

1. Click on any border of a cell you want to customize. A marquee appears within the cell (**Figure 5-52** on previous page) and the Table Inspector displays the Cell tab (**Figure 5-53**).

2. To align text to the cell vertically, choose Top, Bottom or Middle from the Vertical Alignment menu.

3. To align text to the cell horizontally, choose Left, Right or Center from the Horizontal Alignment menu.

4. To cause the selected cell to span several rows, enter **3** in the Row Span field. The result appears in **Figure 5-54**.

5. To cause a cell to span multiple columns, enter **3** in the Column Span field. The result appears in **Figure 5-55**.

6. To color the cell, click the Color checkbox and make a choice from the Color Palette.

7. Click the Header Style checkbox to center cell text, and make it bold (see **Figure 5-56**).

8. Click No Text Wrap if you want to prevent text from wrapping at the end of a line.

9. Use the Add Row/Column buttons to add cells to the table. When you click Add Row, a new row is added above the current cell. New columns are inserted to the left of the current cell (**Figure 5-57**).

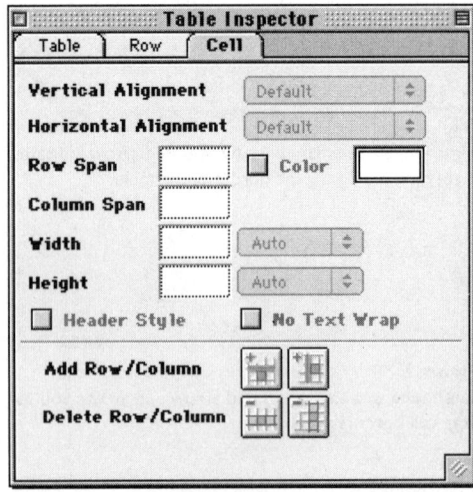

Figure 5-53: The Table Inspector's Cell tab contains tools for customizing individual cells.

1994				December
	January	February	March	April
1995	May	June	July	August
	September	October	November	Decembe

Figure 5-54: A Row Span of 3 looks like this.

1994	Archives begin in December 1994			December
	January	February	March	April
1995	May	June	July	August
	September	October	November	December
1995				
1996				
1997				

Figure 5-55: A Column Span of 3 looks like this.

1994	Digests began in December 1994			December
	January	February	March	April
1995	May	June	July	August
	September	October	November	December

Figure 5-56: Table Headers are centered and appear in bold type.

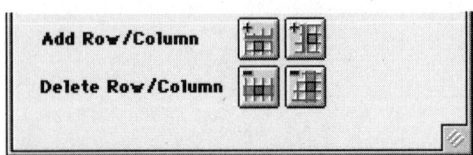

Figure 5-57: You can add or delete individual rows and columns with these buttons. You'll find them under the Table Inspector's Cell tab.

TABLES

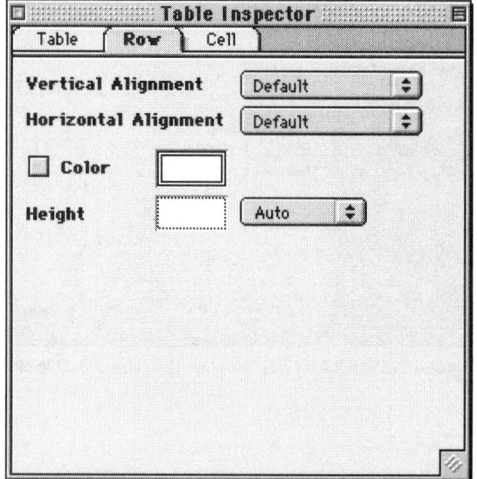

Figure 5-58: The Row tab of the Table Inspector.

✔ Tips

- It is usually easiest to resize cells by dragging their borders, as described in the previous section. But if you want a precise measurement, use the Width and Height fields to resize them. First choose Pixels from the appropriate popup menu, and then enter a value.

- You can format multiple table cells at once by selecting them together. Move your cursor to the border of a table cell and select it. With the Shift key held down, select another cell. Now you can format the cells together, using options in the Table Inspector's Cell tab.

To customize a row:

1. Select a cell within the row you want to customize by clicking on the bottom or right border.

2. In the Table Inspector, choose the Row tab (**Figure 5-59**).

3. Choose an alignment for the row from the Vertical Alignment popup menu. You can align text within the selected row to the top, middle or bottom of the cells.

4. Choose an alignment from the Horizontal Alignment popup menu. You can align text within the selected row to the left, right or center of the cells.

5. Click the Color field to view the Color Picker. Choose a color and drag it to the Color field within the Table Inspector.

6. Choose a custom height for the selected row by selecting Pixels from the Height popup and then typing the height measurement you want.

TABLES

Adding content to a table

HTML tables can include any element you can put on a Web page, including text, images and multimedia objects. You can type directly into the table, use the palette to add objects or drag and drop items into a table.

To add text to a table:

1. Click within a cell of the table.

2. Type the text.

3. Press Tab. The insertion point moves to the next horizontal cell. Tabbing from the last cell in a row moves the insertion point to the first cell in the text row.

✔ Tips

■ When you type text into a table cell, and the text exceeds the visible boundaries of the cell, the cell grows downward to accommodate the text. So, if you're typing the contents of your table from scratch, you should complete the typing before you finish sizing the table cells.

■ When you add an image to a table, either by drag-and-drop or by using the Image Inspector to place the image, the table cell grows to accommodate the image at the size you place it. If you resize the image, the cell's size changes too, though not in direct proportion to the image.

To change the appearance of a table:

1. Select the table by clicking on the top or left border.

2. In the Table Inspector window (under the Table tab), type a value (in pixels) in the "border" field. **Figure 5-59** shows the table with a six-pixel border.

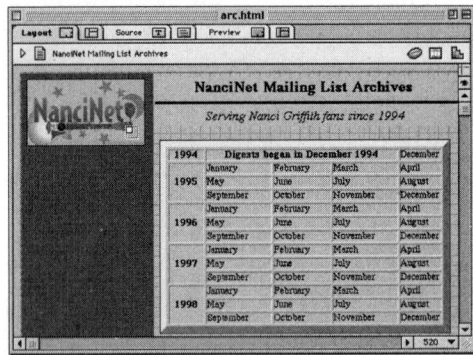

Figure 5-59: A heavy border gives the table a 3-D look.

TABLES

1994	Digests began in December 1994			December
	January	February	March	April
1995	May	June	July	August
	September	October	November	December
	January	February	March	April
1996	May	June	July	August
	September	October	November	December
	January	February	March	April
1997	May	June	July	August
	September	October	November	December
	January	February	March	April
1998	May	June	July	August
	September	October	November	December

Figure 5-60: Even a small amount of padding within a cell provides lots of white space.

Click on a montht link to see a list of daily digest files				
1994				December
	January	February	March	April
1995	May	June	July	August
	September	October	November	December
	January	February	March	April
1996	May	June	July	August
	September	October	November	December
	January	February	March	April
1997	May	June	July	August
	September	October	November	December
	January	February	March	April
1998	May	June	July	August
	September	October	November	December

Figure 5-61: A caption is a cell that spans the full width of the table.

3. Click the Color checkbox and then the Color field to bring up the Color Picker. Choose a color for the table and drag it from the Color Picker into the Color field.

4. Type **2** in the Cell Pad field to create extra vertical space within each cell. **Figure 5-60** shows the table we've been working on, with a two-pixel pad in each cell. The Cell Space field controls the amount of space between cells. By default, tables use a two-cell pad.

5. If you are not using a layout grid, choose an option from the Alignment menu to place the table, relative to the page you're working on. You can align the table to the left or right or leave it unaligned.

To add a caption to a table:

1. Click on the Caption checkbox within the Table Inspector (under the Table tab).

2. Use the adjacent popup menu to place the caption above or below the table.

3. Type a caption in the space created above or below the table (**Figure 5-61**).

✔ Tip

■ When you complete the table, you can choose to convert it into a CyberStudio layout grid. To covert it, click the Convert button in the Inspector window (under the Table tab). When the conversion is complete, the table is replaced by a new layout grid with text frames that include the contents of your table. Be careful when converting tables because this action cannot be undone.

TABLES

Importing table content

You can add content to a table by typing, or by importing the contents of a tab-delimited text file into your CyberStudio document. The fields (which will become table cells) in your file must be separated by tabs, and each record (row) must include a carriage return at the end.

To import table content:

1. Drag the table tool from the Palette into the document window to create a new table.

2. In the Table Inspector, click the Import Tab-Text button.

3. Locate a tab-delimited file in the dialog box that appears. When you click Open, the file's contents appear in the table (**Figure 5-62**).

4. Resize the table, its rows and columns so that the data fits correctly on the page.

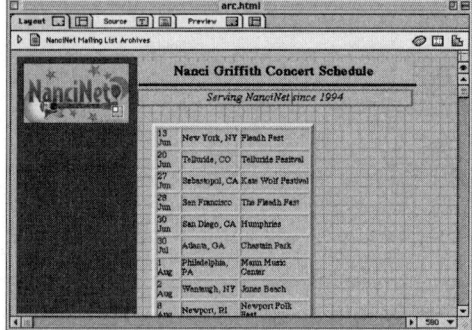

Figure 5-62: When you import text into a new table, chances are that it won't look the way you want it. This newly populated table needs to be resized.

TABLES

Figure 5-63: The Marquee tool.

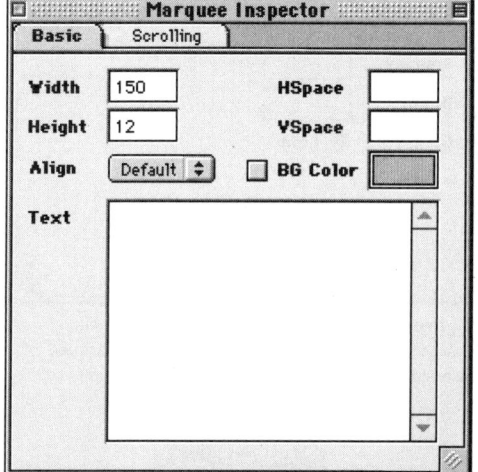

Figure 5-64: The Marquee Inspector opens to the Basic tab when you select a marquee.

These are the archives of the Nanci Griffith Mailing List (Nanci

Figure 5-65: Text appears in the marquee as you type it into the Marquee Inspector window. The marquee need not be as long as the line of text because the text will scroll through the marquee.

- The scrolling marquee is an Internet Explorer-only tag. Only Internet Explorer users can view these elements. If you want to create a marquee-like element that will scroll across the page, use JavaScript and/ or dynamic HTML to do this.

Scrolling marquees

Scrolling marquees actually move. Unlike the other layout tools we've worked with in this chapter, marquees do not just sit there on your Web page. A scrolling marquee is a line of text that scrolls horizontally—à la the famous *New York Times* sign in Times Square—across your Web page.

To create a scrolling marquee:

1. Drag the Marquee tool from the palette to the document window (**Figure 5-63**). You can place it on a layout grid or directly in the window. The Marquee Inspector appears (**Figure 5-64**).

2. With the marquee selected, click on the Inspector window to bring it forward.

3. Type some text into the Text field of the Inspector window. The text becomes visible in the marquee (**Figure 5-65**).

4. To resize the marquee, drag one of its handles or type values (in pixels) into the Width and Height fields in the Inspector window.

✔ Tips

- Because text will be scrolling across the screen, it isn't necessary that the marquee be large enough to display the full line of text. Size the marquee so that it displays the number of words you'd like to be visible at any given time.

- If a marquee is inserted into a text frame, you can align the surrounding text to the top, middle or bottom of the marquee. Choose one of these options from the Alignment popup menu in the Marquee Inspector.

- Use the HSpace and Vspace fields to add horizontal and vertical space, respectively, around the marquee.

To set a marquee's scrolling pattern:

1. Select the marquee in the document window.

2. Click on the Inspector window and choose the Scrolling tab (**Figure 5-66**).

3. Choose a scrolling method for the marquee from the Behavior popup menu (**Figure 5-67**). You can choose from three types of scrolling behavior: *Scroll*: moves the text across the page continuously. *Slide*: moves the text into the marquee box and leaves it there. *Alternate*: moves the text into the marquee and bounces it from side to side.

4. Choose the number of loops you want the marquee to scroll through. You can also click the Forever checkbox to continue scrolling indefinitely. Loops are only available when you choose the Scroll or Alternate pattern.

5. Set scrolling speed by typing a value in the Amount field.

6. Type a value in the Delay field to set the time between loops.

7. Choose a direction to scroll by pressing the Left or Right button.

8. Click on the Preview tab at the top of the document window to view your scroll-ing marquee in action. To change marquee settings, return to the Layout View, select the marquee and open the Marquee Inspector.

✔ Tips

■ If you choose the Alternate scrolling method, make sure that the marquee is wide enough to display the full line of text. Alternate bounces text from one side of the marquee to the other and thus doesn't display text that won't fit in the visible marquee.

■ Try several marquee settings to determine which one best fits your needs. As you set up the marquee, use the Preview View to watch its scrolling method and speed. You should also preview the marquee in one or more Web browsers.

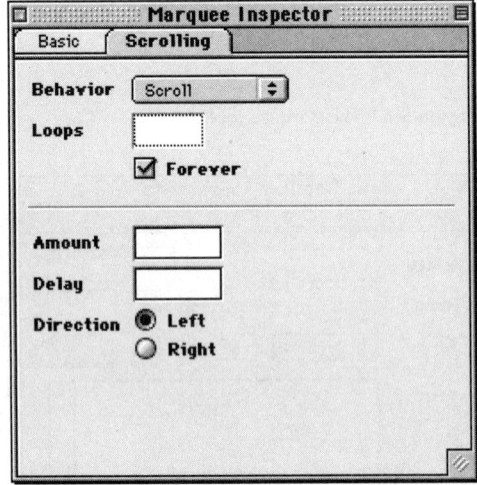

Figure 5-66: Choose the marquee's movement characteristics under the Scroll tab of the Marquee Inspector.

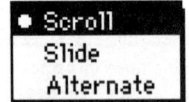

Figure 5-67: The Behavior popup menu.

Figure 5-68: Hold down the Shift key while selecting multiple objects on a layout grid.

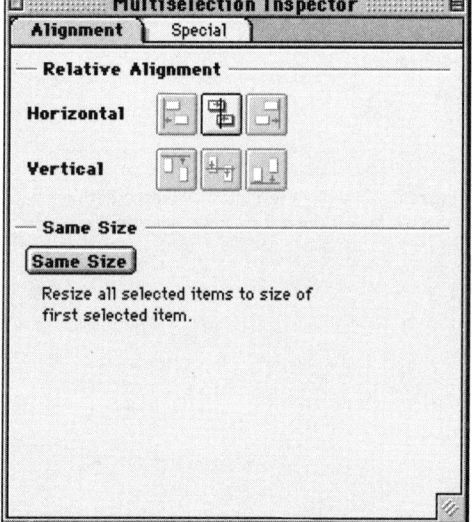

Figure 5-69: The Multiselection Inspector includes tools for aligning objects you've selected.

Figure 5-70: Align objects to the layout grid itself with tools from the Layout Toolbar.

Working with multiple objects

CyberStudio 3.1 includes the very useful ability to select and work with multiple objects on a layout grid. Like most drawing programs, CyberStudio allows you to align and distribute objects in relation one another and group them so that you can work with them together.

To work with multiple objects:

1. Open a document with several objects on a single layout grid.

2. Select one object, then a second, by holding down the Shift key while you click on the objects. Just as you would when selecting any object on a layout grid, be sure that the cursor has changed to a hand before you click on an object.

   With multiple objects selected (**Figure 5-68**) the layout grid toolbar takes the place of the formatting toolbar, and the Multiselection Inspector appears.

3. Use the Relative Alignment buttons in the Multiselection Inspector (**Figure 5-69**) to align the left, center or right edges of selected objects horizontally.

4. Use the top, middle and bottom buttons in the Inspector to align objects vertically.

5. If you want to align the selected objects to the layout grid, use the alignment tools on the toolbar (**Figure 5-70**). You can also use the toolbar to align objects to one another.

✔ Tips

- If you select objects and find that an alignment choice is dimmed, and not usable, it is either because the two objects cannot be aligned with that choice, or because they are already in alignment.

- If you align objects and don't like the results, choose Undo from the Edit menu before you do anything else, and the objects will return to their original position.

To resize aligned objects

1. Choose a group of objects that you want to align and that should also be the same size. This option is useful when you are creating lines, form elements or other objects that form part of a larger layout.

2. Select the object whose size you want the other objects to take on.

3. With the Shift key held down, select the other objects and align them in the Multi-selection Inspector. **Figure 5-71** shows a set of objects at their original size. Note that they are aligned but have different lengths.

4. Click the Same Size button in the Inspector window. The horizontally aligned objects are now the same length (**Figure 5-72**).

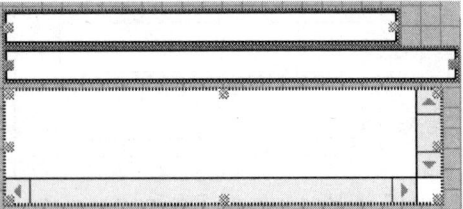

Figure 5-71: These selected objects are aligned, but are of different widths.

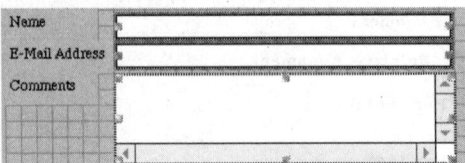

Figure 5-72: Using the Same Size button in the Inspector makes these form fields uniform in size.

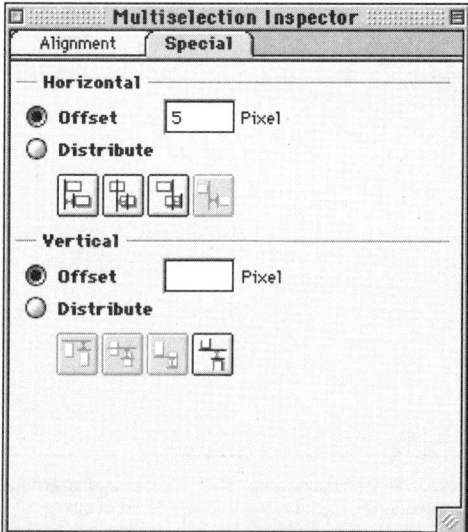

Figure 5-73: The Special tab of the Multiselection Inspector

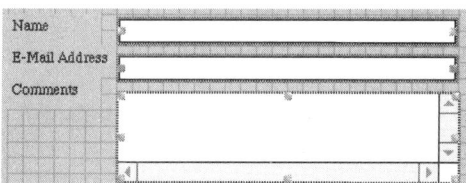

Figure 5-74: An offset adds space between or around selected objects.

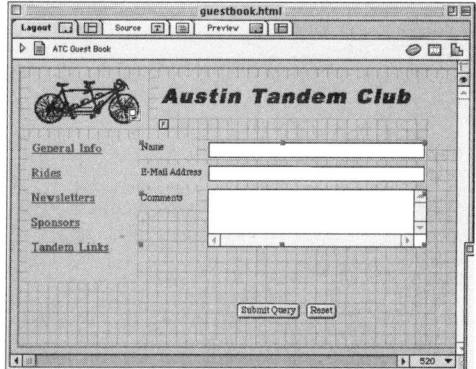

Figure 5-75: Grouped objects has one set of handles, and can be moved as a single object.

To distribute or set objects off from one another:

1. Choose several objects to work with.

2. Click the Special tab of the Multiselection Inspector. It looks like **Figure 5-73**).

3. Click the Offset button under the Vertical label.

4. Enter a number (in pixels). Entering 6 creates 6 pixels of space between the form fields (**Figure 5-74**).

5. Select the labels and enter the same offset, so that labels and fields remain even within another. Because you cannot arrange objects vertically that have a horizontal relationship (and vice versa) we need to offset the field labels separately from the fields themselves.

To group objects:

1. Select several objects and align or distribute them as you like.

2. Click the Group button on the toolbar. The objects' individual selection handles become one large set of handles surrounding the newly grouped object (**Figure 5-75**).

3. Drag the grouped object. All the elements move together, allowing you to position the complete set of objects.

4. When you create a group, the Inspector changes to the Group Inspector. Here, you can choose to lock the group so that its elements will continue to move together.

5. To break up a group, choose Ungroup from the toolbar.

The Custom tab

In addition to the tabs full of tools you can use to add HTML tags and objects to your Web page, the palette contains one tab that's all yours. You can use the Custom tab to store layout grids—and their contents—and other Web page elements that you want to be able to reuse.

To add an item to the Custom tab:

1. In the palette, click on the Custom tab to make it visible (**Figure 5-76**).

2. In the document window, locate an item or group you want to save.

3. Drag the item into the Palette window. An icon representing the item you've chosen appears under the Custom tab.

✔ Tips

■ Saving templates in the Custom tab is another great reason to use several layout grids on your page. You can add all of your standing elements to a single grid, move it to the Favorites tab and reuse it whenever you like.

■ When dragging a layout grid containing lots of items, you may have to click and hold the mouse button for a second or two before the grid begins to move.

To use items under the Custom tab:

1. Open a document where you want to use the saved material.

2. Click the Custom tab of the palette to open it.

3. Drag an icon for the desired item from the palette into the document window.

Figure 5-76: Click on the palette's Custom tab to open it. My custom tab holds images and layout grids.

WORKING WITH LINKS

Hyperlinks are as essential to the World Wide Web as PostScript is to modern desktop publishing. Links between Web pages make it possible to for people to jump instantly (surf) from place to place on the Internet.

Using links effectively is also an integral part of building a useful Web site. You use links to move visitors from page to page and to provide points of reference (in the form of navigation bars and tables of contents) for your site.

GoLive CyberStudio provides several ways to create links and supports the various kinds of links that are standard parts of the HTML language.

In this chapter, I cover:

- How links work.

- Linking to remote sites.

- Local links.

- Using anchors.

- Link warnings.

How links work

An HTML link is basically a pointer from a Web page to another item (Web page, FTP server, newsgroup or e-mail address, for example) on the Internet. Links are usually designated visually on the Web page by underlining and/or a custom color. Images or multimedia files can also be used as links. Links have two parts: a URL (Universal Resource Locator) and a descriptive label. When a Web site visitor clicks on a link's label, the Web browser uses the link's URL to locate the desired item. The browser then displays, downloads or connects to the item. (see **Figure 6-1**).

Links can point to other pages within a Web site, to a remote Web site, or non-Web resources, including FTP servers, newsgroups and e-mail addresses. Some links point to locations on the same page as the link: these links are called *anchors* and are used to make it easier to navigate through long documents (see **Figure 6-2**).

While using CyberStudio, you will find several ways to create each type of link. You will also find that the Site window and Point & Shoot make creating and managing links much easier.

Figure 6-1: Clicking on the PBS link sends a request across the Internet to the PBS site and returns the appropriate Web page.

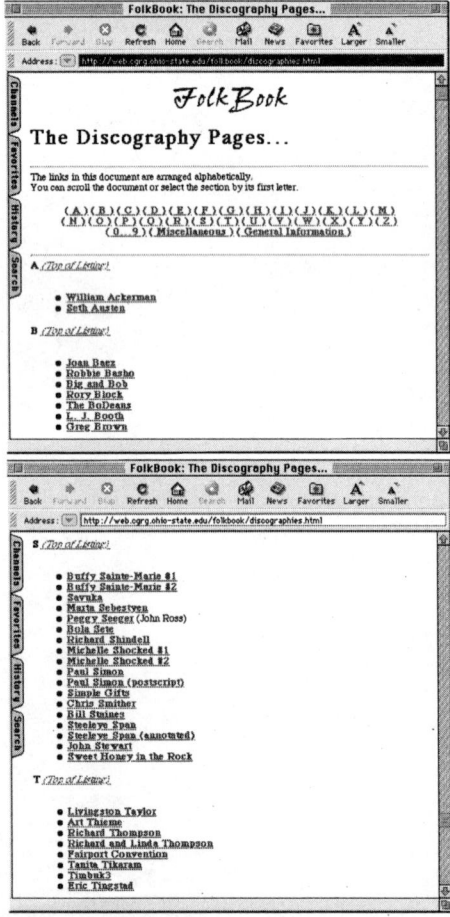

Figure 6-2: The alphabet at the top of the FolkBook Artists' Page includes anchors that connect to the site's roster of artists, all of which are on the same page.

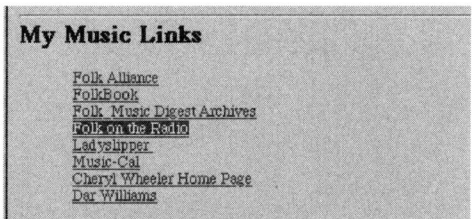

Figure 6-3: Text links should be short but descriptive.

Figure 6-4: Use the Link icon from the toolbar to create a link.

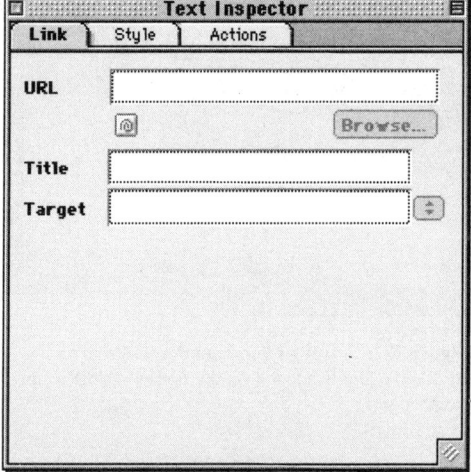

Figure 6-5: Enter your link's URL in the Text Inspector.

Creating remote links

CyberStudio supports two strategies for creating links from your Web site to remote resources, including other sites, e-mail addressees, newsgroups, and downloadable files. These strategies are:

- Creating links manually.

- Using links stored within a site.

To create a link manually:

1. In the Layout view, select some text (a single word or short phrase) or an object that you would like to link to a remote resource (**Figure 6-3**).

2. Click on the Link icon on the toolbar (**Figure 6-4**). The Text Inspector window becomes visible (**Figure 6-5**) and displays the link tab.

3. Type a complete URL in the URL field of the Inspector window.

4. Optionally, you can type the title of the item you are linking to in the Title field.

CREATING REMOTE LINKS

Using links stored within a site

In addition to Web pages and media files, you can store pointers to external URLs and e-mail addressees within a CyberStudio site. Once these resources are part of the site, you can link to them and keep track of them as easily as you do local files. I'll cover creating and importing external resources in Chapter 16, but for now, I'll use Point & Shoot to create a link to an external Web site.

To add a link with Point & Shoot:

1. Open a CyberStudio site.

2. Open a document by double-clicking on it in the Files tab of the Site window.

3. In the Site window, click on the Exteranl tab to display external resources that you have stored there (**Figure 6-6**).

4. If there is a URLs folder under the External tab, open it by clicking the triangle on the left.

5. In the document window, select the text or object that you want to link.

6. Command-click the selection and drag the resulting line to the Site window.

7. Stop dragging when your cursor is over the URL you want to link to and let go of the mouse button (**Figure 6-7**).

8. Verify that the link is complete in the Link tab of the Text Inspector (**Figure 6-8**).

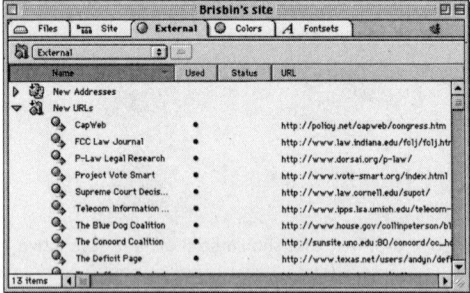

Figure 6-6: Store resources (including Web and FTP site URLs) that you want to use in your site under the External tab in the Site window.

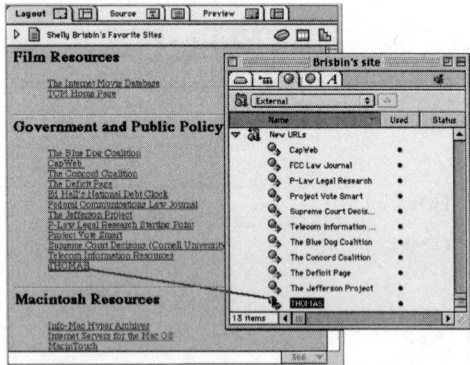

Figure 6-7: Drawing a line from the selection to a URL in the Site window links the text or object to the external site.

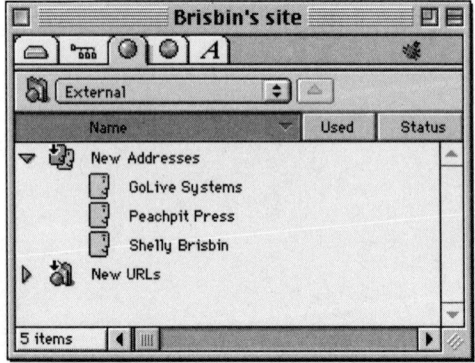

Figure 6-8: With the insertion point positioned within the new text link, the Inspector shows the URL your text is linked to.

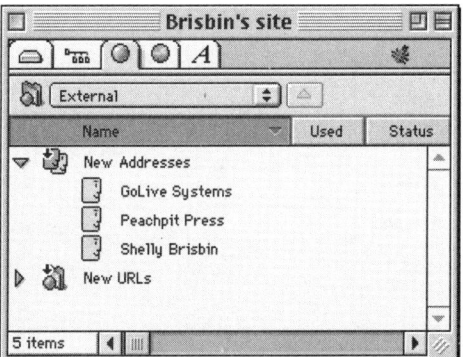

Figure 6-9: The Addresses folder of the Site window stores e-mail addresses you can link to from your Web site.

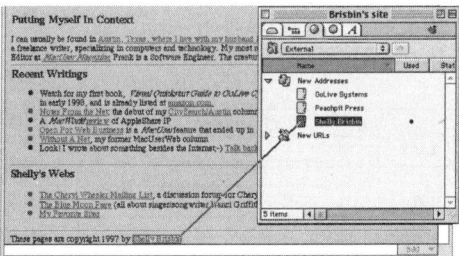

Figure 6-10: Drawing a line from the selection to an address in the Site window will link the text or object to the e-mail address.

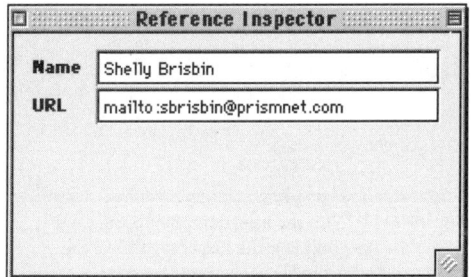

Figure 6-11: With the insertion point positioned within the new text link, the Link Inspector shows the URL for the address your text is linked to.

Linking to an e-mail address

You can create a link between a Web page and an e-mail address with Point & Shoot. When the link is clicked, the site visitor's browser switches to an e-mail interface or opens an e-mail application, depending on how the user's system is configured.

To add an e-mail address with Point & Shoot:

1. Follow steps 1–3 in the preceding section.

2. If there is an Addresses folder under the External tab, open it by clicking the triangle on the left (see **Figure 6-9**).

3. In the document window, select the text or object you want to link.

4. Command-click the selection and drag the resulting line to the Site window.

5. Stop dragging when your cursor is over the address you want to link to and let go of the mouse button (**Figure 6-10**).

6. Verify that the link is complete in the Link Inspector (**Figure 6-11**).

CREATING REMOTE LINKS

Creating local links

Local links are those that connect a Web page to other portions of your Web site, whether they be another page, an image or a multimedia object. In this section, I concentrate on links to other pages. There are three ways to create a local link:

- Use the Link Inspector and toolbar to locate files you want to link.

- Use Point & Shoot to link pages within your project.

- Use the Page icon to link open files.

✔ Tip

- You don't need to be working in a Cyber-Studio site to use the Link Inspector or Page icon method of linking local files. These methods also work when you're editing individual pages, too.

To link files with the Inspector and the toolbar:

1. In the document window, select some text that you would like to link to another file in your Web site.

2. Choose the Link icon from the toolbar. The dimmed fields of the Text Inspector's Link tab brighten up.

3. In the Inspector window, click the Browse button (**Figure 6-12**).

4. In the dialog box that appears, locate the file you want to link to and press Open. The relative URL appears in the URL field of the Inspector window (**Figure 6-13**), and the linked text is underlined in the document window.

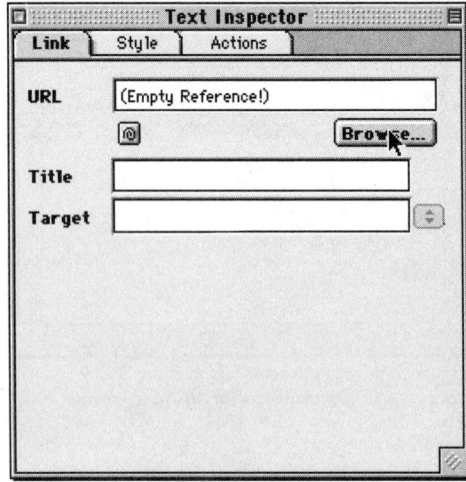

Figure 6-12: Clicking the Browse button gives you access to the files on your hard disk.

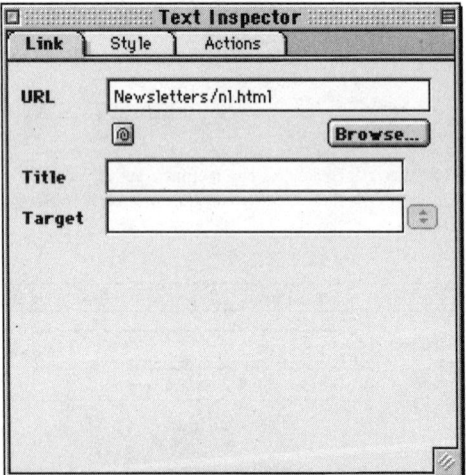

Figure 6-13: With the insertion point positioned within the new text link, the Inspector shows the relative URL for the file your text is linked to.

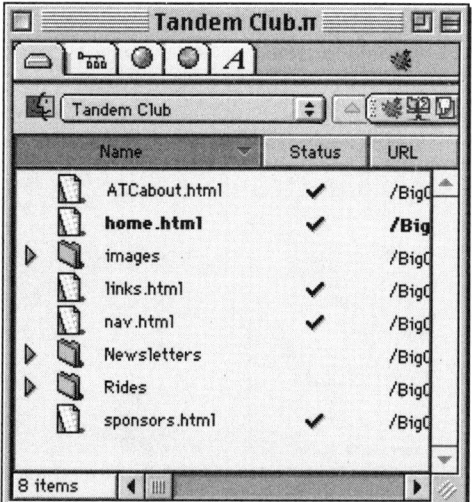

Figure 6-14: The Site window's Files tab contains the pages that make up your Web site.

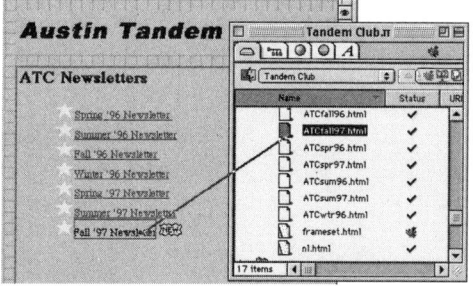

Figure 6-15: Drawing a line from the selection to a file in the Site window links the text or object to another file within your Web site.

✔ Tip

■ *Relative* URLs are those that point to objects within your Web site and that don't include the full **http://www.etc.com** URL. In **Figure 6-13**, the URL indicates that the file it refers to is located in a subdirectory of the file from which it was linked.

To link files with Point & Shoot:

1. Open a CyberStudio site.

2. Open a document by double-clicking it from the Site window.

3. If the file you want to link to is not already part of your site, add it by dragging it into the Site window before proceeding to step 4.

4. In the Site window, click on the Files tab to display pages within your project (**Figure 6-14**).

5. In the document window, select some text or an object that you would like to link.

6. Command-click the text.

7. While holding down the mouse button, drag into the Site window, creating a line as you drag.

8. Stop dragging when your cursor is over the file you want to link to and let go of the mouse button (**Figure 6-15**).

9. You can verify that the link is complete in the Link Inspector.

To create a link with the Page icon:

1. With a document open, select some text or an object that you would like to link.

2. Open another document.

3. Position the new document onscreen so that you can see the portion of the first document that contains the selected text or object.

4. Drag the Page icon at the top of the document window onto the selected text or object in your destination document (**Figure 6-16**). The link is complete.

✔ Tip

■ You can use the Page icon method whether you're working within a project or simply constructing individual pages. If you're working with a Site, using Point & Shoot is an easier way to link.

To edit a local link in the Inspector:

1. Open the file containing the link you want to change.

2. Click on the link. The Text Inspector window is now visible.

3. In the Inspector window, click Browse.

4. Locate the new file you want to link to and click Open. The new link is complete.

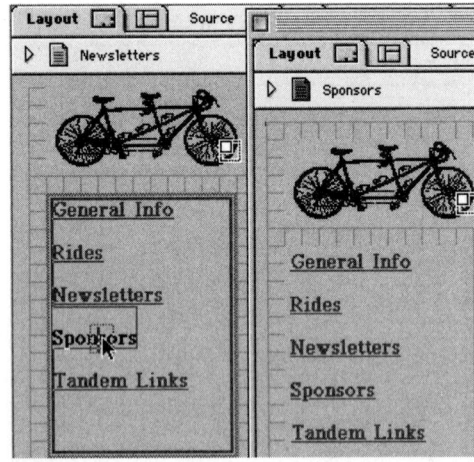

Figure 6-16: Dragging a document's Page icon onto a selection creates a link.

To edit a link from within a site

If you rename or move a page within your site, you will need to relink items that point to it.

1. Open a site, if one isn't already open.

2. Open the file containing the link you want to move.

3. If you are linking to an external URL or an e-mail address, click on the External tab in the Site window. Otherwise, proceed to step 4.

4. In the document window, Command-click on the link.

5. Drag the resulting line to the Site window.

6. Let go of the mouse button when the line connects with the new link point. The new link is complete.

To delete a link:

1. Click on a link so that the insertion point is within the text of the link, or the linked object is selected.

2. From the toolbar, choose the Unlink icon. The link is deleted.

Anchors

Anchors are a special kind of link. Rather than linking one page to another, anchors are usually used to navigate within a single page. Sometimes, they are used to cause a Web page to open to a location in the middle rather than at the top of the page.

You can create an anchor two ways:

■ Use Point & Shoot to create links to an anchor point.

■ Use the palette's Anchor tool to create anchors and link to them.

The link-to-anchor method works best if you're creating a single link that connects to a single anchor. Reversing the process by creating the anchor first is the best choice if you plan to create several links that point to a single anchor point.

To link to an anchor:

1. With a document open to the Layout View, select the text or object you would like to link.

2. Command-click the text or object and drag the resulting line through the document until you reach the point where you would like the anchor to appear (**Figure 6-17**).

3. Release the mouse button. An anchor icon appears (**Figure 6-18**). The Link Inspector is now visible and displays a unique anchor name.

✔ Tip

■ As always, it's a good idea to check your work by previewing it. For best results, open your document in a Web browser rather than CyberStudio's Preview mode.

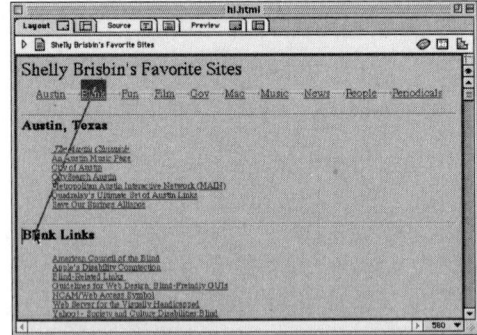

Figure 6-17: Command-click on the link you want to create and drag to the anchor location.

Figure 6-18: When the anchor is complete, the anchor icon appears.

Figure 6-19: The Anchor tool from the palette.

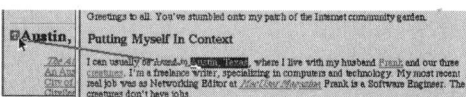

Figure 6-20: Point & Shoot from the link to the anchor.

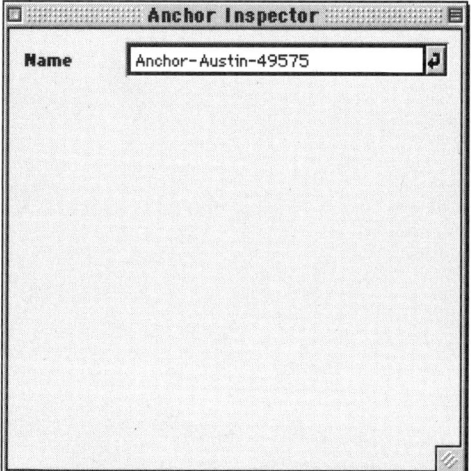

Figure 6-21: The Anchor Inspector appears when you drag the Anchor tag to the document window.

To create an anchor that will support multiple links:

1. Drag the Anchor (**Figure 6-19**) tool from the palette to the document window. An anchor icon appears, and the Anchor Inspector is displayed in the Inspector window (**Figure 6-20**).

2. In the Anchor Inspector window, type a unique, one-word name for the anchor.

3. Locate some text or an object (in the current document or any other document) that you would like to link to the anchor you just created.

4. Select the text or object and Command-click the selection.

5. Drag the resulting line to the anchor you created earlier and release the mouse button (**Figure 6-21**). The link is now complete.

6. Repeat steps 3 and 4 to add links to the anchor you've created.

When a web page visitor clicks on the new link, the anchor point comes into view. If the anchor appears in a different document, that document opens and displays the anchor location.

✔ Tip

■ You can create as many links to a single anchor as you like, from any number of documents. Just Point & Shoot from each link to the anchor.

To move an anchor:

In the document window, click on the anchor's icon and drag it to its new location on the page. Any links you've created will now point to the new location.

To delete an anchor:

1. In a document, click on an anchor icon to select it.

2. Press the Delete key to remove the anchor. Now, you need to remove links to the anchor you've just deleted.

3. Locate a link you have created and click on it, so that the insertion point is within the text or the object is selected.

4. Click the Unlink icon in the toolbar. The link is removed.

✔ Tip

- Removing a link does not delete the text or object you previously linked. It simply deletes the pointer between that item and another.

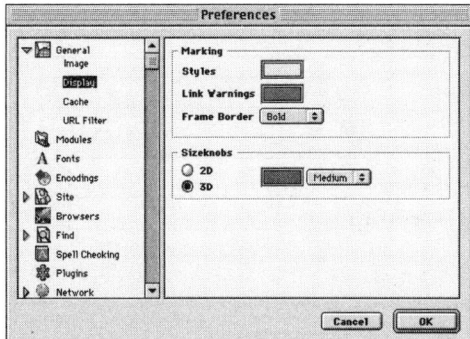

Figure 6-22: Change Link Warning preferences under the General:Display pane of CyberStudio's Preferences window.

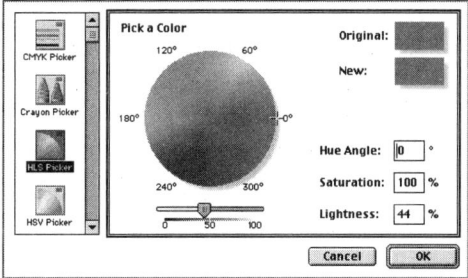

Figure 6-23: Pick a Link Warning color from the Mac OS Color Picker.

Link warnings

CyberStudio can alert you to broken links using a variety of link warnings. You can turn link warnings on and off to determine the status of your links. By default, problem links are highlighted in red.

To change the color of link warnings:

1. Choose Preferences from the Edit menu.

2. Click the triangle next to the General label in the left side of the Preferences window to view more options.

3. Click the Display label. The resulting screen (**Figure 6-22**) includes a color box for changing the appearance of link warnings.

4. Click on the color box. The Apple Color Palette appears (**Figure 6-23**).

5. Choose a color from one of the panels. If you need help with the color picker, see your Mac OS documentation.

6. Click OK. The new color appears in the Link Warnings color box.

7. Click OK to close the Preferences dialog box.

LINK WARNINGS

To locate errors with link warnings:

1. Choose Show Link Warnings from the Edit menu. If the Edit menu command says "Hide Link Warnings" instead, link warnings are already available. Proceed to the next step.

2. Scroll through your document to locate links that are highlighted (in the color you chose when you set Link Warnings preferences).

3. When you locate a broken link click on it to place your cursor within the link. The Text Inspector appears, displaying the broken link and the bug symbol that alerts you to the problem (**Figure 6-24**).

4. Repair the link.

✔ Tip

■ CyberStudio will display link warnings for images and multimedia files, too. The procedure for finding and fixing broken links is exactly the same. When an image or media file link is broken, you'll see a red (or whatever color you want to use for link warnings) border around the image box. Of course, you'll also notice that the image itself is missing, since its link is no longer in place.

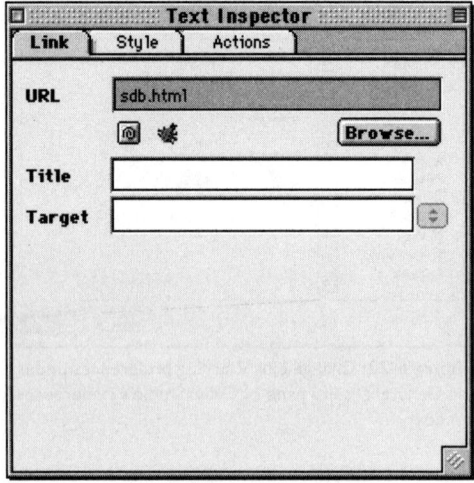

Figure 6-24: The Text Inspector displays the link and the bug icon that indicates the problem.

WORKING WITH FORMS

Forms add interactivity to Web sites. Guest books, search engines and product ordering systems are just a few of the applications that use forms.

Basically, a form is a Web page component that allows a user to send information to the owner of the page. A form can contain one or more elements—text fields, checkboxes, radio buttons, popup menus—that allow user input. Web servers accept the input and return information or confirmation to the Web site visitor.

In this chapter, I describe all of CyberStudio's forms tools and how forms interact with the rest of your Web site.

In this chapter, I cover:

- How forms work.
- Creating forms.
- Configuring forms.
- Using form elements.
- HTML 4.0 form elements.
- HTML 4.0 form features.

✔ Tip

- In order to use forms with your Web site, your Web server (run by your company or an ISP) must have a CGI (Common Gateway Interface) application installed that supports the forms you create. Before you design any forms, be sure that you will be able to use them with your server. If not, you can skip this chapter.

How forms work

To a Web site visitor and, perhaps, to a Web page designer, forms look and behave just like any other Web page element. Most forms are integrated with text and graphics, and their appearance is usually designed to complement the overall look of the page.

What differentiates forms is how they work behind the scenes. When a user enters text in a form, clicks a checkbox, and hits the Submit button, the form's work is done. From that point, the Web server takes over.

As I pointed out in the introduction to this chapter, a Web server must be running a script or CGI application designed to process the information Web site visitors submit. The CGI application transfers data entered into a Web page form into a database on the Web server. If, for example, the site visitor is using a form to reach a search engine, the database sends the search results to the server, which sends it back to the user via the CGI application. The result is an HTML page containing search engine hits.

When you create a form page, you have two tasks: designing the form so that it looks the way you want it to, and creating the hooks that allow your form to work with a Web server and CGI application.

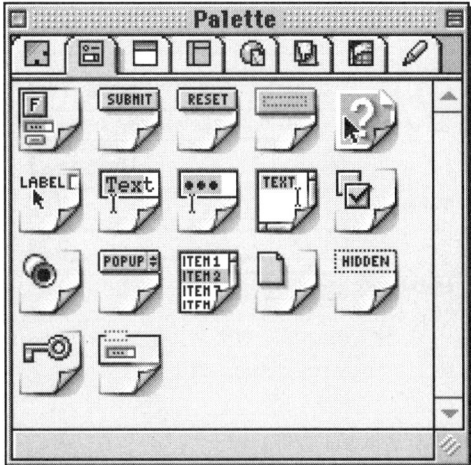

Figure 7-1: The Forms tab contains tools you need to add forms to your Web pages.

Figure 7-2: The Form tool.

Figure 7-3: The Form tag.

Creating forms

All the tools you need to create forms with CyberStudio can be found under the palette's Forms tab.

To locate the Forms tab:

1. With CyberStudio open, make sure that the palette is visible. If it's not, choose palette from the Windows menu.

2. Click on the Forms tab at the top of the palette. It's the second tab from the left. **Figure 7-1** shows the palette with the Form tab selected.

Each Form tab item is linked to a context-sensitive Inspector window, where you will configure the form to work with your Web page and the script or CGI that accepts your form's contents from users.

To create a form:

1. Drag the Layout Grid tool from the palette onto the document window. You can create forms without layout grids, but using a grid greatly simplifies the layout process. Forms elements can be aligned on the page automatically if a grid is present.

2. Click on the palette's Form tab to display the forms-creation tools.

3. Drag the Form tool (see **Figure 7-2**) onto the layout grid. CyberStudio creates a small square with an F, as shown in **Figure 7-3**.

Because the Form tag is the first of several elements you'll be adding to your form, position it on the page so that there is plenty of room to the right and below the Form icon.

Notice that the Inspector window has changed, allowing you to configure your new form. In order for the form to work, you must connect it to a CGI script on your Web server and tell the server a few things about how to work with the data that will be transferred from the form. That's where the Inspector comes in, creating hooks in your form's HTML that point the form to the server.

To configure the form:

1. Click the Form icon that you dragged to the layout grid to make the Form Inspector visible (**Figure 7-4**).

2. Type a name for the form into the name field.

3. In the Action field, type the URL of the CGI application which will process data entered into the form. If you're working on the same network as your Web server, you can find the correct file by navigating to your Web server's CGI folder. It's safest to type the full URL, so that links do not become accidentally broken as pages move around.

4. Choose an encryption method from the popup menu.

5. The Method field specifies the way the form's output will be returned to the user. From the Method popup menu, choose Post or Get. Post is usually the better choice.

✔ Tip

■ The Post method returns form responses (such as search results) separately from the rest of the Web page, pasting the data into the page that's generated for the user. Get, on the other hand, appends the form response to the URL of the results page, making the URL long and cumbersome.

You've just linked your form to the Web server, making it possible for the form to send and receive information. You've also set up a container for all the elements that will become part of your form. In order for your form to be useful, you now need to add fields, buttons and other elements with which your Web page visitors can interact.

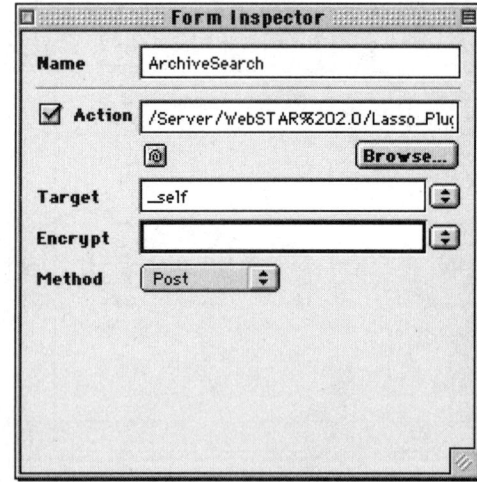

Figure 7-4: The Form Inspector window connects your form to the CGI script on your Web server.

Form elements

Think of the Form tag you just created as a container; it encloses the rest of the items that make up your Web page form and includes instructions (the Method and Action elements) that indicate how the form's input and output should be handled. Every element of the form must fall between the <FORM> and </FORM> HTML tags. You'll see these tags only if you examine the Web page with CyberStudio's Outline View or Source View. When you add form elements in the Layout View, be sure that they appear after the Form tag.

CyberStudio includes palette tools for fifteen different form elements:

- Text field.

- Password.

- Text area.

- Submit and Reset buttons.

- Checkbox.

- Radio button.

- Popup.

- List box.

- File browser.

- Hidden.

- Input image.

- Key generator.

- Button.

- Label.

- Field Set.

In this section, I go through each form element type and describe how to add it to your layout and how to use the Inspector to configure it.

Text and password fields

Text fields allow users to enter a line of text into a form. Text fields can contain names, addresses, search engine queries or just about anything else that can be expressed in a single line of text. If you need to accommodate multiple lines of text, use the Text Area field, described later in this chapter. The Password Field element is identical to the Text Field except that it supports password entry, which conceals text as it is entered.

To create a Text or Password field:

1. With a Form tag in place and configured as discussed earlier in this chapter, drag the Text Field tool (**Figure 7-5a**) from the palette to the main window.

2. The field is displayed in the main window and the Inspector window changes so that you can configure the Text field element. (**Figure 7-5b**).

3. Type a name for the field in the Name field.

✔ Tip

■ When you choose a name for your field, and other form elements, keep in mind that the field names are used by your Web server's CGI application to connect the form to the underlying database. Your field names should match the field names of your database and be intuitively linked to the form you're working with.

4. If you want the field to contain default text (such as "Type Your Search Request Here"), enter it in the Content field. If not, leave the Content field blank.

5. In the Visible field, enter the number of characters you want to be visible to the user.

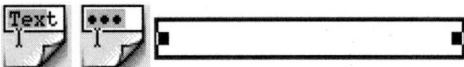

Figure 7-5a: The Text Field and Password Field tools, and a text field.

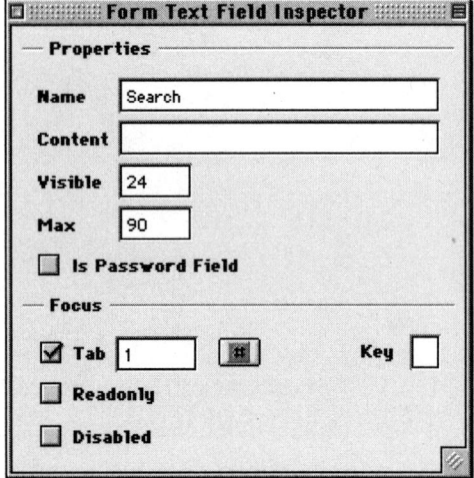

Figure 7-5b: The Form Text Field Inspector window.

6. Enter a larger number in the Maximum field if you want to give the user more room to type but don't want the entire field to be visible.

7. Leave the "Is Password Field" checkbox unchecked, unless you're creating a password field.

✔ Tips

■ You create a password field using exactly the same procedure you did to make the Text field. When you drag the Password field tool onto the main window, the Inspector selects "Is Password field."

■ When you choose a name for your text field and other form elements, keep in mind that the field names are used by your Web server's CGI application to connect the form to the underlying database. Your field names should match the field names of your database and be intuitively linked to the form you're working with.

■ You have two choices when designing Web page forms: to label or not to label. To give each form element (such as a text field) a label, you'll need to create a text frame for it and leave room in your page for the label. Alternatively, you can use the Content and Value fields found in most form elements to label the fields internally. The choice you make depends on your page design.

■ You can resize a text field by dragging one of the field's two handles. As you drag, the value in the Inspector window's Visible field changes.

Checkboxes and radio buttons

Adding a set of checkboxes or radio buttons to your form provides a way for site visitors to choose from a number of options. Radio buttons allow users to choose an option from a group of several options. Checkboxes allow the user to pick one or more items from a group.

To create a checkbox:

1. Drag the checkbox tool from the palette to the main window. A checkbox appears (**Figure 7-6a**).

2. In the Checkbox Inspector (**Figure 7-6b**), type a name for the checkbox.

3. Enter an optional descriptive name for the checkbox.

4. If you want the box checked by default, click the Is Selected checkbox.

To create a radio button:

1. Drag several radio buttons from the palette to the main window (**Figure 7-7a**).

2. Instead of a name for a single checkbox or field, the Radio Button Inspector window (**Figure 7-7b**) asks for a group name, which represents all the radio buttons you will use as part of this series. Type a group name.

3. Type a descriptive name for this button in the Value field, if you like.

4. Repeat steps 2 and 3 for each button you created, choosing the group name that applies to all of them from the popup menu as you go (**Figures 7-7b**).

Figure 7-6a: The checkbox tool and a checkbox.

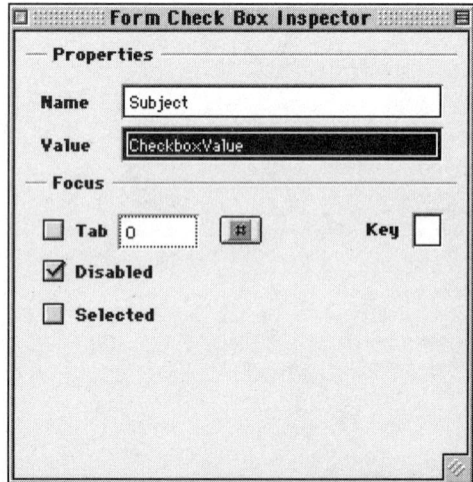

Figure 7-6b: The Form Check Box Inspector window.

Figure 7-7a: The Radio button tool and radio buttons.

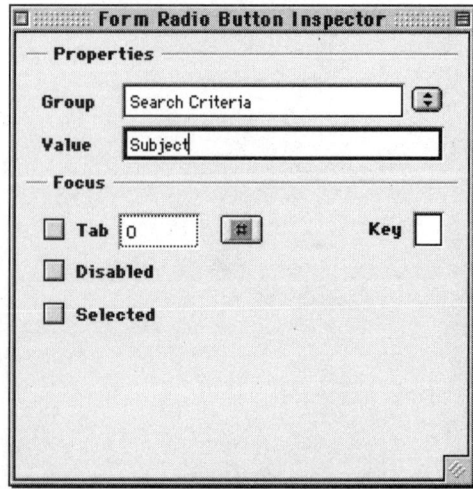

Figure 7-7b: The Form Radio Button Inspector window.

Figure 7-8a: The Submit and Reset button tools and the buttons they create.

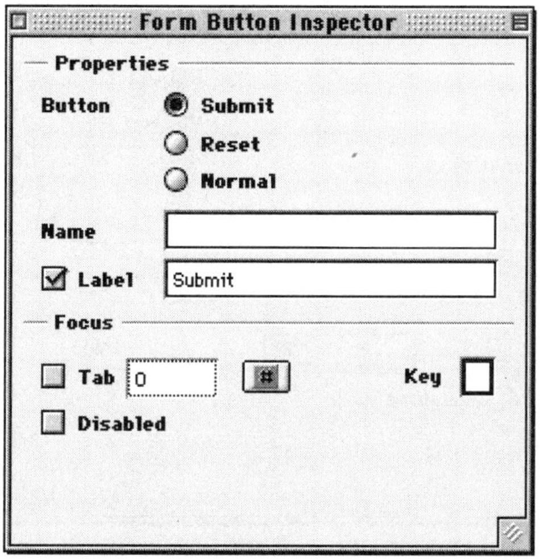

Figure 7-8b: The Form Button Inspector window.

Submit and Reset buttons

The Submit and Reset buttons make your forms truly interactive. After filling out your form, the user presses the Submit button, sending the information off to the server. A Reset button clears the form, which is useful if the site visitor decides to erase the form information he or she has filled out.

To create a Submit or Reset button:

1. Drag the Submit button tool from the palette to the main window **(Figure 7-8a)**.

2. In the Inspector window **(Figure 7-8b)**, choose a name for the button.

3. If you want the button text to say something other than "Submit Query," click the Label checkbox and type your new label.

   Because you used the Submit Button tool, CyberStudio has chosen Submit as your button's type. Leave it unchanged.

✔ Tip

■ You create a Reset button using exactly the same procedure you did to make the Submit button. When you drag the button onto the main window, the Inspector selects Reset, rather than Submit, as the button type.

Input Images

Instead of the usual Submit button, you can dress up your form by using an image as a button. It could be a spinning ball, an icon representing a letter—whatever seems to work with your design. You can manipulate Input Images just as you can any other image that's part of your Web page. For details on working with images, see Chapter 5.

To create an Input Image:

1. Drag the Input Image tool from the palette to the main window (**Figure 7-9a**).

2. The Inspector window (**Figure 7-9b**) displays the Form Image Inspector. Locate an image with the Browse button, or, if you're working within a project, use Point & Shoot.

3. Click on the tab of the Image Inspector. Note that the Form checkbox is selected. Type a name for the Input Image.

✔ Tip

- When you use an image as a submit button, be sure that your site visitors know that this is the image's purpose. Create a label or some instructions that tell the visitor that clicking on the button will send the data in the form to the Web server.

Figure 7-9a: The Input Image tool and Image icon.

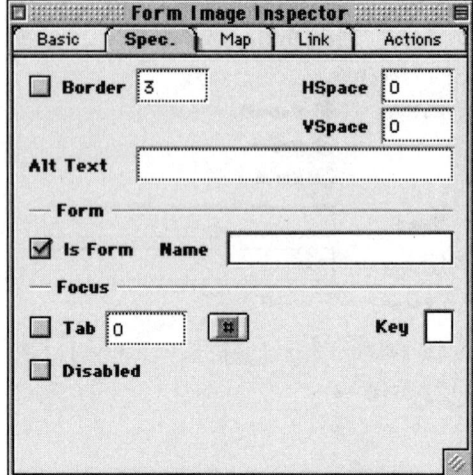

Figure 7-9b: The Special tab of the Form Image Inspector window.

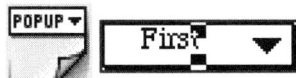

Figure 7-10a: The Popup tool and a popup element.

Form List Box Inspector

— Properties

Name Yeas

Rows 1 ☑ Multiple Selection

— Focus

☐ Tab 0 [#]

☐ Disabled

— Data

✓	Label	Value	
	First	one	▲
	Second	two	▼
☐			

[Delete] [Duplicate] [New]

Figure 7-10b: The Form Popup Inspector window.

Popups and list boxes

You can display a list of choices within your form using a popup menu or a list box. They perform the same basic function but look a bit different from one another.

✔ Tip

■ Popups and list boxes can be used like checkboxes and radio buttons, but they're much easier to configure as a group. They also take up less space on the page—a design bonus or drawback, depending on the look you're trying to achieve.

A popup menu looks just like a Macintosh popup menu. (Windows users call them drop-down menus.) Only a small rectangle is visible until you click on it to pull down the menu. List boxes, on the other hand, display all or part of their contents on the Web page. Simply clicking on an item from the list box selects it.

Configuring the two form elements is similar, too.

To create a popup:

1. Drag the Popup tool from the palette to the main window (**Figure 7-10a**).

2. Name the popup in the Form Popup Inspector (**Figure 7-10b**).

3. If you want site visitors to see more than one popup item, enter that number in the Rows box.

   Note that making multiple rows visible makes your popup virtually identical to a list box and defeats the purpose of having a popup. The same goes for the Multiple Items checkbox, which lets users select more than one item from the popup.

4. By default, the Inspector shows three items that you can edit and include in a popup menu. You modify them, add items, or delete items. To modify an item, first select it.

5. Notice in **Figure 7-11** that the Name and Value of the item are now visible in boxes at the bottom of the Inspector window. Rename the items with names you want to use in the popup menu.

6. To select the item by default, click the checkbox to the left of the Label name at the bottom.

7. Repeat Step 6 with each item you want to use.

8. To add an item, click New and type the new item's Name and Value.

To create a list box:

1. Follow steps 1-3 of the Popup section, above.

2. Because the whole idea of a list box is to view several options, use the Rows box to enter the number of items you want to be visible on the list.

✔ Tips

■ List boxes have scroll bars, allowing you to display some rows and make others available by scrolling. Choose the number of rows you think will look best on the page and display the items you think will be most popular, saving most site visitors the trouble of scrolling down the list.

■ You can change the number of visible rows either by using the Inspector or by dragging the handle on the list box downward.

3. Click "Multiple Selections" if you want the user to be able to pick several options from the list.

4. Follow steps 5-9 of the Popup section, above.

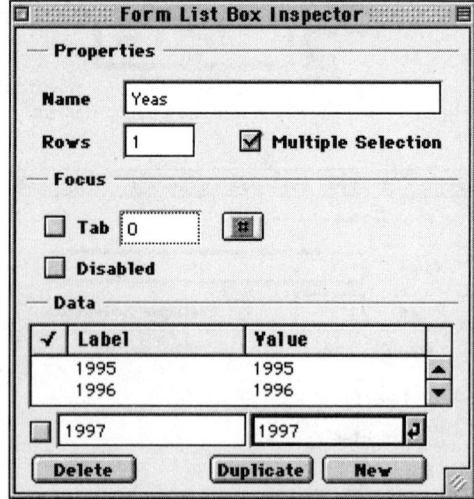

Figure 7-11: Change the default names of items in the Inspector to create a customized popup menu.

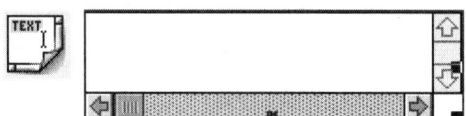

Figure 7-12a: The Text Area tool and a text area.

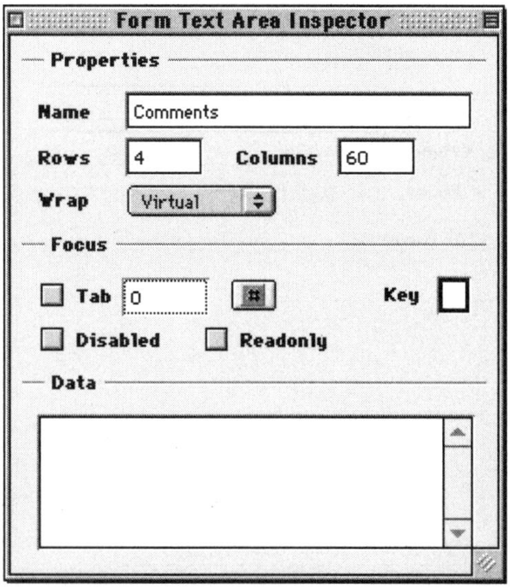

Form Text Area Inspector

— **Properties**

Name | Comments

Rows | 4 | **Columns** | 60

Wrap | Virtual ▾

— **Focus**

☐ **Tab** 0 | [#] | **Key** ☐

☐ **Disabled** ☐ **Readonly**

— **Data**

Figure 7-12b: The Form Text Area Inspector window.

Text areas

Whereas text fields contain a single line, text *areas* allow you to provide multiple lines in which a user can enter information. You can use text areas to give users a place to add comments on your site, for example.

To create a text area:

1. Drag the Text Area tool from the palette to the main window (**Figure 7-12a**).

2. Click on the Inspector window. (**Figure 7-12b**).

3. Name the text area.

4. If you want to change the default size of the text area, do so by raising or lowering the values in the Columns and Rows boxes or dragging the text area's handles to alter the field's size.'

5. Use the Wrap popup menu to tell the form whether or not to wrap the text at the end of each line.

Hidden elements

As the name implies, hidden elements are not a visible part of your form. Instead of holding information entered by a form user, hidden elements store information that has already been collected.

For example, if your Web site includes a form that asks for a user's name and address, among other things, and a second form where the user can place an order, a hidden field can link the information on the two forms by providing the user's name and address to the second form.

To create a hidden element:

1. Drag the Hidden tool from the palette to the main window. The Hidden element is represented by a small H, as shown in **Figure 7-13a**.

2. In the Form Hidden Inspector (**Figure 7-13b**), type a name in the Name field. The name should match the name of the field you are copying from one form to another.

3. Type a value (the specific information you want to copy) only if it is the same for each iteration of the form submitted.

4. Create a hidden element for each item that you wish to transfer from one form to another. Do this by repeating steps 1–3 above.

Figure 7-13a: The Hidden tool and the Hidden element.

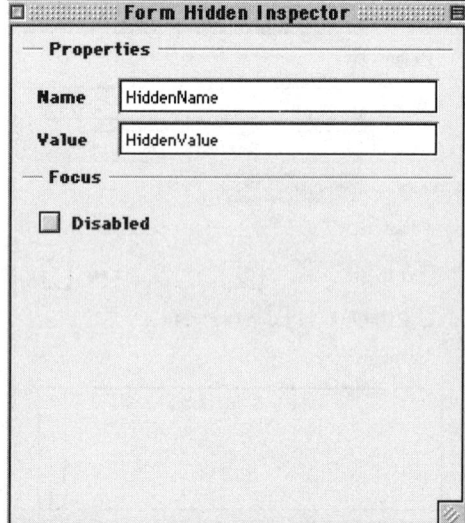

Figure 7-13b: The Form Hidden Inspector window.

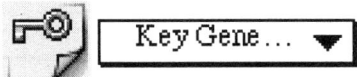

Figure 7-14a: The Key Generator tool and item.

```
┌─────── Form Keygen Inspector ───────┐
│  ┌ Properties ─────────────────────  │
│                                      │
│   Name    │KeyGenName            │   │
│                                      │
│   Challenge │publickey           │   │
│  ┌ Focus ──────────────────────────  │
│                                      │
│   ☐ Tab  │0    │   │ # │   Key ☐    │
│   ☐ Disabled                         │
│                                      │
│                                      │
│                                      │
│                                      │
│                                      │
│                                      │
└──────────────────────────────────────┘
```

Figure 7-14b: The Form Keygen Inspector window.

Key Generators

Key Generators are used to insert an encryption key into the transaction between Web site visitor and Web site owner. Keys are often used when forms contain financial transactions or personal information. When a site visitor submits a form, the Web server sends a dialog box to the visitor, asking the visitor to accept or decline the key so that the transaction can be completed.

To create a Key Generator:

1. Drag the Key Generator from the palette to the main window. The Key Generator item appears (**Figure 7-14a**).

2. Name the key in the Inspector window (**Figure 7-14b**).

3. Enter the type of encryption (such as Public Key) that your server software supports in the Challenge field.

File Browser

The File Browser element lets you open a window to the FTP directory on your Web site. Using a File Browser, site visitors can look for and download files, provided that the Web server has a CGI application that supports this.

To create a File Browser:

1. Drag the File Browser tool from the palette to the main window. The File Browser field and button appear. (**Figure 7-15a**).

2. Type the directory path of the server's CGI application in the Name field. (**Figure 7-15b**).

3. In the Visible field, type the number of characters that you would like be visible onscreen.

Figure 7-15a: The File Browser tool, field and button.

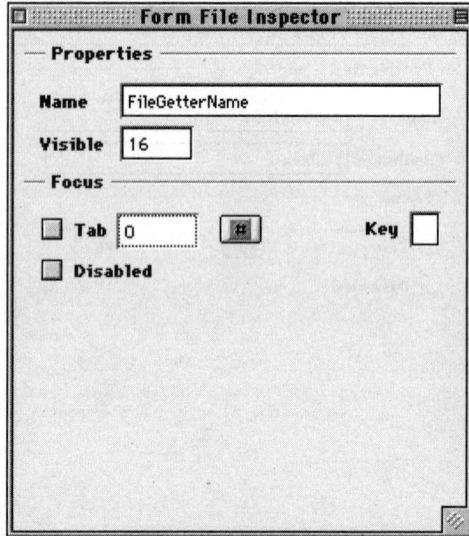

Figure 7-15b: The Form File Inspector window.

Figure 7-16a: The Button tool, and a button.

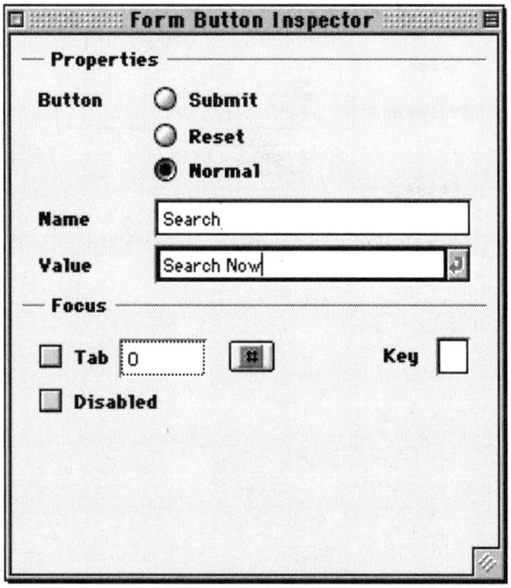

Figure 7-16b: The Button Inspector window.

HTML 4.0 Forms

The latest version of the HTML spec includes several new form tags and a couple of new form features that will help users navigate your forms. The catch is that your Web site's visitors' must use a 4.0 browser to view and use the new tags and features.

Button

An HTML 4.0 button is like the Submit and Reset buttons I described earlier in this chapter, except that you can customize its appearance and function with the Text Inspector.

To create an HTML 4.0 button:

1. Drag the Button tool from the palette to the main window (**Figure 7-16a**).

2. Drag your cursor over the button until it changes from a hand to an I-beam. You can now type text in the button and customize that text just as you would any other text in your document. If you click on the text, notice that the Inspector window displays the Text Inspector, allowing you to add a link or other attribute of your choice.

3. Click on the border of the button to select the entire button. The Button Inspector appears.

4. In the Inspector window (**Figure 7-16b**), choose a name and value for the button.

HTML 4.0 FORMS

Label

It seems like a pretty simple matter to create a text label for a form element such as a radio button or checkbox. HTML 4.0's Label form element is a nifty way of connecting label with button or box, however, because clicking on the label activates the other form element, much as clicking on a label in the CyberStudio Inspector activates the button or box associated with it.

To create a label element:

1. Create or locate a checkbox, radio button, or any other form element you would like to label. Make sure that you have configured your form elements before trying to create a label.

2. Drag or double-click the Label item (**Figure 7-17a**) from the palette to the document window.

3. Double-click the label to select the text and type the label.

4. Position the label element near the item you want to connect it to.

5. Command-click the label (not the text inside it) and drag the resulting Point & Shoot line to the box, button, or other element you want to link to. Note that the Label Inspector window becomes visible (**Figure 7-17b**), and that it now displays an ID number that connects your label to the form element.

✔ Tip

■ Just like an HTML 4.0 button tag, you can format label text when it (not the label) is selected. Formatting makes it easier to ensure that the labels you create fit into your page layout.

Figure 7-17a: The Label tool, and a button.

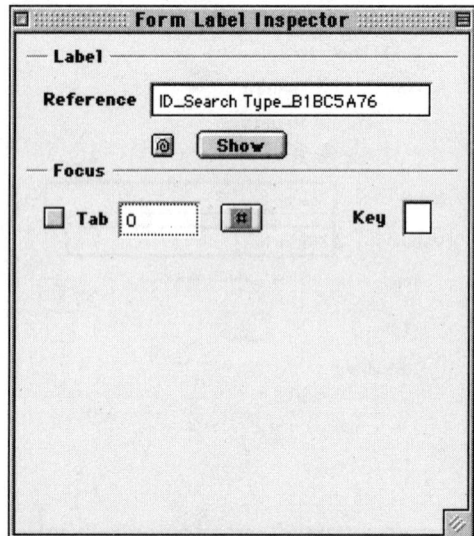

Figure 7-17b: The Label Inspector window.

Figure 7-18a: The Fieldset tool, and a button.

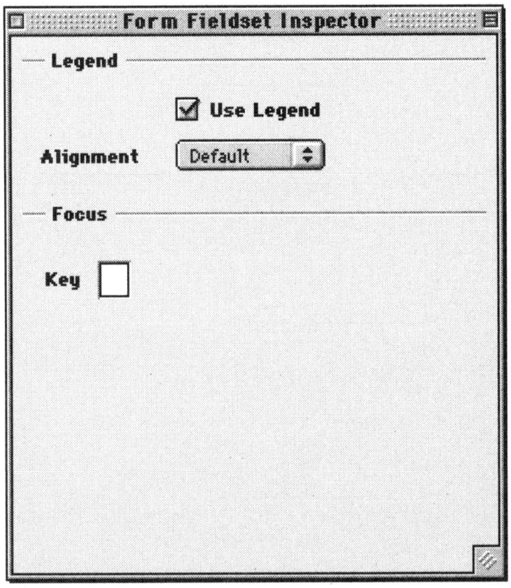

Form Fieldset Inspector

Legend

☑ **Use Legend**

Alignment | Default |◆|

Focus

Key ☐

Figure 7-18b: The Fieldset Inspector window.

Fieldset and legend

The Fieldset and legend element provides a physical grouping for other form elements. You can work with and move a group of buttons, checkboxes, or radio buttons around together, once they've been added to a Fieldset. The legend option allows you to label the group.

To create a field set:

1. Drag the Fieldset item (**Figure 7-18a**) from the palette to the document window.

2. In the Fieldset Inspector, choose an alignment for the Fieldset legend or uncheck the Legend box to disable this feature.

3. If you plan to use a legend, click the word Legend in the main window and change the word Legend to a title of your choice.

4. Drag a table (either one you've worked on already or a new one from the palette) into the Fieldset box you just created. The Fieldset box expands to hold the table.

5. Drag some checkboxes into the Fieldset box and table. Add labels to the table.

HTML 4.0 FORMS

HTML 4.0 form features

Filling out a long online form is much easier if you can move from one field to the next using the Tab key. CyberStudio and HTML 4.0 give you, as a Web author, a way to create and control the order in which users move from field to field.

You may have noticed several items under the Focus label of many form element inspector windows. These items specify the 4.0-specific features I'll cover in this section.

HTML 4.0 form features supported in Cyber-Studio 3.1 are:

- Tab chains.

- Access keys.

- Read-only elements.

- Disabled elements.

✔ Tip

- The navigation method covered in this section is currently available only to users of Microsoft's Windows version of Internet Explorer.

Form elements that support *tab chains* are:

- Tab chains.

- Text and password fields.

- Text areas.

- Submit and Reset buttons.

- Checkboxes and radio buttons.

- Popup menus and list boxes.

- Labels.

To create a tab chain:

1. Open a document that contains fields that require the user to make a text entry; such as a text field, password field, or text area.

2. Choose Start Tabulator Indexing from the Special menu. Small yellow boxes with numbers appear next to the indexable fields in your form.

3. Click the boxes in the order you want the tabs to appear. The numbers change to reflect your clicks.

4. Choose Stop Tabulator Indexing from the Special menu.

✔ Tip

■ You may have noticed a checkbox and a field labeled Tab in the Inspector window of some form elements. You can check on or change the tab order of fields within your forms in this Inspector field.

Access keys

Defining an access key within a form element allows the user to activate the element or field by typing a certain character.

Form elements that support access keys are:

■ Text and password fields.

■ Text areas.

■ Submit and reset buttons.

■ Checkboxes and radio buttons.

■ Labels.

■ Legends.

HTML 4.0 FORM FEATURES

To create an access key:

1. Choose a supported element. If it's not already placed within a form, drag it to the document window and configure it.

2. In the Inspector, type an alphanumeric character in the Key field.

3. Test your new key in a browser that supports access keys, such as Internet Explorer for Windows.

✔ Tip

■ It's a good idea to include some sort of label or other visual cue on the page, so that your visitors will know that the form field includes an access key.

Read-only elements

You can use read-only elements to prevent visitors from editing the contents of a form field. If, for example, you want to limit the visitor to submitting a pre-defined text string, you could create a field that includes it.

Form elements that support read-only elements are:

■ Text and password fields.

■ Text areas.

■ Submit and reset buttons.

■ Checkboxes and radio buttons.

■ Popup menus and list boxes.

To create a read-only element:

1. Select the element you want to make read-only, in your document.

2. Add text that you would like to appear in the field.

3. In the Inspector, click the Read-Only checkbox.

Disabled elements

You can disable any form element. while it may seem kind of silly to create an element, only to disable it, you can use scripts to bring disabled elements to life conditionally. In other words, the item will be disabled unless a script activates it. You could, for example, disable fields in an order form until your e-commerce system has verified a credit card number. Once the affirmative result is returned to the Web server, a script re-enables the form fields, and your customer can complete the order.

To disable a form element:

1. Choose the form element you wish to disable.

2. Write or edit a script (CGI, JavaScript, AppleScript or other script supported by your Web server) to provide for enabling the element, when appropriate.

3. Select the element in the document window.

4. In the Inspector, click the Disabled checkbox.

HTML 4.0 FORM FEATURES

WORKING WITH FRAMES

Think of frames as multi-paned windows to your Web site. Instead of a single, scrollable page full of text and images, framed pages display two or more pages within the same browser window. Usually, framed pages (*frame sets*, in HTML-speak) contain a main pane and one or more smaller ones. Panes may include scroll bars that move you through the frame independently of the other elements on the page. Some frames remain stationary in the browser as you click through other pages within a Web site.

Many Webmasters use frames as navigation tools. A frame can display a table of contents for the entire site alongside each individual page. Other sites use frames to force visitors to view advertisements or other banner content.

In this chapter, I cover:

- How frames work.
- Creating frames.
- Adding content to frames.
- Adding frames and frame sets.

How frames work

Most Web pages consist of a single HTML file. Frame-based Web pages, on the other hand, actually display several HTML documents at once, each in its own pane of the browser window. **Figures 8-1a** and **8-1b** are examples of the wide variety of design choices available using frames.

To use frames, you'll need to create and link several files. Although the files you need will vary based on the arrangement of your frames, these are the most basic ones:

- A frames set document.

- A contents document.

- A main page document.

The frames set document contains instructions on how the browser window and its panes should look by default, and how they are positioned on the page. Whatever frame setup you choose, the frames setup document is required. The frames set document does not contain HTML that is displayed. It forms the structure for your framed page.

The contents document, as its name implies, provides a listing (including links) of pages that can be displayed on your frames-based page. The contents document appears along with every page within your Web site.

The main page document is basically a place-holder for HTML pages that will appear in the main frame of your Web page.

To add a banner, a group of navigation buttons, or another type of frame, you'll need to create additional frame documents.

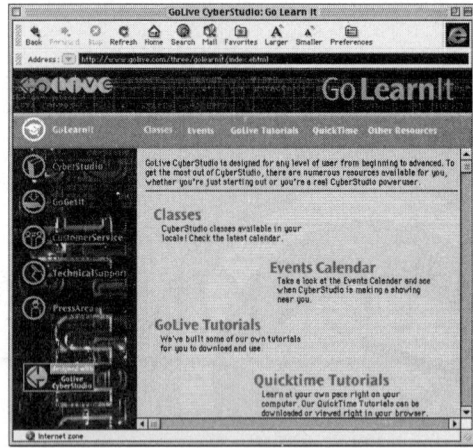

Figure 8-1a: GoLive Systems' site uses a pair of frames to wrap its navigation metaphor around the contents of individual pages, making it easy to find everything on the site.

Figure 8-1b: ZD Internet magazine's three frames include a table of contents and scrollable feature article, plopped smack dab in the middle of the page.

Frame caveats

Frames are not really a full-fledged part of the HTML standard. Netscape Communications introduced frame tags as an extension to HTML at about the time version 2 of the company's Navigator Web browser was released. At this writing, only Netscape browsers (Navigator and Communicator) and Microsoft Internet Explorer support frames. Although browser software from Netscape and Microsoft dominates the marketplace, Webmasters who use frames run the risk of creating pages that users of other browsers cannot view. The solution, for some, is to create both frame-filled and no-frames versions of their Web sites.

Even when site visitors use browsers that support them, frames can be a challenge to Web site visitors. Although frames make it possible to look at large portions of your site at once, they also limit the user's ability to use mouse and cursor to move freely. For example, if you're used to using the PageDown key to scroll a Web page, you'll find that impossible to do in some framed pages.

Frames also decrease the amount of screen space available to display Web site content. Contents areas and navigation frames leave less room for the main pane. To be fair, though, the same is true of other templated site design methods that use tables to create navigation and contents elements. The challenge is to leave as much space as possible in the main pane while retaining readability within smaller frames.

HOW FRAMES WORK

Creating frames

Once you've decided what portions of your Web site belong in frames, you can create a page with one or more *frame sets*. Frame sets specify the way a group of frames on the page will look and interact.

All the tools you need to create and customize frame-based pages can be found on the Frames tab of the palette.

To locate the Frames tab:

1. Make sure that the palette is visible. If it's not, choose Palette from the Windows menu.

2. Click on the Frames tab at the top of the palette. It's the fourth tab. **Figure 8-2** shows the palette with the Frames tab selected.

To create a frame document:

1. Open a new CyberStudio document.

2. Switch from the Layout View to the Frames View. The result looks like **Figure 8-3**.

3. Choose the Frame tab from the palette. You see a number of different frame configurations that you can choose from.

4. Drag a Frame Set icon (all but the upper, leftmost icon are frame sets) from the palette onto the main window.

   The configuration I chose is displayed in **Figure 8-4**, along with the corresponding frame set icon from the palette.

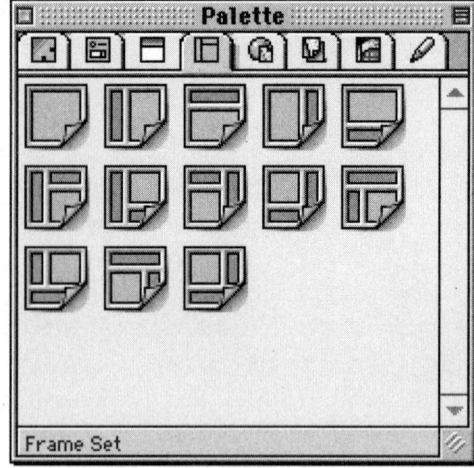

Figure 8-2: The Frames tab contains tools you need to add forms to your Web pages.

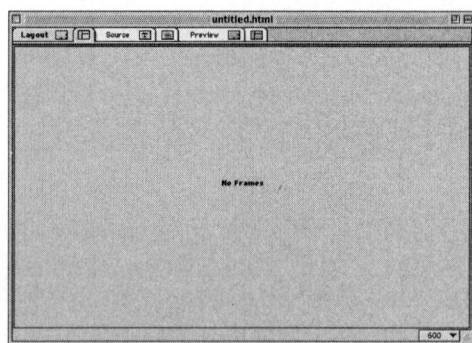

Figure 8-3: The Frames View only displays the structure of frames on a Web page.

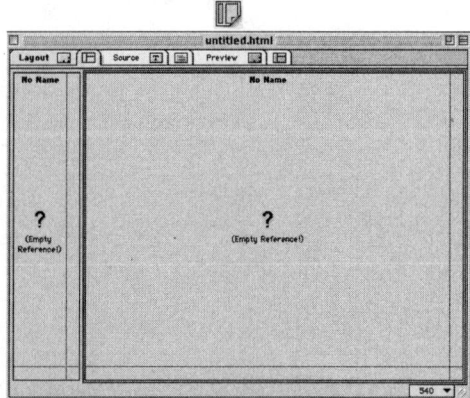

Figure 8-4: Here is a simple, two-frame set, as created by the palette item above.

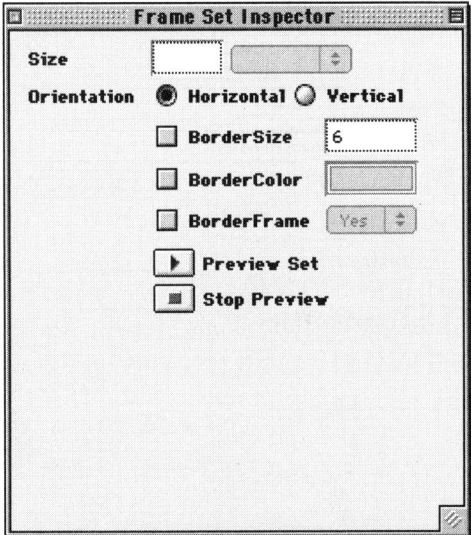

Figure 8-5: The Frame Set Inspector sets display preferences for all frames in a set. You probably won't spend much time configuring it.

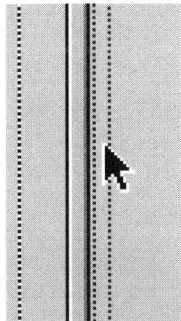

Figure 8-6: When you attempt to resize a frame, be sure that your cursor is positioned on the border between the two adjacent frames, and not inside a frame or scroll bar.

5. Click on the border between the two frames to bring up the Frame Set Inspector in the Inspector window (**Figure 8-5**). If you don't see the Inspector window, choose Inspector from the Windows menu.

Options you choose here apply to all frames within the frame set. You can change the set's orientation, specify the thickness the border, the border color and whether there should be a border frame. You can also tell CyberStudio whether or not to allow frame previewing within the Frame View.

To arrange frames:

1. Click and hold the mouse button inside one of the frames on your page and drag the mouse to the right, across the main window. When the frame you've selected reaches the other frame onscreen, the two change places. Drag the frame to the left to return it to its original position.

2. By default, the smaller frame, sometimes called a sidebar, is very narrow. To widen it, click and drag the border of the frame to the right. I'll need the extra space, because I'm going to use the frame as a table of contents for a Web site.

✔ Tip

■ Be careful to position your cursor on the border of the frame, as shown in **Figure 8-6**, rather than the outline of the scroll bar (to the left of the cursor). As we've seen, dragging from inside a frame moves the entire frame. All you want to do at this point is resize it.

CREATING FRAMES

To configure frames:

1. Click within a frame. The Inspector window now displays the Frame Inspector (**Figure 8-7**).

2. Type a name for the frame in the Name field.

   Give your frames simple and descriptive names. The name will be used to identify the frame later on, as you build connections to items within your Web site. I'll name the sidebar frame contents.html.

3. Choose Yes or No in the scrolling popup menu to determine whether your contents frame will have scroll bars. In this example, I'll turn off scrolling because the table of contents won't be long enough to require scrolling. Leaving off the scroll bars also conserves valuable screen real estate.

4. Save your frame document. Again, give it a descriptive name, one that conforms to the HTML naming convention: name.html. Because this example Web site uses only one Frame Set configuration, I'll call the file frame.html. Remember, this document won't contain any Web page content, just instructions for the display of other pages.

I named the page frame.html so that it would be obvious which document we were working with. Chances are, though, that you'll want to use a different name if your new framed look will be the home page of your site.

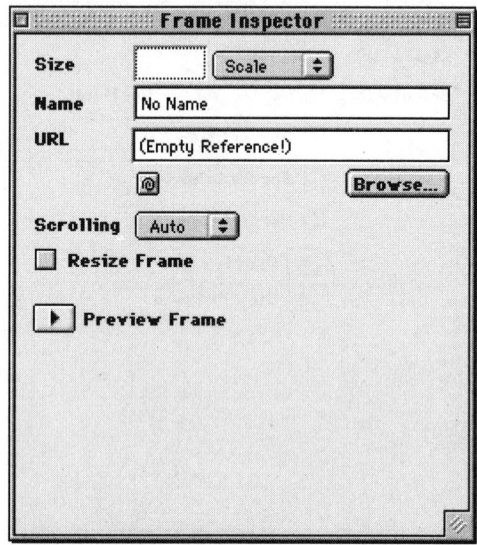

Figure 8-7: Name and configure individual frames in the Frame Inspector.

✔ Tips

- If you want to use a frames-based page as your home page, consider naming it index.html, home.html or some other name that your Web server recognizes as your default Web page.

- Even if your server doesn't care how your page is named, Webmasters redesigning existing sites will want to preserve their previous home page URLs by giving the frame page the same name as the previous home page.

- Some Webmasters avoid this naming headache (as well as problems caused for people whose Web browsers don't support frames) by offering framed and non-framed versions of their home page. In that case, name the page where that choice is offered home.html and let site visitors click on the version of their choice. In that case, you can name your framed document anything you like—as long as there's an .html or .htm suffix at the end.

Adding content to frames

With a framework in place (pun intended), it's time to dress up those window panes with some content. Although frames can simply provide windows to individual Web pages, they are much more powerful when used as a navigation tool for your entire site. The example frame structure I'm using in this chapter does that. The contents frame offers a list of available pages within our site, and the larger frame (I'll call it the body frame) displays a page your site visitors request from the table of contents.

Like the frame document itself, the body frame is a container for information. It displays when called for by the table of contents.

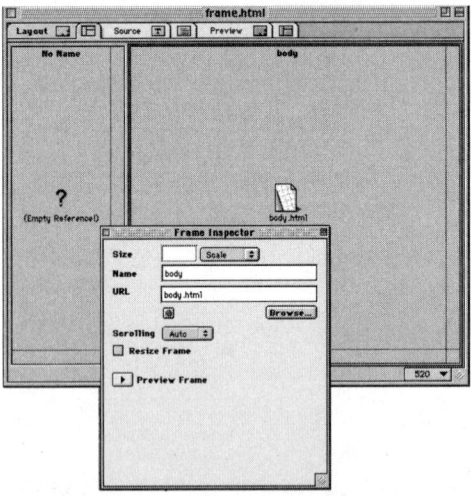

Figure 8-8: With the body frame Inspector completed, the question mark in the body frame changes to an icon, and the frame's name appears at the top of the page.

To add a body page to your frame set:

1. Open a new document.

2. Click on your new document's title bar (currently labeled "Welcome to GoLive CyberStudio3") and change the title to "body."

3. Save your document as body.html.

4. Open the frame.html document you created in the preceding section. Switch to the Frames View.

5. Click in the larger of the two frames to select it.

6. Using Point & Shoot, or the Frame Inspector's Browse button, locate the body.html file and link it to your frame.

7. In the Frame Inspector, name the frame "body." If you want to add scroll bars to the frame, choose that option. **Figure 8-8** shows the completed body frame Inspector window and the frame itself.

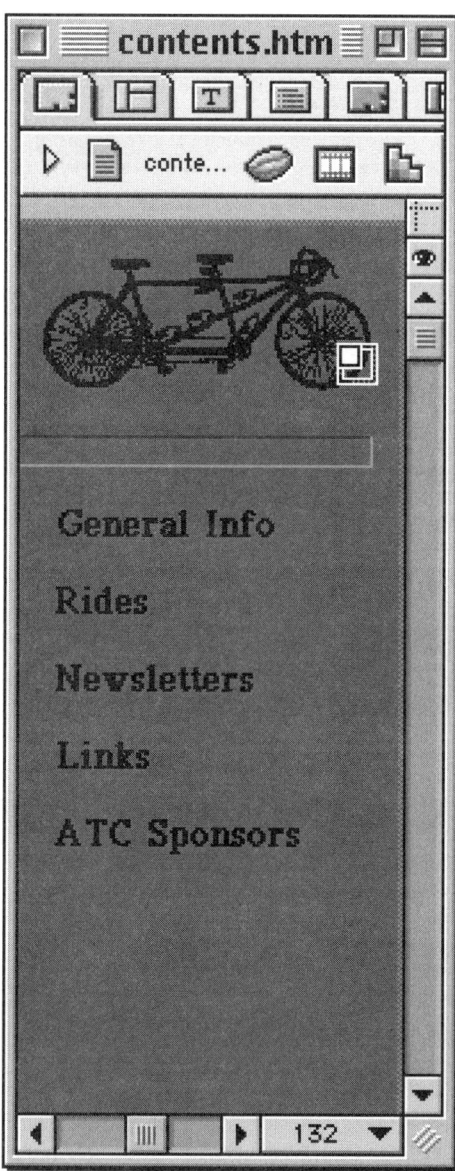

Figure 8-9: The contents.html file includes the TOC for the Austin Tandem Club site. I made the window narrow so that the display would resemble the contents frame where this page will be viewed.

If you check Resize Frame, those who view your page will be able to shrink or enlarge the frame in their browser windows. Otherwise, the frame is always the same size you created for it.

Unlike the body frame, the contents frame contains visible HTML in the form of links that activate the body frame. You can also add other text, graphics or any other element you'd like to appear on your contents page.

✔ Tip

■ When you're designing your contents frame, remember that it will proabably be quite narrow. Limit your text elements to headings and listings, and keep logos and graphics small. Of course, you can make your contents frame as wide as you like, but you'll be sacrificing valuable body frame screen space with every expansion of the contents frame.

To add a contents page to your frame set:

1. Create a new CyberStudio document.

2. Title your new document "contents" and save it as contents.html.

3. Now type the text for your table of contents. **Figure 8-9** shows my contents page.

I included several elements: headings, listings (including links to individual pages) and spacers. Your next task is to create hyperlinks that connect the listed items to the body frame. Although connecting frames together is very much like creating links or anchors for a normal page—with one added wrinkle: the target.

To create targeted links:

1. Open contents.html. Be sure that frame.html is also open.

2. In contents.html, select an item from your table of contents list.

3. Choose Link from the toolbar.

4. In the Inspector window or the Site window, locate the file your contents item should link to and complete the link.

5. Next, connect the link to the main frame of your frame set (frame.html) by filling in the Target field of the Inspector. Because this is the first frame link you've created, you need to type the word **body** (the name you gave to your main frame) in the Target dialog box. The completed Inspector window looks like **Figure 8-10**.

6. Save the contents.html document.

7. Bring frame.html to the front.

8. In the main window, choose the Frames Preview tab. You should see the contents document in the left frame and an empty pane on the right (**Figure 8-11**).

9. Click on the link you just created in the contents frame. The page you've linked appears in the body frame (**Figure 8-12**).

10. Repeat steps 2-5 for each table of contents element you'd like to connect to the main frame.

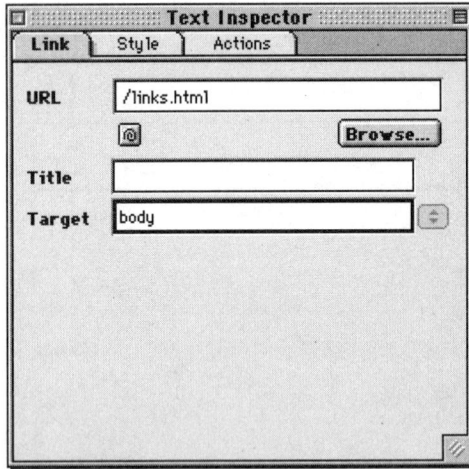

Figure 8-10: You must create a target in the Link Inspector in order for links on the left to display properly on the right.

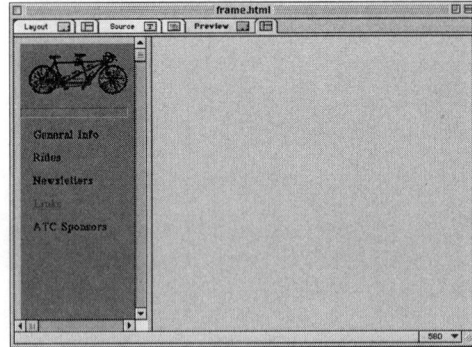

Figure 8-11: With the contents.html file linked to frame.html, you can preview the table of contents in the Frames Preview.

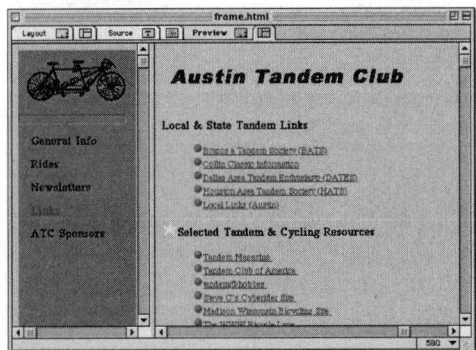

Figure 8-12: Clicking on a properly configured link in the table of contents brings up the requested page in the body frame.

✔ Tip

■ When you choose targets in the Link Inspector, use the popup menu. Once you create the first link you'll notice that it now includes the word *body*. Creating the first body target added this item to the menu. This shortcut does not work, however, unless the frame set document (frame.html) is open.

Does the contents frame look right to you in Preview mode? Do the line breaks occur where you want them to? If not, you can adjust the contents frame's width in the Frames view. Here's how.

To tweak the contents frame:

1. Open frame.html and choose the Frames View.

2. Click on the contents frame.

3. In the Frame Inspector window, click the Preview Frame button. Contents.html pops into the contents frame.

4. To adjust the width of the frame, drag the border to the left or right (depending upon whether you think the contents frame is too wide or too narrow) and note the impact the movement has on line breaks and available space within the body frame.

5. For that extra measure of accuracy, click the Frames Preview tab and verify the look of your frames.

ADDING CONTENT TO FRAMES

Adding frames and frame sets

GoLive CyberStudio allows you to create frame sets in a wide variety of configurations. The Frames tab of the palette suggests a number of options, including the simple two-frame arrangement I've been using in this chapter. You can also modify existing frame sets by adding new frames, one at a time. You can even use multiple frame sets on the same page.

To add a single frame:

1. Open the frame.html document you've been working with.

2. Switch to the Frames View.

3. Drag the Frame item (**Figure 8-13**) from the palette to the main window, dropping it into the body frame. A new frame appears.

4. Click on the new frame and drag it upward so that it switches places with the body frame, as shown in **Figure 8-14**. I'm going to use this frame for a banner.

5. Click on the new frame. Now I'll use the Frame Inspector to resize it.

6. In the Size popup of the Frame Inspector, note that the default setting is Scale. Choose Percent from the menu. You can now enter a number (try 25) that states the frame's size as a percentage of the available vertical space. The upper frame shrinks. Now you're ready to add content to your new frame by dragging an HTML file into it.

Figure 8-13: The Frame icon adds a single frame to an existing frame set.

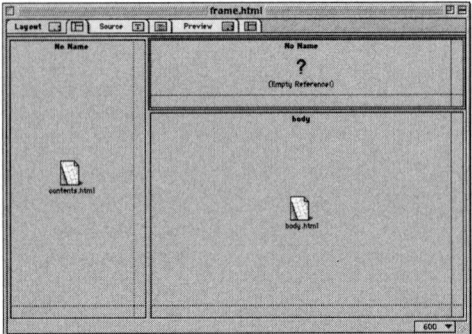

Figure 8-14: By default, a new frame is as large as the existing frame onto which you drag it.

✔ Tip

■ If you'd rather use the mouse than the keyboard, you can resize the frame by dragging its border, so long as either Pixel or Percent are chosen in the Frame Inspector's Size popup menu.

If you want to add a group of frames to an existing frame-based page, simply drag a frame set from the palette to the main window. Each frame set on a page operates as a separate entity, meaning that the preferences you set for one frame set do not apply to other sets on the same page.

ADDING FRAMES AND FRAME SETS

Working with Plugins

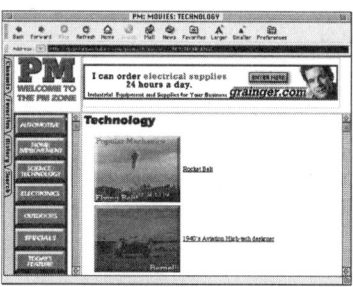

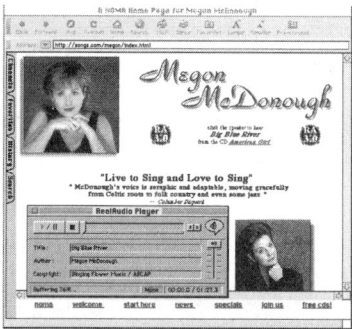

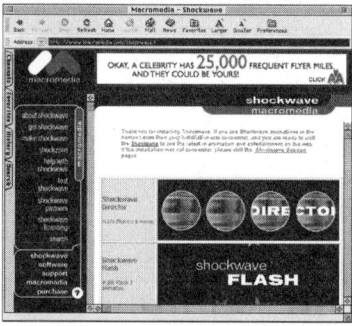

Figure 9-1: Here are (a) QuickTime movies from *Popular Mechanics* (b) RealAudio music from the National Online Music Alliance and (c) ShockWave animation from Macromedia.

You can add multimedia to your Web site in much the same way you add GIF or JPEG images. Like images, some multimedia files are displayed inline—as part of the Web page. Others are displayed externally.

Multimedia formats supported on the Web include QuickTime video, QuickTime VR, RealAudio and a number of other sound, video, animation and publishing formats. In order for the user to view multimedia files, Web browsers must either directly support the appropriate format or support *plugins*. Plugins are software that is automatically activated when a multimedia file is called for and which can play or display the files. **Figure 9-1** shows three Web pages that include plugin items.

CyberStudio allows you to add plugin-based content and to configure the files' appearance and behavior within a Web page.

In this chapter, I cover:

- Setting up plugins.
- Setting plugin preferences.

Setting up plugins

CyberStudio includes support for configuring and displaying several popular plugin formats.

Displaying plugin content

CyberStudio supports a variety of plugins. QuickTime plays a number of audio and video formats, including standard QuickTime movies and QuickTime VR movies. Like a Web browser, CyberStudio can display new plugins once you have installed plugin software in the CyberStudio Plugin folder. Just drop the plugin into the Plugins folder, inside the CyberStudio folder.

Adding plugin content

Adding a plugin file to a Web page is much like inserting an image. The differences between plugins and static images, and between different types of plugins, become clear as you configure them.

To add a plugin file to a Web page:

1. Open a CyberStudio document.

2. Drag the Plugin tool (**Figure 9-2**) from the palette to the document window. A plugin icon with a question mark appears, and the Plugin Inspector is displayed in the Inspector window (**Figure 9-3**).

3. In the Inspector window, click Browse.

4. Locate a media file that you want to use and click Open to select it. (If you are working within a CyberStudio site, use Point & Shoot to select a media file.) The plugin placeholder in the document window now contains the name of the media file (**Figure 9-4**).

Figure 9-2: The palette's Plugin tool.

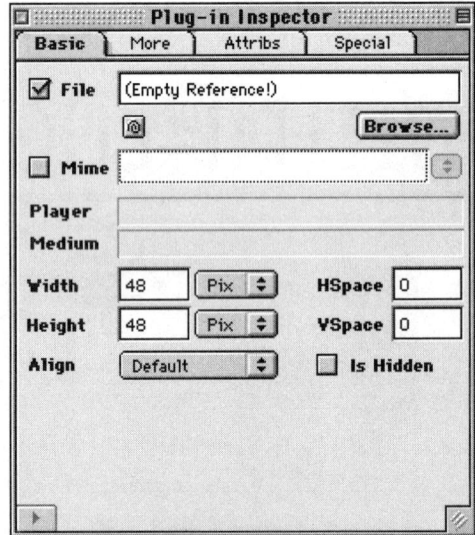

Figure 9-3: The Plugin Inspector.

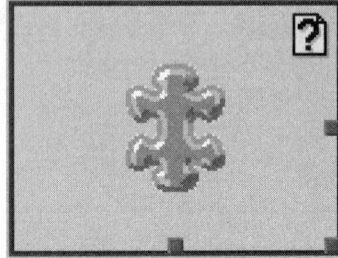

Figure 9-4: The Plugin placeholder contains the name of the media file you've chosen.

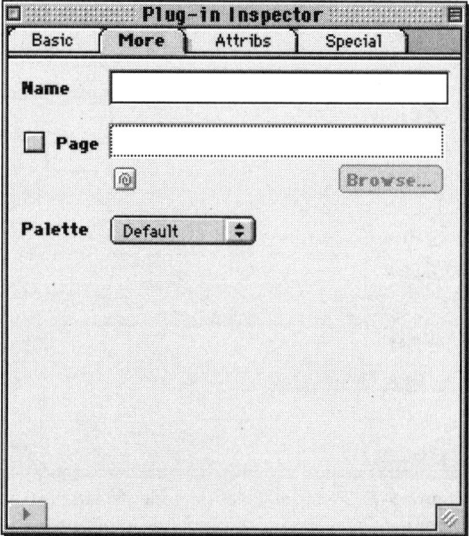

Figure 9-5: The More tab includes several optional settings for the plugin object.

Figure 9-6: The Play button starts playing the selected plugin file in the document window.

To set up a plugin file:

1. If it isn't selected, click on a plugin place-holder to select it. The Plugin Inspector appears.

2. Resize the plugin placeholder by dragging one of its handles or by typing new height and width values in the corresponding Plugin Inspector fields.

3. If you are not using a layout grid, add horizontal and vertical space between the plugin and other items on your Web page by entering values (in pixels) in the Plugin Inspector's HSpace and VSpace fields.

4. Align the plugin placeholder to Web page text with the Alignment popup menu. The same rules that govern the alignment of images to text apply when using plug-ins. For a full description of alignment options, see Chapter 5. Like the spacing options, alignment choices are only available when a plugin is outside of a layout grid or when the plugin is inside a text frame.

5. Name the plugin by clicking on the More tab in the Inspector window (**Figure 9-5**) and typing a unique name in the Name field.

✔ Tip

- You can play or display a media file at any time while you are configuring it by clicking the Play button at the bottom of the Plugin Inspector window (**Figure 9-6**). Click the button again to stop playback.

Configuring specific plugins

GoLive CyberStudio has built-in support for a number of popular plugin formats, including QuickTime and QuickTime VR. When you link a supported media file to a plugin placeholder, the Plugin Inspector displays not only generic plugin configuration tools, but also a tab that supports the file's specific format. If you link a media file that isn't supported, the tab is simply labeled Special and is empty.

To configure a QuickTime file:

1. Select a plugin placeholder containing a QuickTime file that you have already placed.

2. Click the QuickTime tab in the Plugin Inspector window (**Figure 9-7**).

3. Choose the Show Controller checkbox to display the QuickTime audio/video controls at the bottom of the movie as it plays on screen.

4. Choose the Cache checkbox to tell the browser to cache the movie.

5. Leave the Autoplay checkbox selected if you want the movie to play automatically when the page is opened. Otherwise, uncheck the box.

6. Click the Loop checkbox to play the movie continuously. If you choose a loop, checking the Palindrome option will play the move in reverse on every other loop.

7. Click the BGColor checkbox, and choose a Color from the Color Palette if you want the movie to have a background color. (For details on using the Color Palette, see Chapter 13).

8. Type a value (as a percentage of 100) in the volume field to change the movie's sound level. Leave the field blank to use the default value.

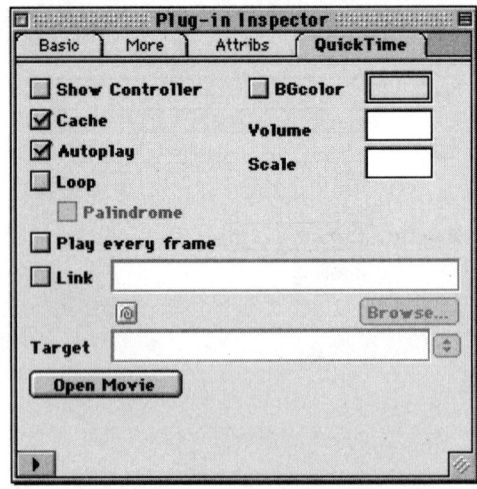

Figure 9-7: Configure QuickTime-specific settings under the QuickTime tab of the Plugin Inspector.

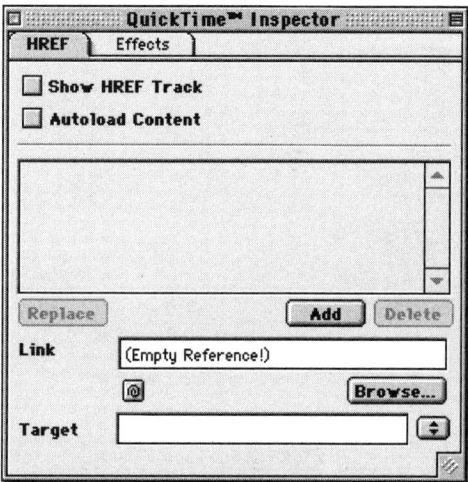

Figure 9-8: The QuickTime Inspector.

9. Type a value (as a percentage of the movie's current size) in the Scale field to shrink or enlarge the movie's play area. Leaving the field blank displays the movie at its original size.

10. Click Play Every Frame to prevent the browser from dropping frames. Frames are dropped to improve playback speed.

11. Click the Link checkbox and locate an image that you want to appear as a poster in the Plugin window. Browse or Point & Shoot your way to the poster image, to complete the link.

12. Choose the _self option from the Target popup menu.

Editing QuickTime movies

With QuickTime 3.0 installed on your Mac, CyberStudio allows you to play and edit QuickTime movies. You can play movies with any version of the QuickTime plugin, but you'll need QuickTime 3.0 to edit them.

To edit a movie:

1. Add a QuickTime movie to your page, as described in the previous section.

2. In the Plugin Inspector's QuickTime tab, click Open Movie. The movie appears in its own QuickTime window, and the QuickTime Inspector (**Figure 9-8**) appears.

3. Click Show HREF Track to add a URL. The browser will jump to the URL at a specified time during playback of the movie..

4. Click Autoload Content to cause the URL to load automatically, rather than waiting for a click.

5. Use the Add button to insert occurrences of the HREF track into your movie's playback sequence.

SETTING UP PLUGINS

✔ Tip

■ You can also open and edit a movie by simply double-clicking the plugin from within CyberStudio.

To add visual effects:

1. With the movie in the foreground, click the Effects tab of the QuickTime Inspector.

2. Click Apply to open the Effects window (**Figure 9-9**).

3. Click on an effect to edit its properties. Options specific to that effect appear in the window. When you click on an effect, the preview version of the movie takes on that option's characteristics.

4. When you have finished creating effects, click OK to close the window. A Save dialog appears.

5. Save the movie.

To configure a QuickTime VR file:

1. Select a plugin placeholder containing a QuickTime VR file that you have already placed.

2. Click the QuickTime VR tab in the Plugin Inspector window (**Figure 9-10**).

3. Click Show Controller to display a QuickTime VR console within the displayed image.

4. Choose the Cache checkbox to tell the browser to cache the movie.

5. Enter a percentage in the Volume box if the VR movie has sound.

6. Scale the movie (as a percent of 100) to resize it onscreen.

7. Choose a background color for the movie (if desired) by clicking the BGColor checkbox, and choosing a color from the Color Palette.

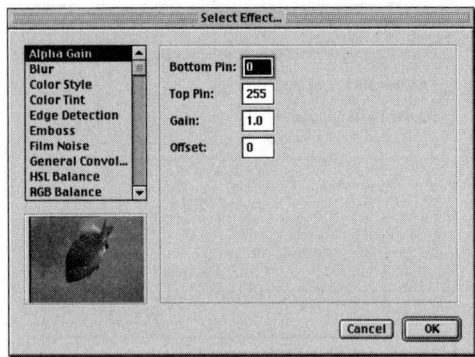

Figure 9-9: The QuickTime Effects window.

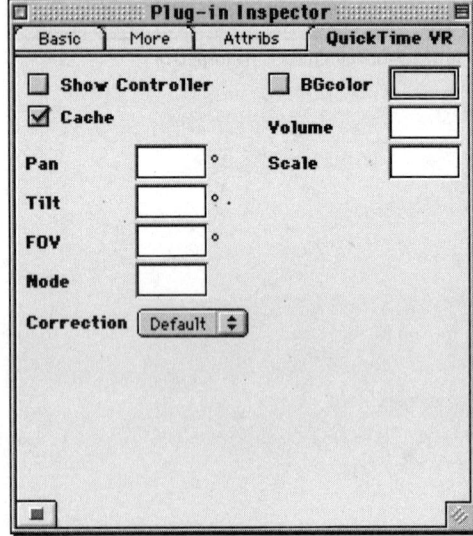

Figure 9-10: The QuickTime VR tab contains settings that are specific to the VR plugin format.

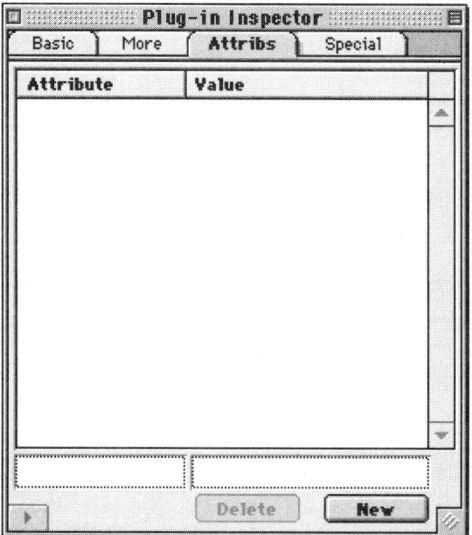

Figure 9-11: The empty Attributes tab of the Plugin Inspector window.

Figure 9-12: Enter the name and value of an attribute in the Attribs tab.

8. Enter values (in degrees) in the Pan, Tilt and POV fields to change the way a VR image moves when a Web site visitor manipulates it.

9. Choose a Node value.

10. Make a choice from the Correction popup menu to affect the amount of correction applied to the VR movie as it is manipulated.

QuickTime and QuickTime VR are just two of the plugin types supported by CyberStudio. You can also configure audio files.

Adding plugin attributes

Many plugin formats have attributes similar to those specified in the QuickTime or Quick-Time VR plugin definitions. You can add these attributes manually to plugins you place in your pages. Each plugin format is a bit different. In this example, I use a plugin to add a sound to a Web page. The sound plays when the page is opened.

To add attributes manually:

1. Select a plugin placeholder pointing to a media file that you have already placed on the page.

2. In the Plugin Inspector window, click on the Attribs tab (see **Figure 9-11**).

3. Click the New button to set up a new plugin attribute. A pair of fields appears in the Attribs window. The Attribute field is selected.

4. Type **autostart** in the Attribute field and press Tab.

5. Type **true** in the Value field and press Enter. The attribute is complete and it appears in the upper portion of the window (**Figure 9-12**). The new autostart attribute tells a Web browser to play the sound associated with this plugin when the page is loaded.

SETTING UP PLUGINS

149

6. Click the New button again.

7. Type **loop** and **three** in the Attributes and Value field, respectively. Adding a loop attribute means that the sound plays continuously. I chose to play it only three times, so as not to annoy the site's visitors. If you had typed **true** instead of **three**, the sound would play continuously.

✔ Tips

■ Each category of plugins (sound, video, virtual reality) is supported by a specific group of plugin attributes. To learn more about how to create custom plugin configurations, visit each plugin developer's Web site.

■ Microsoft's Internet Explorer browser has a few IE-specific plugin attributes. To learn about these, check out Microsoft's Authors and Developers' site at **http://www .microsoft.com/ie/authors/**.

■ CyberStudio includes a feature that enables you to create interfaces to new plugins as they become available. Once you create and save the definition for a user-defined interface, the Plugin Inspector's Special tab includes the interface attributes. You need to study each new plugin's requirements and attributes before you can create these custom interfaces.

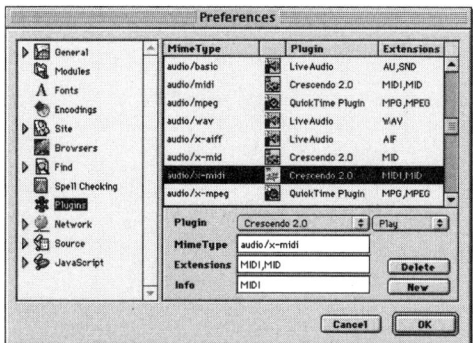

Figure 9-13: When an attribute is completed, it appears in the upper portion of the window.

Figure 9-14: The Plugin Preferences window shows the media formats you can play from within GoLive CyberStudio and allows you to choose a plugin with which to display the content.

Setting plugin preferences

Most Web browsers that support plugin playback allow you not only to use plugins but to choose which file formats are read by each plugin. Some of these choices are automatic. Besides movies, the QuickTime 2.0 plugin (the current version at this writing, and the one included with CyberStudio) supports a variety of sound files that are listed in CyberStudio's plugin preferences window. CyberStudio automatically associates a plugin with each file format it knows about, and vice versa.

You can change these relationships if you would rather use different plugins to play files of a given format. You can also tell CyberStudio not to play the media files at all, if you choose.

To change plugin/media relationships:

1. Choose Preferences from the Edit menu.

2. Click on the Plugin Preferences icon. Scroll through the window to find it, if necessary. It is displayed in **Figure 9-13**. The Plugin Preferences panel shows plugin formats, the plugin used to play the format and the file extension associated with each format.

3. Click once on a media format to select it. The current settings for the chosen format are displayed and can be edited.

4. Click on the Plugin popup menu and choose the Crescendo plugin. **Figure 9-14** shows that there are three installed plugins (Crescendo, LiveAudio and QuickTime) that can read and play the audio/midi format.

5. Leave the Play/Don't Play menu alone so that MIDI files play when you open a Web page that contains them.

✔ Tips

■ All the formats listed in the Plugin Preferences window were entered there automatically by the plugins stored in the CyberStudio plugins folder. To use a plugin with CyberStudio, you must copy the plugin software into the Plugins folder or place an alias of the plugin file there.

■ You can use the Plugin Preferences window to create entries for new media formats, but that is usually not necessary. When you add a new plugin to the Plugins folder and launch CyberStudio, the plugin software registers the media formats it supports and displays them in the Plugin Preferences window.

■ The Plugin popup menu in the Preferences window is a good way to remember which plugins support which formats. When you select a format and click on the menu, only those plugins that support the format you've selected are available.

■ Version 2.0 of the QuickTime Plugin supports a large number of audio and video formats. You may be able to reduce the number of different plugins you use by selecting QuickTime whenever it is available.

JavaScript, Java and ActiveX

10

GoLive CyberStudio includes support for Netscape's JavaScript, Sun Microsystems' Java, and Microsoft's ActiveX. Each of these formats makes it possible for Web pages to come to life in one way or another and to take on some of the characteristics of a computer program. In CyberStudio, you can insert or edit scripts and create pointers from your Web page to Java applets and ActiveX controls.

In this chapter, I cover:

■ JavaScript.

■ Java applets.

■ ActiveX controls.

JavaScript

Netscape created JavaScript as an adjunct to the Java language. JavaScript can be used to give life to a Web page with moving banners, animation and other decorative touches. JavaScript can also be used to give instructions to Java applets or link multiple applets together. Unlike Java, JavaScripts are composed of code within your Web page or stored with it. Java applets are actually programs that are run on the Web server, with output sent to a Web browser.

CyberStudio allows you to add JavaScript to a Web page and includes tools that allow you to create and edit scripts yourself.

To add an existing JavaScript to a Web page:

1. Open a CyberStudio document to the Layout View.

2. Drag the JavaScript tool (**Figure 10-1**) from the palette to the document window. A JavaScript placholder appears, and the Body Script Inspector is displayed in the Inspector window (**Figure 10-2**).

3. Name the script.

4. Choose a language (based on the target browser you want to support) from the Language popup menu. CyberStudio enters a JavaScript dialect to match your choice in the dialect field.

5. Click the Source checkbox to light up the Reference field and Browse button.

6. Use the Browse button to locate a JavaScript or, if you're working in a CyberStudio site, use Point & Shoot to find one.

✔ Tips

- To ensure the widest possible browser compatibility for your JavaScript, choose an older browser. The tradeoff, of course, is that older browsers and script dialects

Figure 10-1: The JavaScript palette tool.

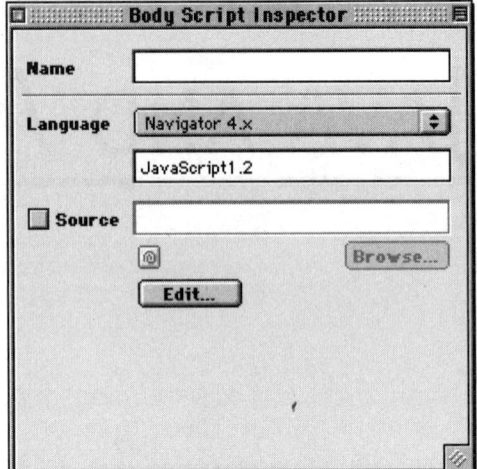

Figure 10-2: The Body Script Inspector.

Figure 10-3: Click the Java Bean to open the JavaScript editor.

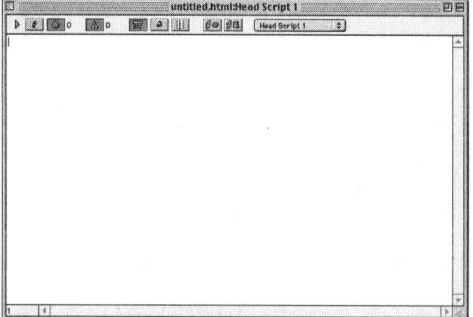

Figure 10-4: The JavaScript Editor.

Figure 10-5: Click the New Script button on the JavaScript editor's toolbar.

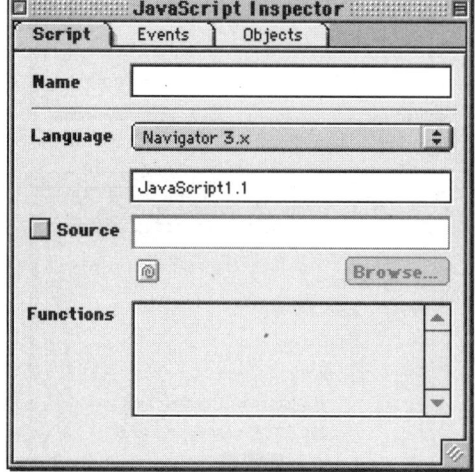

Figure 10-6: The JavaScript Editor.

don't include all of the features of newer offerings. At this writing, I recommend choosing Navigator 3.x (JavaScript1.1) as a compromise between widely used Java-Script and the most advanced feature set.

■ If you want to use a later version of JavaScript, consider creating a page that supports older browsers, or doesn't use JavaScript at al. You can implement this either by detecting the user's browser (with a DHTML browser switch action) or simply by asking the user to click to reach a non-JavaScript page.

Creating JavaScripts

CyberStudio includes a full-fledge JavaScript editor, where you can write your own scripts. The editor includes a variety of drag-and-drop tools and selectors for creating the script.

There are three ways to reach the JavaScript editor. They are:

■ Drag the JavaScript item from the palette to the document window and double-click the icon.

■ With a JavaScript item selected in the document window, click the Edit button in the Body Script Inspector..

■ Click the Java Bean icon in the document window.

I'll use the Java Bean.

To create a JavaScript:

1. Click on the Java Bean, near the upper-right corner of the document window (**Figure 10-3**). The JavaScript Editor (**Figure 10-4**) and JavaScript Inspector appear.

2. Click the New Script Item on the toolbar in the JavaScript Editor (**Figure 10-5**).

3. In the JavaScript Inspector (**Figure 10-6**), name the script, and choose a language, as described in the previous section.

JAVASCRIPT

4. Click the Events tab of the JavaScript Inspector (**Figure 10-7**). The Events tab includes the items (window and document) that can support events. Under these items are the events that the item can support.

5. Click the Objects tab of the JavaScript Inspector (**Figure 10-8**).

6. Click the triangle next to the Other Objects item, and then on a subsequent item, to reveal a list of specific objects you can add to a script.

7. Click on an item in the window. The item is highlighted, and a description appears at the bottom of the Inspector window (**Figure 10-9**).

8. To add events and objects to your script, drag and drop individual item into the JavaScript editor window.

9. When you've finished adding items, save the script.

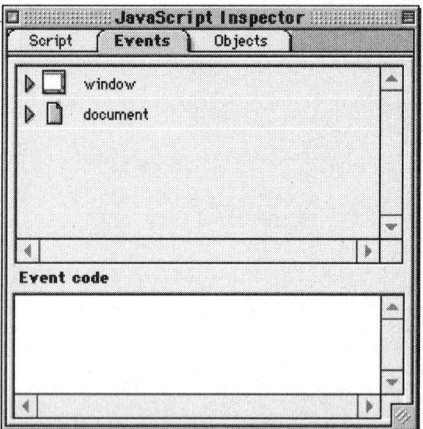

Figure 10-7: The Events tab of the JavaScript Inspector.

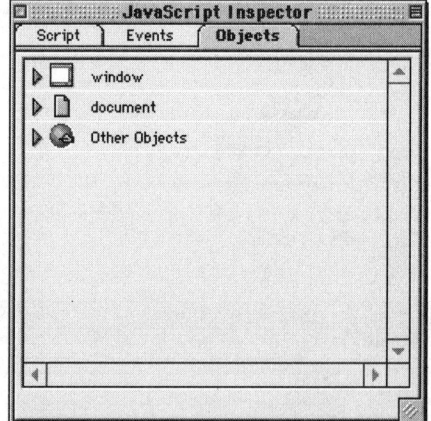

Figure 10-8: The Objects tab of the JavaScript Inspector.

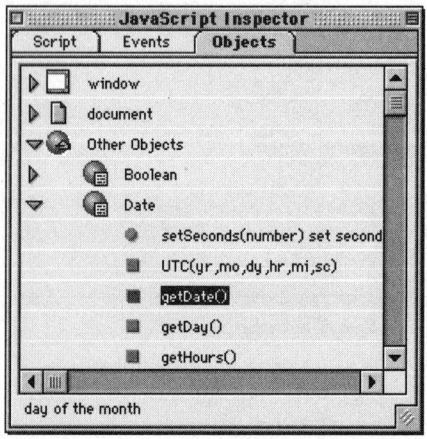

Figure 10-9: Click on an event or object to view a description.

JAVASCRIPT

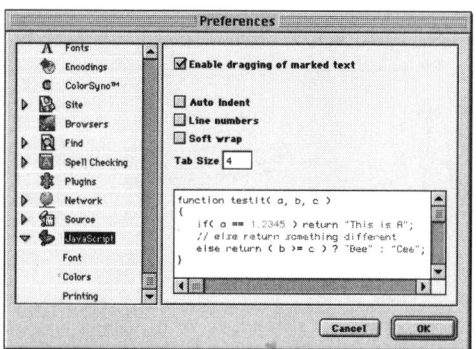

Figure 10-10: The JavaScript Preferences window's General tab.

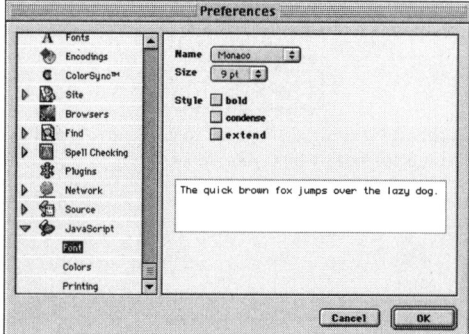

Figure 10-11: The JavaScript Font Preferences window.

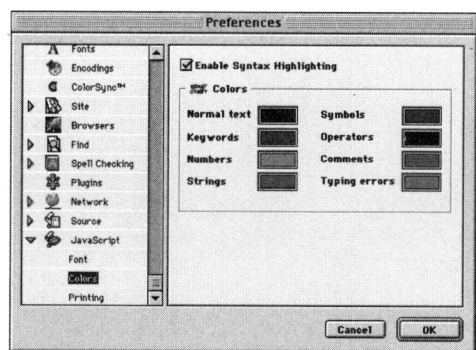

Figure 10-12: The Color tab of the JavaScript Preferences window.

To set general JavaScript preferences:

1. Choose Preferences from the Edit menu.

2. Click on the JavaScript item. Scroll through the window to find it, if necessary. JavaScript preferences appear (**Figure 10-10**).

3. Leave the "Enable dragging of marked text" box checked to support drag-and-drop within the Script Editor.

4. Leave "Auto-Indenting" checked if you want lower-level tags indented by default.

5. Check "Soft Wrap" to cause JavaScript code to wrap to subsequent lines.

To set JavaScript font preferences:

1. Click the triangle to the left of the Java-Script item, to reveal more preferences.

2. Click the Font tab in the JavaScript Preferences window (**Figure 10-11**).

3. Choose a typeface, size and style.

To set JavaScript color preferences:

1. Click the Color tab in the JavaScript Preferences window (**Figure 10-12**).

3. Leave the "Syntax Highlighting" box checked to use colors to highlight elements and errors in your scripts.

3. Click a color field to apply color to a specific type of script code. The Apple Color wheel appears.

4. Choose a color and click OK.

To set JavaScript printing preferences:

1. Click the Printing item under the JavaScript preference item (**Figure 10-13**).

2. Click "Printer specific settings" to light up several choices that relate to display of items when you print scripts.

3. Click "Use special font for printing" to choose font, style and size options.

Checking a script for errors

With JavaScript:Colors preferences set, you can use colors to display syntax and errors within a script.

To check a script:

1. With a script visible in the JavaScript Editor, click the Syntax Highlighting button on the toolbar (**Figure 10-14**). CyberStudio highlights any syntax errors found within your script.

2. Click the Display Errors button and/or the Display Warnings button to list the number of errors in your script.

3. If errors in your script were highlighted, click the triangle next to the Syntax Highlighting button to view errors in a pane of their own.

✔ Tip

■ Display preferences that you choose here do not affect the appearance of your Web page, even if elements of a JavaScript you create are visible to those viewing your page.

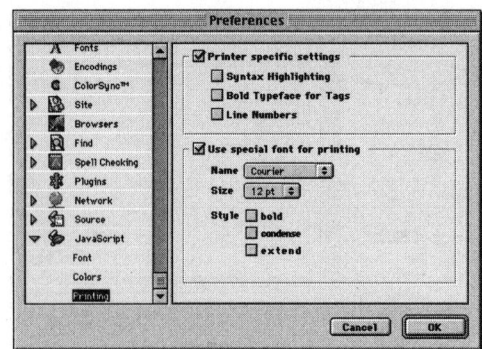

Figure 10-13: The JavaScript Printing Preferences window.

Figure 10-14: Highlight syntax to locale errors and incomplete items within your script.

Figure 10-15: The Java Applet tool.

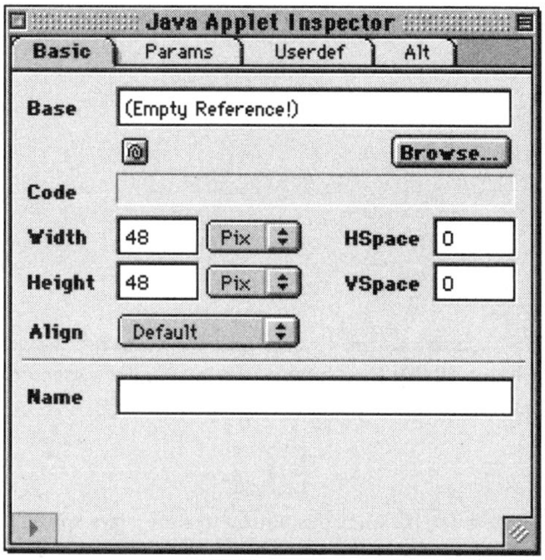

Figure 10-16: The Java Applet Inspector window.

Java applets

Despite the similarity of their names, Java-Scripts and Java applets are not the same thing at all. As I pointed out earlier, JavaScripts are usually fairly simple structures that are embedded in a Web page's HTML code. Java applets, on the other hand, are complete programs, written in the Java language, that are called by, and may even appear within, a Web page but are not part of that page. Java applets can be database interfaces, games or any number of other applications.

You don't write Java applets in GoLive Cyber-Studio. You connect existing applets to the pages you create, specifying the appearance of the applet primarily within the applet itself. HTML (and CyberStudio) allow you to specify basic size, spacing and alignment options, but the rest is up to the applet developer. You can preview applets in CyberStudio, because, like newer Web browsers, CyberStudio supports Java.

To add a Java applet to a Web page:

1. Open a CyberStudio document.

2. Drag the Java Applet tool (**Figure 10-15**) from the palette to the document window. The Java Applet Inspector appears in the Inspector window (**Figure 10-16**).

3. Locate a Java applet on your hard disk with the Browse button or Point & Shoot. The applet's location (Base) and Code appear in the Inspector window.

4. Resize the applet if you want, either by dragging the placeholder's handles in the document window or by typing new dimensions in the Inspector's Width and Height fields (in pixels).

5. If the applet is not on a layout grid, or if it is within a text frame, you can add horizontal and vertical space between the applet and adjacent text with the Hspace and Vspace

fields. You can also use the Align popup menu to align the applet to adjacent text.

6. Name the applet by typing a unique (not in use by any other applet on the page) name in the Name field.

7. To add alternative text or HTML that will be displayed by browsers that support Java but whose Java option is disabled, click on the Alt tab of the Java Applet Inspector (**Figure 10-17**).

8. Type the alternative text in the Alt Text field.

9. If you want to display an HTML object instead, click the "Show Alternative HTML" box.

10. Return to the document window and click on the Java applet placeholder. Drag the palette tool of your choice into the placeholder and configure the HTML object (text, image, plugin, etc.) you want to appear when Java is disabled.

✔ Tip

■ You can view the contents and action of a Java applet in two ways: click the Play button in the Java Applet Inspector (**Figure 10-18**) or view your document with the Preview View.

To add Java parameters:

1. Select a Java applet in the document window.

2. In the Java Applet Inspector, click the Params tab. The Params window appears (**Figure 10-19**). Parameters are applet-specific attributes.

3. Click New to set up a new parameter.

4. Type the name of the parameter in the Param field when it appears. Press Tab.

5. Type a value for the parameter in the value field. Press Return to confirm your entry. The new parameter appears in the window, above.

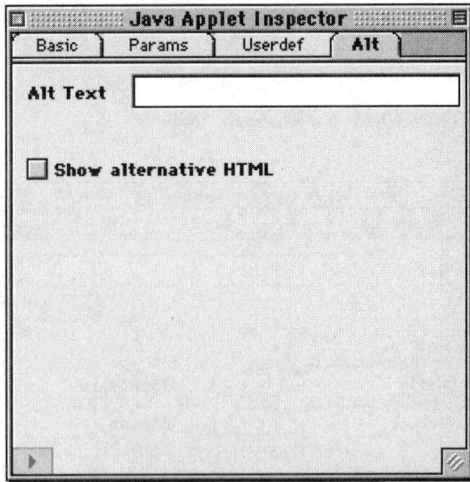

Figure 10-17: The Alt tab of the Java Applet Inspector.

Figure 10-18: Click this button to view a Java applet.

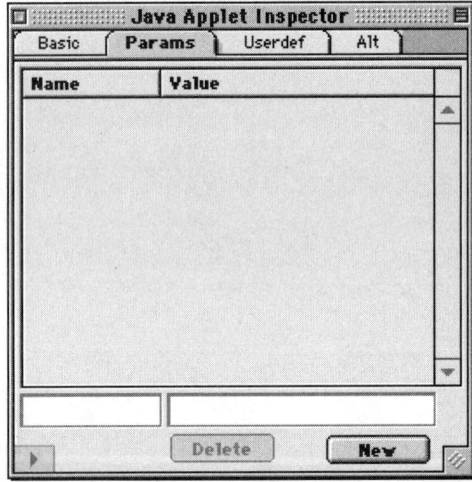

Figure 10-19: The Java Applet Inspector's Params tab.

Figure 10-20: The ActiveX Control panel tool.

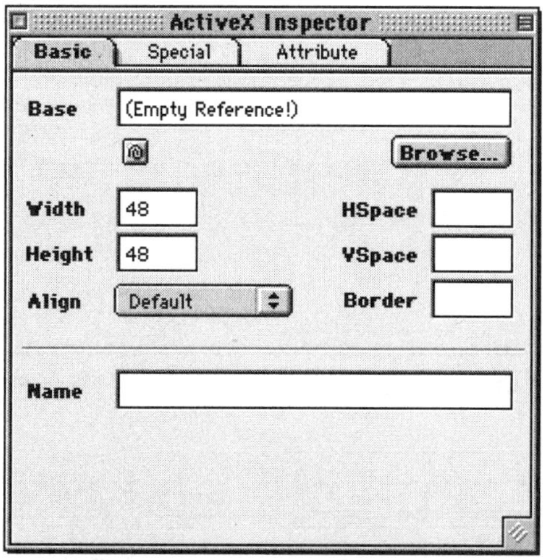

Figure 10-21: The ActiveX Inspector.

ActiveX

Microsoft developed ActiveX as an alternative to Sun's Java language, as an improvement on current plugin technology, and as a way to add interactivity to Web sites. Unlike Java, ActiveX is not platform-independent. It's a proprietary technology that is used primarily with the Windows 95 operating system version of Microsoft's Internet Explorer browser.

You can add ActiveX *controls*—the ActiveX equivalent of plugins—to a Web page in CyberStudio, but you won't be able to view them without an ActiveX-compatible browser.

Note: Although a version of Microsoft Internet Explorer is available for the Macintosh, there are very few ActiveX controls for the Mac.

To add an ActiveX control to a Web page:

1. Open a CyberStudio document.

2. Drag the ActiveX Control tool (**Figure 10-20**) from the palette to the document window. The ActiveX Inspector appears in the Inspector window (**Figure 10-21**).

3. Locate an ActiveX control on your hard disk with the Browse button or Point & Shoot. The control's location (Base) appears in the Inspector window.

4. Resize the control if you want, either by dragging the placeholder's handles in the document window or by typing new dimensions in the Inspector's Width and Height fields.

5. If the control is not on a layout grid, or if it is within a text frame, you can add horizontal and vertical space between the control and adjacent text with the Hspace and Vspace fields. You can also use the Align popup menu to align the control to adjacent text.

ACTIVEX

6. Name the control by typing a unique (not in use by any other control on this page) name in the Name field.

7. Click the Special tab in the ActiveX Control Inspector window (**Figure 10-22**).

8. In the Data field, enter the URL for a resource to be used when the ActiveX is activated. Press Tab.

9. In the Linktype field, type the link that the control should use to transfer data to the target location. Press Tab.

10. The Target is the page where ActiveX control data will appear. Type the name of the file or application to receive ActiveX control data. Press Tab.

11. Type a message in the Standby field if you want a message to appear on the page as the ActiveX control loads.

To add ActiveX attributes:

1. With an ActiveX control selected, click the Attribute tab in the ActiveX Inspector to display the Attributes window (**Figure 10-23**).

2. To create a new attribute, click New.

3. Type the attribute's name in the Name field and press Tab.

4. Type a default value for the attribute in the Value field. Press Return to confirm the attribute.

5. Repeat steps 2–4 to add additional attributes.

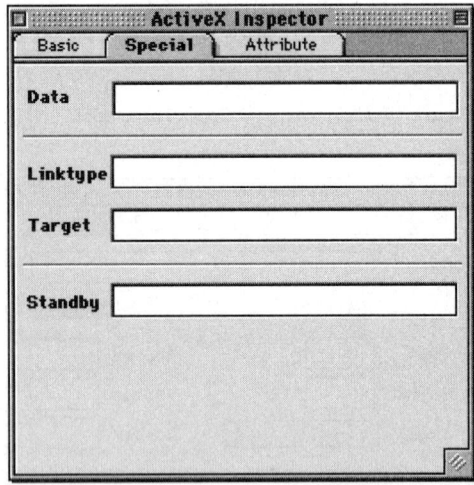

Figure 10-22: The Special tab of the ActiveX Inspector.

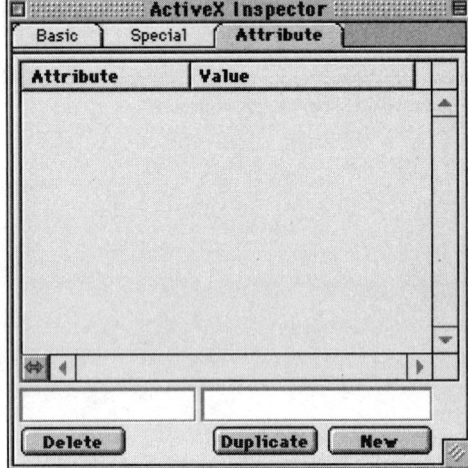

Figure 10-23: The Attribute tab of the ActiveX Inspector.

ACTIVEX

Working with Style Sheets

You can do a lot with basic HTML tags; you can arrange objects and format text, but you can't position text precisely, and you can't always format it exactly as you need to. If you're used to using style sheets in word processing software and desktop publishing tools, HTML's limitations can be frustrating.

CyberStudio 3 includes support for Level 1 Cascading Style Sheets (CSS1), an HTML-standard method of creating formatting instructions and saving them for use with all of your documents. You can use Cyber-Studio's familiar tools and fill-in Inspector windows to avoid most of the coding normally associated with creating style sheets.

In this chapter, I cover:

- How style sheets work.
- Types of style sheets.
- Creating style sheets.
- Selectors.
- Properties.

How style sheets work

Cascading style sheets consist of files and tags that contain instructions on how to format text on the Web. Style sheets contain individual styles that specify new formatting for an HTML tag throughout a site, or they can alter a single block of text. There are lots of variations in between, that I'll describe throughout this chapter.

Like other HTML pages and tags, style sheets require a certain syntax to work, and that syntax varies depending upon the way the style sheet is intended to work with your document. Similarly, individual styles use syntax to tell a Web browser how to interpret it, and what changes to make in text display and position.

What style sheets are good for

First of all, style sheets allow you to create and save sets of formatting instructions for blocks of text within your Web pages. This makes it easier to establish a consistent design for your pages, and to apply it quickly throughout your site without having to remember the parameters you need.

Finally, and most importantly, style sheets provide some capabilities that have, up to now, been unavailable to Web authors. You can use them to specify the precise position of text on the page, and to set measurements for margins and vertical and horizontal spacing. Without style sheets, the position of your text is subject to the interpretation of each visitor's browser.

Style sheet syntax

It's easiest to think of style sheets and their components as a hierarchy. Style sheets are documents that contain styles, also known as style rules. Each style is defined by its *selectors, properties* and *values.*

A selector describes how the style interacts with the documents to which you apply it. Properties identify the type, display or positioning elements that you wish to format with the style. Finally, each property supports *values* that specify the way the element will appear, including relevant measurements.

Using CSS1 correctly

Cascading style sheets are part of the HTML 4.0 specification, approved by the W3C; the organization that attempts to create and enforce HTML standards. In order for a Web browser to recognize and properly interpret style sheets, it must support CSS1 tags. Even within CSS1, there are a few style elements that version 4.0 browsers don't support. That's because both Netscape and Microsoft have developed their own CSS1 versions. As I proceed through this chapter, I'll note these inconsistencies, so that you can plan for them when constructing your own style sheets.

HOW STYLE SHEETS WORK

Types of style sheets

All style sheets support the same kinds of content formatting (properties) and most of the same style rules (selectors) but they differ in the way they connect to, or work with Web pages. *Internal* style sheets format the content of a single HTML document, while *external* style sheets can change the appearance of a group of documents.

Internal style sheets

There are two types of internal style sheets; *embedded* and *inline*. Both are actually part of the HTML page it supports. An embedded style sheet is included in the document's header section. Embedded style sheets are useful if you want to change formatting for all occurrences of a given type of text formatting (usually an HTML tag) within a single document.

Inline style sheets are included in the body of an HTML document, and apply styles to specific items only. In other words, if you create an inline style to change an <h2> heading from black to blue, the style would appear next to the heading you want to change, and would apply only to that instance of the heading. To make all <h2> headings in a document blue, you would need to add an embedded style sheet to the header section of the document.

External style sheets

You can use external style sheets to apply styles to a group of documents—your whole Web site, for example. The two types of external style sheets are: *linked* and *imported*.

Linked style sheets are the easiest to understand. All styles for a site can be included in a single style sheet document that you link to each document where its styles should be applied.

Imported style sheets use both internal and external style rules by importing the rules associated with local pages along with global ones that you create within an external style sheet page.

✔ Tip

■ CyberStudio supports imported style sheets, in that it can display them in the style sheet window, and preview their results correctly, but you can't use CyberStudio tools to create an imported style sheet.

TYPES OF STYLE SHEETS

Creating style sheets

Though there are a number of style sheet types, selectors and properties, the process of creating all style sheets in CyberStudio is basically the same. Here are some basic steps, which will get you acquainted city CyberStudio's style sheet tools.

To create a style sheet:

1. With a document open, click the Style Sheet button, located above the main window, at the right edge of the title bar (**Figure 11-1**). A new Style Sheet window appears (**Figure 11-2**).

2. Save the style sheet by choosing Save from the File menu. Leave the style sheet's name as CyberStudio created it. The name refers to the document the style sheet supports.

To add a style to the style sheet:

1. With the style sheet file open (the style sheet window should be visible), choose New Class, Net Tag or New ID from the toolbar (**Figure 11-3**). A new item appears in the Style Sheet window, under the appropriate heading.

2. To begin configuring the style, locate or open the Inspector window, which contains the CSS Selector Inspector (**Figure 11-4**).

3. Name the style.

Figure 11-1: Click the Style Sheet button to open the Style Sheet window.

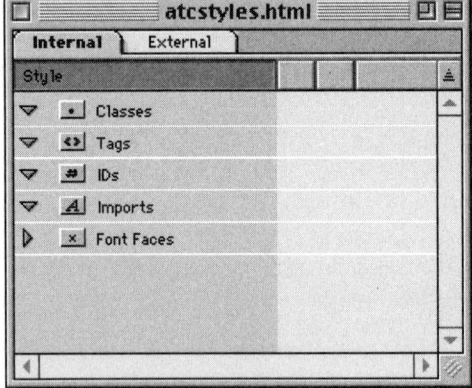

Figure 11-2: The Style Sheet window

Figure 11-3: Choose New Class from the toolbar to add a class selector to a style sheet.

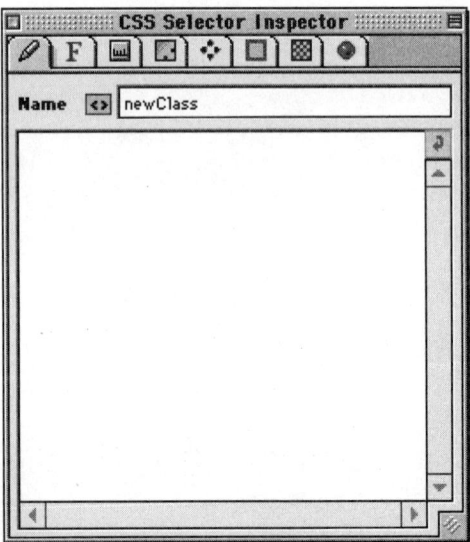

Figure 11-4: The CSS Selector Inspector includes the tools you'll use to configure style properties.

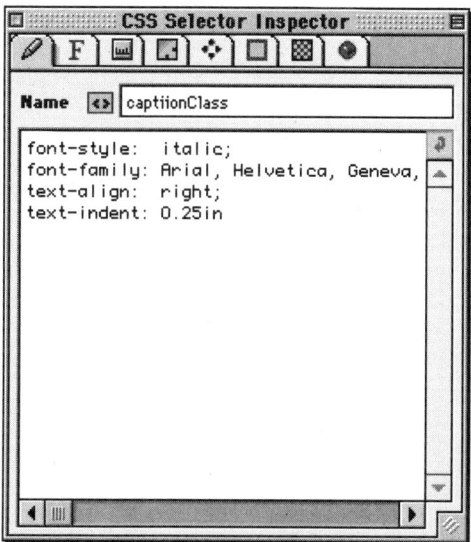

Figure 11-5: Once you've configured a style, its properties appear in the Inspector.

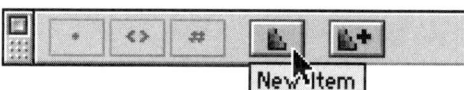

Figure 11-6: Add an external style sheet reference by choosing New Item from the toolbar.

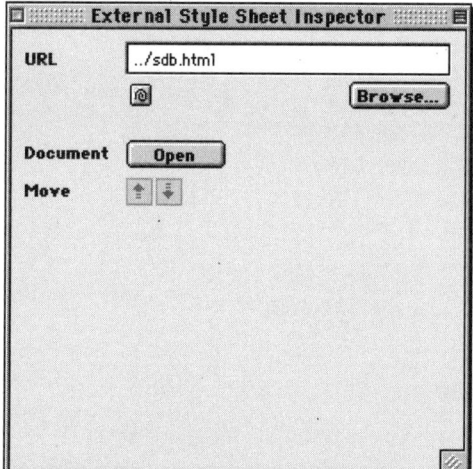

Figure 11-7: Choose the file to refer to with the External Style Sheet Inspector.

4. Click on the other tabs in the CSS Selector Inspector to configure the style's properties.

5. Once you've configured one or two properties, click on the Pencil tab (where you named the style) in the Inspector. Notice that your properties appear in the pane below the name of your style (**Figure 11-5**)

To refer to an external style sheet:

1. Open a document to which you want to add external style sheet references.

2. Open the local style sheet (whether or not you've already created one) by clicking on the Style Sheet button.

3. In the Style Sheet window, click the External tab.

4. Choose New Item from the toolbar (**Figure 11-6**). A new item appears in the External tab of the Style Sheet window.

5. Click in the Inspector window, which has changed to become the External Style Sheet Inspector.

6. Click the Browse button (or use Point & Shoot) to locate a document with styles you want to use in the current document. The finished Inspector appears in **Figure 11-7**.

7. Meanwhile, the Style Sheet window now includes the name of the document, a checkmark indicating that the link is valid, and the URL (**Figure 11-8**).

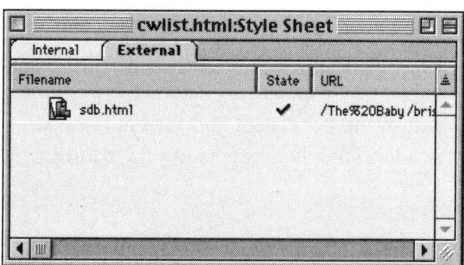

Figure 11-8: The external reference has been successfully linked in this image of the Style Sheet window.

Selectors

Style sheet selectors tell the style sheet how an individual style will interact with the sheet and the documents it supports. Different selectors offer

CyberStudio recognizes three types of style sheet selectors. They are:

- Tags.
- Classes.
- IDs.

Tag Selectors

Tag selectors allow you to apply style rules to any HTML tag within a document. Applying a tag selector tells CyberStudio (and the browser a visitor uses to view your page) to style all occurrence of the tag according to style properties you specify.

✔ Tip

- An important advantage of tag-based styles is that they are fully compatible with browsers that can't read CSS1 information. Visitors whose browsers can view style sheets will see the enhanced formatting, while those with older browsers simply see the tag's normal formatting.

You can use tag selectors with all four types of CSS1 style sheets.

To create a tag selector:

1. Open a new or existing style sheet document, along with a document to which you want to apply a tag selector. Type some text in the document and format the text as a level one heading, using the toolbar.

Figure 11-9: Choose New Tag from the toolbar to create a tag selector.

2. Choose New Tag from the toolbar (**Figure 11-9**). The new tag appears in the Style Sheet window.

3. In the CSS Selector Inspector, type **H1**. Do not include the usual < and > brackets. You can create a tag selector for any HTML tag that uses the <tag> </tag> syntax.

4. Configure the new style's properties under the Property tabs of the Inspector window. Notice that the text in your document changes as you specify style options.

Class selectors

Unlike tags, class selectors apply style formatting to specific instances of a text block, rather than all instances that share a common HTML tag. Classes use conditional rules (if x exists and meets these criteria, then style should be applied). You could, for example, create a class that colors an H2 heading blue, but only when it's also indented from the left margin.

To create a class selector:

1. With a style sheet window open, choose New Class from the toolbar.

2. In the CSS Selector Inspector, name the class. You can use any name you like, because classes don't depend on, or expect to see an HTML tag as the identifier within the style sheet code.

3. Configure the class style with the properties tabs of the Inspector.

Applying classes

Unlike tag styles, which apply automatically to all matching HTML tags in a document, classes, which apply to specific, or conditional instances of text, must be specifically applied.

To apply class styles to text:

1. With a class style created and configured, open the document to which you want to add the style.

2. Click on some text to display the Text Inspector.

3. Click the Style tab, to display classes available to this document.

4. To apply a style to a specific text block with an inline class, select the text you want to format. In the Inspector, select the style you want and click under the Inline label (**Figure 11-10**) to apply it. A checkmark appears, and the style is applied.

5. To apply a style to a paragraph with a Par class, click within the paragraph and locate the style you want in the Inspector. Click in the Par column to display a checkmark.

6. To create a style that divides the styled section from the rest of the HTML page allowing you to align it separately, click within a paragraph, choose the style you want, and click in the Div column.

7. To create an Area style, that applies a class to the entire body section of an HTML page, click anywhere within the document's text and choose a style. Click in the Area column to apply it.

ID Selectors

ID selectors apply a chosen style to only one item. They don't include conditions for applying a style to tags, or to other parts of a document. Even if you aren't interested in creating an elaborate system of style sheets to manage a Web site, ID-based style are a great way to take advantage of the powerful text formatting capabilities CSS1 offers.

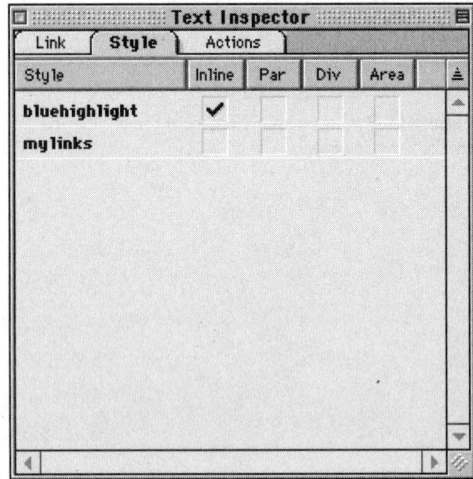

Figure 11-10: Click to select an inline style in the Text Inspector.

Figure 11-11: Choose New ID to create a new ID selector.

To create an ID selector:

1. With a style sheet window open, choose New ID from the toolbar (**Figure 11-11**).

2. In the CSS Selector Inspector, name the ID. You can use any name you like.

3. Configure the ID style with the properties tabs of the Inspector.

Applying IDs

Unlike most operations in CyberStudio, applying an ID style requires you to edit HTML code. You'll need to locate the text you want to style, modify the existing formatting slightly, and add the ID tag. Here we go!

To apply an ID selector:

1. With an ID created and configured, click on the Source tab in the document window to display the Source view.

2. Locate the text you want to format with an ID.

3. To apply an ID to all text enclosed within HTML tags, insert the ID selector within the start tag of your text block, by adding ID=idname. Here are two examples:

   Original code:

   ```
   <H2>One Day Sale!</H2>
   <P>All bicycles 50 percent off, today only.</p>
   ```

   With IDs added:

   ```
   <H2 ID="salebanner">One Day Sale!</H2>
   <P ID="redandlarge">All bicycles 50 percent off, today only.</P>
   ```

4. To apply an ID only to a portion of a text that falls within tags, use this syntax:

   ```
   <P>All bicycles <SPAN ID="salebanner">50 percent</SPAN> off, today only.</P>
   ```

SELECTORS

Properties

Throughout this chapter, I've referred to style sheet properties. Properties are the specific formatting elements you use to change the appearance of text with style sheets. All style sheet types and selectors use the same set of properties.

Properties are truly the nuts and bolts of style sheets, because they add formatting capabilities that are otherwise unavailable to Web authors who use standard HTML. For example, using a style sheet property, you can specify that all level 2 headings should be 18 point Helvetica, with 36 points of leading above the heading. Try doing that with basic HTML.

The seven categories of style sheet properties supported by CyberStudio are:

- Font.
- Text.
- Box.
- Positioning.
- Border.
- Background.
- List.

✔ Tip

- Just because you can create a property doesn't mean that it will work with all 4.0 browsers. Unfortunately, browser vendors are inconstant about the way the support properties. It's important that you test style sheets with all major browsers before making your pages live.

In this section, I'll describe how to configure style sheet properties. First though, I need to explain a couple of unique configuration elements; measurements and color-handling.

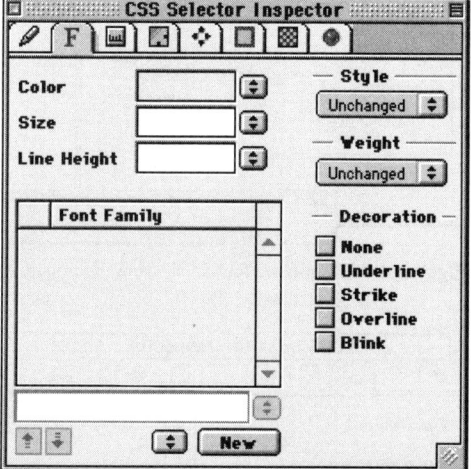

Figure 11-12: The Font properties tab of the CSS Selector Inspector.

Measurements

Style sheet properties support a measurement and color application scheme that is different from standard HTML. While they do support the familiar pixel and percentage measurements, for example, you'll also find that style sheets accept measurements in picas, centimeters, inches and more.

Units of measure supported by style sheets are:

- *Absolute measurements*: point, pica, millimeter (mm), centimeter (cm) and inch.

- *Relative units*: em, ex and pixel. Em measures the item relative to the height (in points) of the current font. Ex measures text relative to the letter X, also in the current font. Pixels are relative to the resolution of the screen.

- *Percent unit*: expresses styled text as a percentage of the default.

- *Keyword units*: ranging from XXSmall to XXLarge measure text, like standard HTML size tags, relative to the default size.

Color

Colors are also handled differently within style sheets. Style sheets support only 16 colors from the W3C RGB color palette. They are named on popup menus within the Properties tabs of the CSS Selector Inspector, or you can drag them from the Color Palette.

To set font properties:

1. Open a style sheet and create a style.

2. In the CSS Selector Inspector, click the Font tab. It appears in **Figure 11-12**.

3. Choose a font color (if you want to change it) from the popup menu, or drag a color from the Color Palette. CyberStudio will interpret the color you choose from the Palette to conform to the 16-color palette.

PROPERTIES

175

4. Type a number in the Font Size field, and choose a unit of measure from the popup. Note that, unlike ordinary HTML text formatting, you can choose an absolute point size for your text, if you wish.

5. Type a Line Height and choose an option from the popup, using the one of the same measurement units. Line Height is referred to as leading in the print publishing world.

6. To apply a new typeface, choose a font family from the popup at the bottom of the Inspector window (**Figure 11-13**), or click New to add a new family.

7. Choose font style, and/or decoration options in the Inspector.

8. To change the font's weight, choose a number from 100 to 900 from the popup. Choosing Normal applies a weight of 400, while Bold equals a weight of 700. Font weights are absolute but the Bolder and Lighter options are relative to the default, or to any existing style that this new style inherits properties from.

To set text properties:

1. Click the Text tab in the CSS Selector Inspector. It appears in **Figure 11-14**.

2. Edit Text Indent, Letter Spacing and Word Spacing the same way you chose numerical font properties, above.

3. Choose an option from the Vertical Alignment popup to relate the styled text to the rest of the text on the page.

4. Use the Font Variant and Transformation options to further customize the text within your style. Both allow you to change the case of styled text.

5. Like standard HTML alignment options, the Alignment popup under the Text properties tab aligns text to the page horizontally.

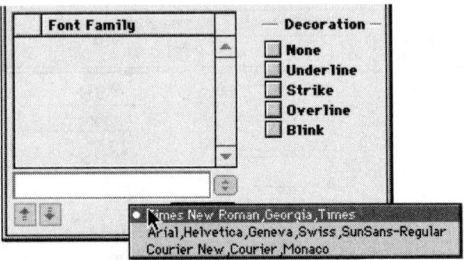

Figure 11-13: Choose a font family from the popup.

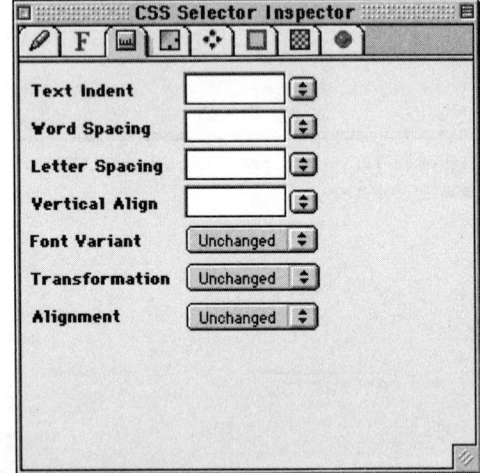

Figure 11-14: The Text Properties tab of the CSS Selector Inspector.

PROPERTIES

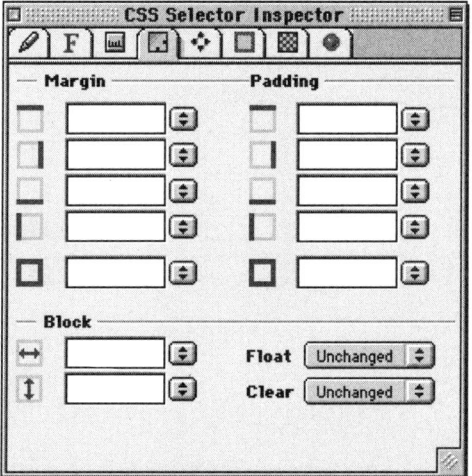

Figure 11-15: The Box properties tab of the CSS Selector Inspector.

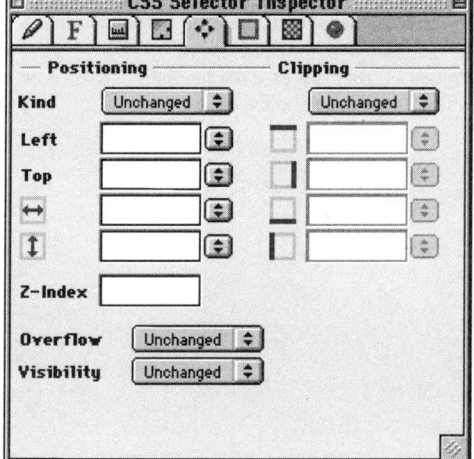

Figure 11-16: The Positioning tab of the CSS Selector Inspector.

To set box properties:

1. Click the Box tab in the CSS Selector Inspector. It appears in **Figure 11-15**. The "box" defines the area of the document controlled by the style you are creating. If you don't change box properties, the boundary is the text itself. If you do, there will be space between styled text and other elements of the page.

2. Choose margins for the box, to create it. You only need to choose margins for those boundaries you want to extend.

3. Choose padding to create space between the styled text and the margin you've created.

4. You can use the Block option (horizontal and/or vertical) to define width and height of the box. This property is most useful when you need to include an image within the styled box.

To set positioning properties:

1. Click the Positioning tab in the CSS Selector Inspector. It appears in **Figure 11-16**. Positioning is used with floating boxes to apply their attributes to styled elements. Positioning properties determine where on the page the styled element will appear. You can position the element absolutely (measuring its location from the top and left of the page) or relatively (according to the element's proximity to other items on the page.

2. Choose the type of positioning you want to use. Absolute sets a precise location on the page. Static positioning allows the styled element to flow with the main body of text on the page. Relative positions the styled element with respect to a parent element.

3. Specify the position numerically. Pixels are the best measurement choice.

4. Choose a Z-Index value to control how the element behaves when another floating element lands on top of it. The element with the higher Z-Index will appear on top.

5. Change the Clipping option to specify how a style element reacts when another object runs into it.

6. Choose an overflow option to address a text block that outgrows the floating box you have specified for it. You can choose the Visible (expand the box), Scroll (add scroll bars), Hidden (don't show the excess content) or Auto (allows the visitor's Web browser to choose).

To set border properties:

1. Click the Border tab in the CSS Selector Inspector. It appears in **Figure 11-17**. Unlike the box properties we created earlier, which create an invisible boundary around the element you are styling, border properties specify a visible border for the styled element.

2. Choose left, right, top and/or bottom border thickness by typing values and using the popups to choose a measuring unit.

3. Choose colors for borders from the popup, or with the Color Palette.

4. Choose the type of border (solid, dotted, etc.) from the popup menus.

5. If you want a four-sided border with the same thickness, color and line style, use the box field and popup (**Figure 11-18**).

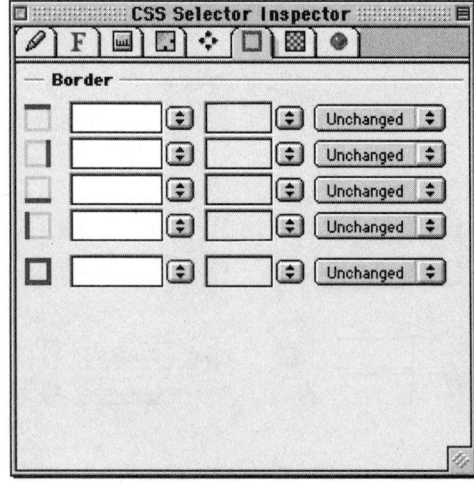

Figure 11-17: The Border tab of the CSS Selector Inspector.

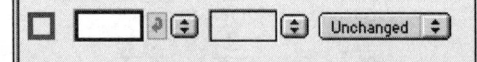

Figure 11-18: Make your border uniform on all sides with the box options in the Border tab.

PROPERTIES

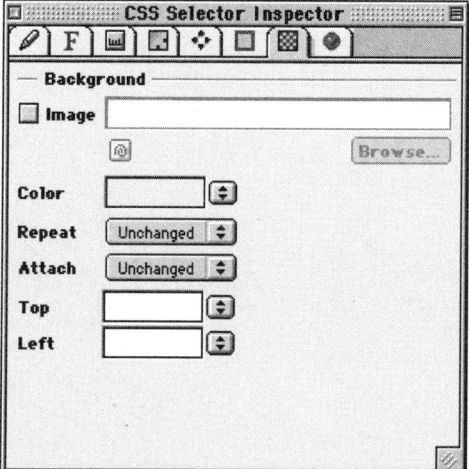

Figure 11-19: The Background properties tab of the CSS Selector Inspector.

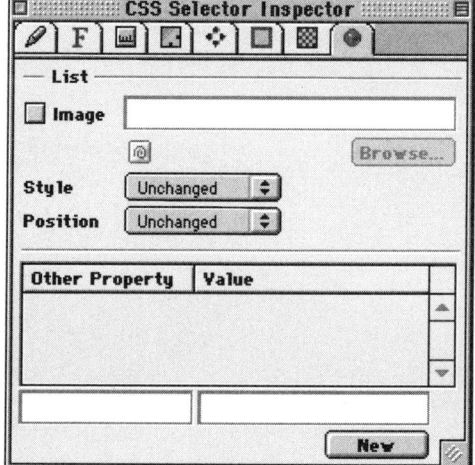

Figure 11-20: The List tab of the CSS Selector Inspector.

To set background properties:

1. Click on the Background properties tab in the CSS Selector Inspector. It appears in **Figure 11-19**. Use these options to add a background color or image to the box that surrounds your styled text.

2. Click the checkbox and then Browse (or use Point & Shoot) to locate an file you would like to use as a background image.

3. Choose a Repeat option to tile the background image within the box. Repeat X tiles the image horizontally; Repeat Y tiles it vertically.

4. Choose an Attach option to specify whether or not a background image should scroll as a visitor scrolls within the browser window.

5. Choose Top and Left measurements to position a background image relative to the box in which it is located.

6. To create a colored background, choose a color from the Color Palette or the popup menu.

To set list properties:

1. Click the List tab in the CSS Selector Inspector. It appears in **Figure 11-20**. List properties allow you to customize bullets or other list item markers that appear within HTML lists.

2. Click the image checkbox, and locate an image to use as an alternative list item marker.

3. From the Style popup, choose an HTML list style to use.

4. From the Position popup, chose Inside (to set the list item marker and subsequent lines of text flush) or Outside (to set the list item marker apart from the remaining lines of text.

WORKING
WITH DYNAMIC HTML

HTML 4.0 extends the palette of tools and options available to Web authors beyond simply formatting text and image placement. Of course, previous versions supported the embedding of JavaScript and other code that you can use to animate or bring your page to life. HTML 4.0's *dynamic HTML* (DHTML), though, adds a new dimension. You can use HTML tags, along with JavaScript and Cascading Style Sheets to animation and other dynamic elements to your pages.

CyberStudio 3.0 includes DHTML tools that use scripting and style sheets, but shield you from the coding process. Of course, if you really want to roll your sleeves up and dig into DHTML coding, CyberStudio supports your efforts with the Source Editor and Web Database.

It's important to note that DHTML features will only be visible to users of 4.0-compatible browsers, like Netscape Communicator and Microsoft Internet Explorer 4.0. Users of older browsers won't be able to see or use them.

In this chapter, I cover:

- DHTML tools.

- Using pre-built DHTML objects.

- Actions.

- Animation.

DHTML Tools

CyberStudio 3 includes several tools that
you can use to create and modify DHTML
elements:

- The CyberObjects palette tab.

- Floating boxes.

- The Actions tab.

- The timeline editor.

The CyberObjects palette tab

CyberStudio provides several pre-built DHTML
objects, available simply by dragging s palette
tool from the CyberObjects tab (**Figure 12-1**)
onto a Web page.

Floating Box tools

A principle benefit of dynamic HTML is the
ability to position items precisely on the page,
using movable, stackable layers—called *floating
boxes* in CyberStudio. To establish an item's position, DHTML allows you to add page content
to the box, then position the box relative to the
origin of the page. You can then apply scripts
to floating boxes, causing them to more, or
take other actions within the page, or act relative to other floating boxes. For more about
floating boxes, see Chapter 5.

The Actions tab

You can apply DHTML actions to text, buttons
and images. You configure DHTML actions in
the Actions tab of the Inspector associated with
the object. You add actions to an animation in
the Actions track of the timeline editor.

The timeline editor

If you've ever used Macromedia Director, or
a similar tool, you're familiar with timelines.
Timelines are used to control the elements of
an animated presentation. The CyberStudio
timeline editor (**Figure 12-2**) performs the
same function for DHTML animation.

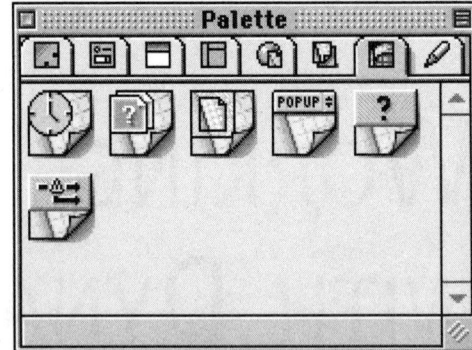

Figure 12-1: The CyberObjects palette tab.

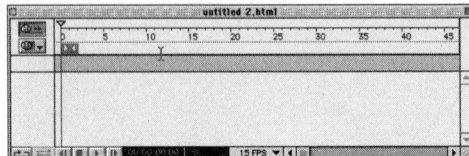

Figure 12-2: The timeline editor controls the pace of
animations within a Web page.

Figure 12-3: The Date & Time tool.

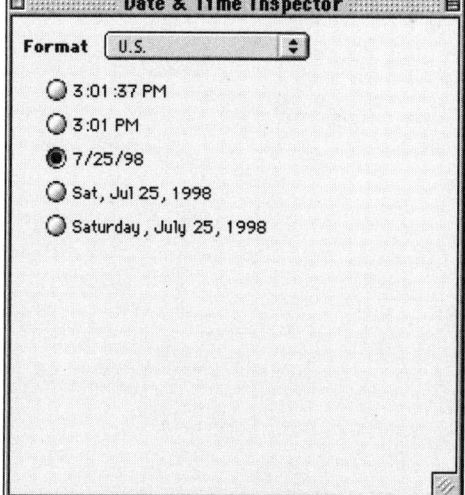

Figure 12-4: The Date & Time Inspector.

Using pre-built DHTML objects

You'll find several ready-to-use objects under the CyberObjects tab of the palette. Each uses DHTML to add a feature to your Web page. Drag one onto your page, configure it with the associated Inspector window, and you've added dynamic HTML to your Web site. The items available from the CyberObjects tab are:

- Date & time stamp.
- Button image.
- Dynamic component.
- URL popup.
- Action item.
- Browser switch item.

Date & time stamp

As the name implies, a date & time stamp adds the current date and time to your Web page. "Current" means the date and time at which the page was saved.

To add a date & time stamp:

1. With a document open in the Layout view, locate the position where you want to add a date and/or time stamp. You can embed the stamp within a block of text, or set it apart on the page. If you want to display both the date and time, you will need to find locations for two stamps.

2. Drag the Date & Time tool (**Figure 12-3**) from the palette's CyberObjects tab into the main window. A date & time stamp appears.

3. In the Date & Time Inspector (**Figure 12-4**), choose a display format by clicking on one of the radio buttons.

4. To change the language of your stamp, choose one from the Language popup menu in the Inspector window. When you alter the language or format of the stamp, the sample in the document window changes, too.

5. In the document window, select the stamp as if it were text, by clicking and dragging across it. You can edit the stamp's appearance, just as you would any text item, with the toolbar or the Text Inspector, which appears when you select the contents of the stamp.

6. To add a second stamp, repeat the previous steps, and choose a time format if your first stamp included the date, or vice versa.

✔ Tips

■ You can use a date & time stamp just as you would any other HTML element: drag it onto a layout grid or into a text box, to relate it to other items on your page.

■ Many Web page authors create date and time stamps that display the current date and time when a user visits the page. To do this, the Web server must be running a CGI that supports that function, and the Web page must contain code that links to the CGI.

Button images

A button image is probably the easiest form of animation to create. With a button image, you can cause a button to change its appearance when a visitor moves the mouse over the button, or clicks on it.

Before you can add the animated image to your page, you'll want to decide how the image should change when your visitors mouse over it, and when they click it. You will probably choose to create slightly different versions of a single image, though you might decide to

Figure 12-5: The Button Image tool.

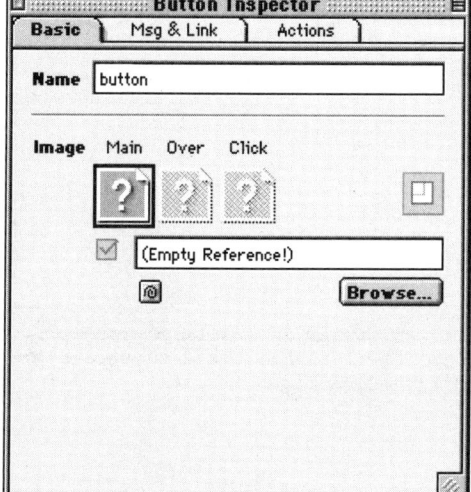

Figure 12-6: The Button Inspector.

display a completely different one when the user moves across it. If you decide to use a variant of one image, you will need to create them using a graphics editing tool, like Adobe Photoshop. Start with the original image, and edit it, saving each version at the same size and resolution as the first image, to make the transitions look smoother. When you have three images (the original, the version that appears when a user mouses over it, and a final one that appears when the user clicks on the image), you're ready to animate it with the CyberStudio button image tool.

To set up a button image:

1. With a document open in the Layout view, drag the Button Image tool (**Figure 12-5**) from the CyberObjects tab to the document window. The image tag that appears looks like a standard image placeholder.

2. In the Button Inspector, name the button.

3. Click on the square marked Main (**Figure 12-6**).

4. Use the Browse button or Point & Shoot to locate an image.

5. When you have finished placing the original image, click the box labeled Over. The checkbox next to the Image Path field lights up.

6. Click the checkbox and Browse or Point & Shoot to the image you want users to see when their mouse moves over the first image you created.

7. With the second image in place, repeat steps 4 and 5 with the Click box to place an image that will replace the original when a visitor clicks on it.

8. To use the image as a link, click on the Msg. and Link tab in the Button Inspector. You *can* link an image to a file or URL, even if you're also displaying a new version of the image when a user clicks it.

9. Click the Ref. checkbox, to light up the adjacent field (**Figure 12-7**).

10. Browse or Point & Shoot to a page you want to link to, or type in a complete URL.

11. You can cause a message to appear when a visitor mouses over the link, by clicking on the Msg checkbox and typing in a short message.

✔ Tips

■ If you want to add button image properties to an image that already appears on your Web page, do so by dragging the Button Image tool over the image. Then, configure the button as described in steps 5–11.

■ You don't have to create both a mouse over image, and a click image. You can use one or both options with your button.

■ If you decide to use completely different images for the three elements of a button animation, you should at least make sure the images are the same size. If they aren't the same size when you create them, they may be stretched or "smooshed" to fit into the image placeholder you've created for them in your document. If you want to try to reach a happy medium when working with images that are different in size, you can experiment, using the Size box in the Button Inspector (**Figure 12-8**). With your two or three images placed and configured, click on the one whose size most closely matches the image size you have in mind. Now, click the Size box. The placeholder box changes to fit the image you've selected. See how everything looks by clicking the Preview tab. Mouse over your image, then click on it. If an image is out of proportion, go back to your graphics software.

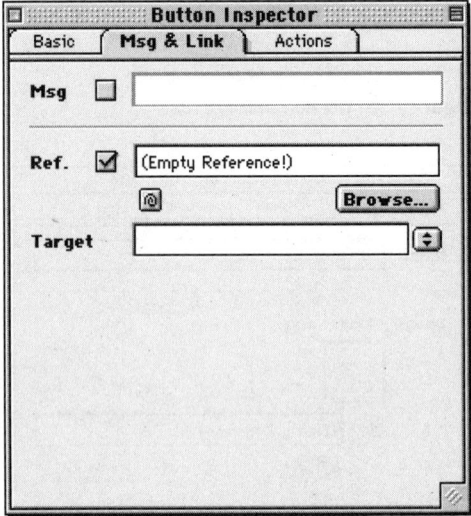

Figure 12-7: The Msg and Link tab allows you to place a link behind your image.

Figure 12-8: The Size box in the Button Inspector window allows you to view all button images at the size of the image you've selected.

USING PRE-BUILT DHTML OBJECTS

Figure 12-9: The Component tool.

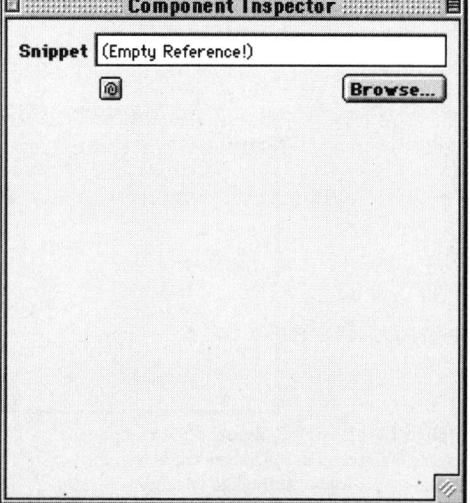

Figure 12-10: The Component Inspector.

Components

DHTML components are a lot like master elements in desktop publishing: you can use a component throughout a site, to provide a header, footer, logo or other standing element. Unlike other CyberStudio methods of creating standard elements, such as storing a layout grid full of text and images in the Custom tab of the palette, components allow you to make changes to one source file, and apply them to all files that use the component automatically, simply by saving each file. Components work by inserting HTML fragments into other documents. If you look at the Source view of a file with a component, you'll see the HTML fragment within the file.

To use components, you must create the source file, then add component objects to each file that will use the component. While you can use components outside CyberStudio's site metaphor, the Site window does offer special support for components, as you'll see in this section.

To create a component source file:

1. Open a CyberStudio site.

2. Create a new document and add the text and items you want to use as a component.

3. Save the file to the Components folder within the folder that contains your site. You can reach the Components folder quickly by clicking on the popup menu near the upper right corner of the Save dialog box.

To apply a component:

1. Open a new document, or locate an existing document to which you would like to add a component.

2. Drag the Component tool (**Figure 12-9**) from the palette to the document window. A large, horizontal rectangle appears, and the Component Inspector (**Figure 12-10**) appears.

3. Browse, or Point & Shoot to the component file you want to use. The component appears in your document.

Though it's easier to browse to a component, you Point & Shoot if you can get to the Site window's second pane. Open it by clicking the button on the right side of the window (**Figure 12-11**). When you drag the Point & Shoot line into the Site window, move it over the Extras tab on the right side of the window, and onto the Components folder. When it opens, connect to the file you want, as shown in **Figure 12-12**.

✔ Tips

■ Once you've created and save components in the Components folder of your site, each appears in the Site extras tab of the palette. To locate them, click on the tab, and make sure that the Components item on the popup menu at the bottom of the window is showing. You can drag components from the palette to the document window.

■ Components may be different shapes and sizes, but they cannot be displayed on the same horizontal line as another object. For that reason, they are best suited to serve as headers, footers and other elements that use the entire width of the page.

■ You can edit a component file. the changes you make will be transferred to all files that contain references to it. You will need to re-upload each file that uses the changed components to the Web server, before changes will take effect.

Figure 12-11: Click the button at the right edge of the site window to open its second pane.

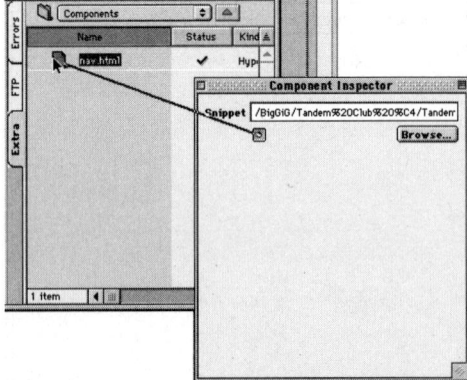

Figure 12-12: Point & Shoot to the component source file, stored in the Extras tab, within the Components folder of the Site window.

Figure 12-13: The URL Popup tool.

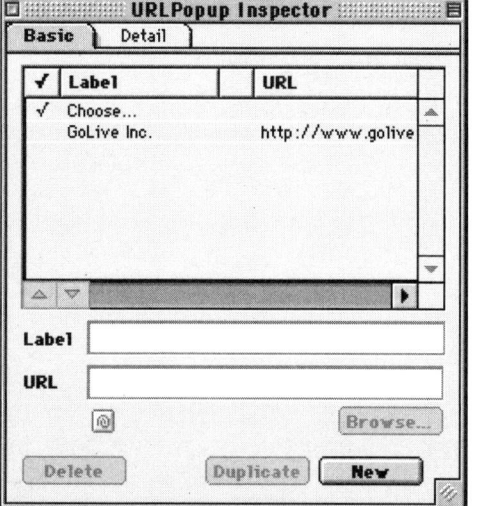

Figure 12-14: The URL Popup Inspector.

URL popups

URL popups are another navigation aid: you can use one to provide visitors a menu of places to go within your site.

To create a URL popup:

1. With a document open, drag the URL Popup tool (**Figure 12-13**) from the palette to the document window. A small popup box, and the URL Popup Inspector appear.

2. In the URL Popup Inspector (**Figure 12-14**), click on the line that says GoLive Inc.

3. In the Label field, GoLive Inc. with text of your own, describing the page or site the visitor will see when that item is chosen.

4. Press tab and type a URL to match the label. If the destination is local, use Browse or Point & Shoot to fill in the URL.

5. Click New to add another item to the popup.

6. Type a label and URL for the new item.

7. Repeat steps 5 and 6 for each additional item you want to add.

Action items

Actions are an important component of DHTML. You can use actions to do everything from opening a window to playing a sound or displaying a special image. We'll cover the full range of CyberStudio-supported actions later in this chapter. For now, I'll concentrate on creating an action that appears in the header of an HTML document. Adding an action to the header causes it to be invoked before the page is loaded.

To add an action:

1. Open a new or existing document.

2. Open the document's header by clicking on the small triangle to the left of the page icon, near the top of the document window. The header pane appears.

3. Drag the Action Item tool (**Figure 12-15**) from the palette to the header pane of the document window. An action item icon appears, and the Action Item Inspector (**Figure 12-16**) becomes visible.

4. Choose an action from the menu. Actions are arranged in the categories displayed in **Figure 12-17**.

5. If necessary, finish configuring the action, using the options that appear in the Action Item Inspector.

Browser Switch Item

Adding a Browser Switch item to the header of a document can help you accommodate visitors whose browsers do not support DHTML elements. When a browser switch detects a non-compatible browser, it switches the user from the current page to one you select.

Like other header action items, a browser switch is invoked before the page loads, speeding the changeover from one page to another. Of course, to use a switch, you'll need to create a page or pages that exclude DHTML, or other 4.0-specific elements that are not supported by older browsers.

Figure 12-15: The Action Item tool.

Figure 12-16: The Action Item Inspector.

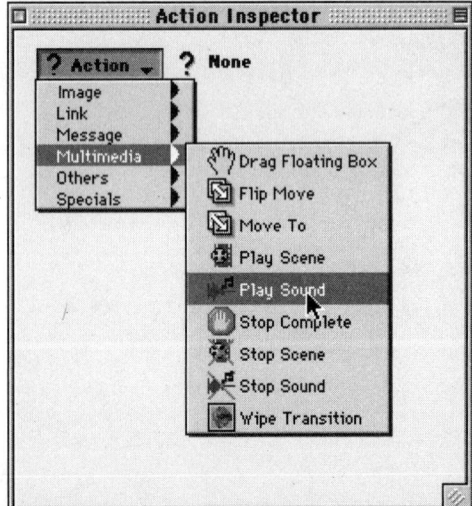

Figure 12-17: Choose an action from the Action Item Inspector's menus.

Figure 12-18: The Browser Switch Item tool.

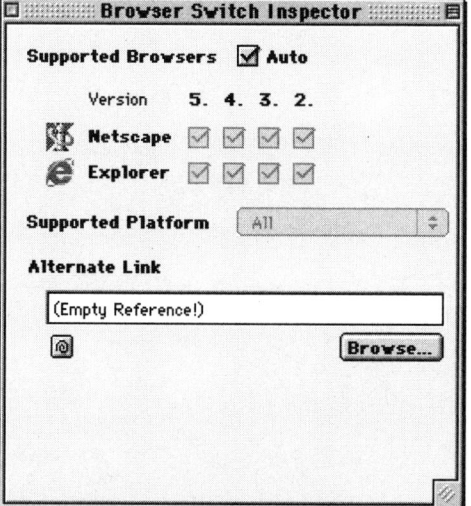

Figure 12-19: The Browser Switch Item Inspector.

To create a browser switch:

1. Open a new or existing document includes DHTML elements.

2. Open the document's header by clicking on the small triangle to the left of the page icon, near the top of the document window. The header pane appears.

3. Drag the Browser Switch tool from the palette to the header pane of the document window (**Figure 12-18**). A browser switch icon appears, and the Browser Switch Inspector (**Figure 12-19**) becomes visible.

4. If you want your page (using the script that the Browser Switch item creates) to determine a browser's compatibility, leave Auto checked in the Inspector.

5. Specify a platform (Mac or Windows).

6. To choose specific browsers to support, uncheck Auto and click on the browser versions that you think are compatible with your DHTML page. The presence of a browser version you don't check will send the user to an alternative page.

7. Browse or Point & Shoot to the alternative page, using the Alternative Link field.

USING PRE-BUILT DHTML OBJECTS

Actions

Actions are scripted events that can be made to occur when a *trigger* is activated on a page. You can use actions to change the display of a page or its elements, to open alert windows, play media files and much more. CyberStudio 3 includes a large collection of pre-built actions, that you can add to pages, animations, text and images, using mouse- and keyboard-related triggers.

You will find action tabs in several Inspector windows. You can apply also apply actions to animations using the action track in the Timeline editor. In this section, I'll use the Inspector as the interface to CyberStudio actions. In the Animation section of this chapter, I'll explain how you can add actions using the timeline editor.

About triggers

An action consists of a trigger and an event. When the trigger is applied, the event you specify occurs. CyberStudio provides nine event triggers that you can use to invoke actions. They are:

- Mouse click.
- Mouse enter.
- Mouse exit.
- Double click.
- Mouse down.
- Mouse up.
- Key down.
- Key press.
- Key up.

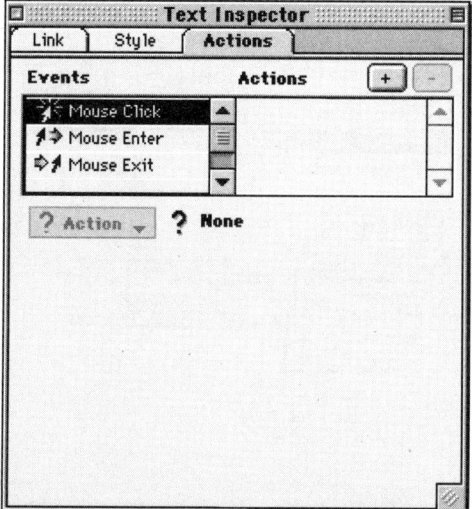

Figure 12-20: The Action tab of the Text Inspector contains trigger options when you choose linked text.

Figure 12-21: Add actions by clicking the Plus button.

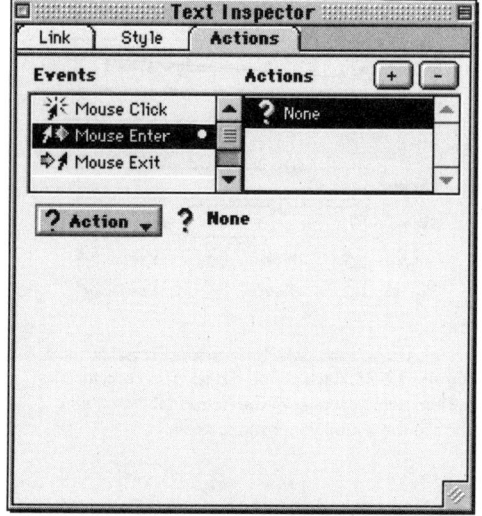

Figure 12-22: The Actions menu lights up when you add an action item to the Inspector.

Elements that support actions

You will find support for actions in the Text and Image Inspectors, as well as in the Button Image and Action Items described earlier in this chapter. As discussed earlier, you'll also find support for animation actions in the Timeline editor.

Adding an action

Because the process of adding an action is identical, regardless of the specific events and triggers you use, I'll describe the general procedure, and then move on to specific explanations of what each type of action does and how to use it.

To add an action via the Inspector:

1. Open a document and locate an item that supports actions (text, an image, or a button image, for example). The item you choose must be a hyperlink. To add an action to an image, for example, the image must have a URL associated with it.

2. Click the item you want to activate, revealing its Inspector.

3. Click the Actions tab (**Figure 12-20**). A list of triggers and a pane for new actions appear.

4. Choose a trigger from the list by clicking on it. Let's try Mouse Enter, which will trigger an action when the visitor moves the mouse over the text or image we're working with.

5. Click the Plus button (**Figure 12-21**) to add an action item, which appears in the right pane of the window. The Action popup menu lights up (**Figure 12-22**).

6. Click on the popup, displaying the categories of actions available.

7. Navigate to the category you want, and choose an action. I've chosen Open Window from the Link menu (**Figure 12-23**). When combined with the Mouse Enter trigger I've previously set, this action will open a window when a visitor's mouse passes over the link. Now, I need to configure the action. With the action chosen, the Inspector displays configuration options. For the Open Window action, they look like **Figure 12-24**.

8. To create a second action for the text or image you've selected, repeat steps 4 through 7.

9. To delete an action, select it in the Action pane and click the Minus button.

Kinds of actions

The following pages describe the actions CyberStudio includes. You can create your own actions, if you know JavaScript, but using an included action shields you from any need to know about scripting. In this section, I'll describe the function and configuration required for each of the actions CyberStudio includes.

As described in the section that deals with adding actions, you begin configuring the action by choosing a linked object and deciding on the trigger you will use. Please review this section before beginning to work with specific actions. The steps used to configure specific actions assume that you've already chosen the object, assigned a trigger and created an action item in the Actions pane.

✔ Tips

■ Although the general rule of thumb for actions is that your visitor must be using a 4.x or later browser, there are some actions that support 3.x browsers. You can

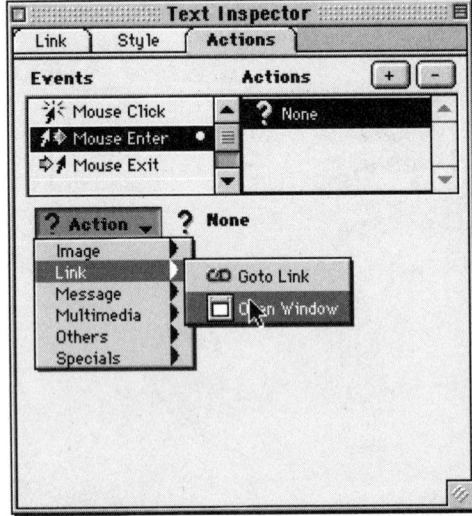

Figure 12-23: Choose a category and a specific action from the popup menu.

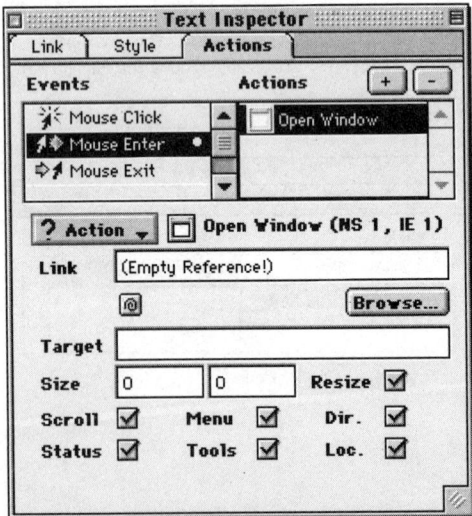

Figure 12-24: Each action has its own configuration options, which appear in the Action tab when you choose the action you want to apply.

ACTIONS

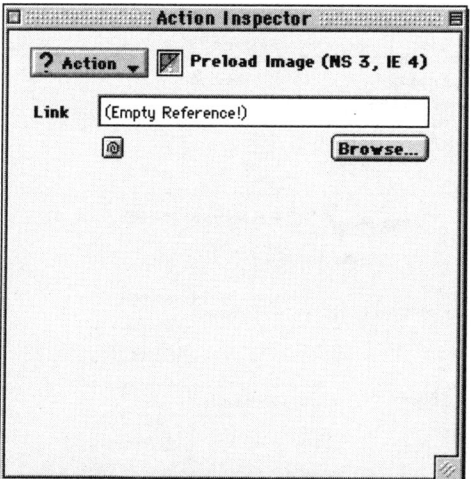

Figure 12-25: Configure a Preloaded Image in the Action Item Inspector.

find one indication of which browsers the action will work with right in the Action tab of the Inspector: when you've chosen an action, CyberStudio will display a label indicating the browsers supported.

■ The second, and most important way to ensure browser compatibility is to test each action you create in as many browsers as you can. Testing is also important, because CyberStudio cannot display all of the results of the actions you create. I recommend that you test each action immediately after creating it in at least one browser (CyberStudio gives you easy access to browsers from the toolbar, as described in Chapter 2) to be sure that everything works the way it should.

The actions CyberStudio includes are divided into categories, as follows:

Image Actions

■ *Preload Image*: is a header action, that caches images used in a mouse rollover. It slows the loading of the page, but makes the animation run more quickly.

■ *Random Image* replaces the image to which you attach an action with a random image from among several you specify.

■ *Set Image URL* exchanges the current image for another, based on the trigger you specify.

To preload an image:

1. Use the palette tool to add an Action Item to the header of a document.

2. In the Action Item Inspector, choose Image: Preload Image from the Actions menu.

3. Use Browse or Point & Shoot to locate an image to preload. See **Figure 12-25**.

To add a random image action:

1. Add a trigger and an action to an image. Be sure that the image is configured with a link.

2. Choose Image: Random Image from the Actions menu. Several image selection fields appear (**Figure 12-26**).

3. Browse or Point & Shoot to locate an image you want to appear randomly when your trigger is activated.

4. Repeat the previous step for up to two more images. Enlarge the Inspector window if needed, to show all three URL fields.

To set an image URL:

1. Choose an image you want to exchange. If it doesn't already have a name, give it one in the Form section of the Spec. tab of the Image Inspector.

2. Add an action to linked text, or to a button image.

3. Choose Image:Set Image URL from the Action menu.

4. Choose the named image from the popup menu.

5. Browse or Point & Shoot to an alternative image to add its URL. The completed Action tab looks like **Figure 12-27**.

Link Actions

■ *Goto Link* actions send a visitor to a URL you select.

■ *Open Window* actions, as the name implies, open a new window when triggered, displaying the link you attach to the action.

To create a goto link:

1. Add an action to text or an image.

2. Choose Link:Goto Link from the Actions menu in the Actions tab of

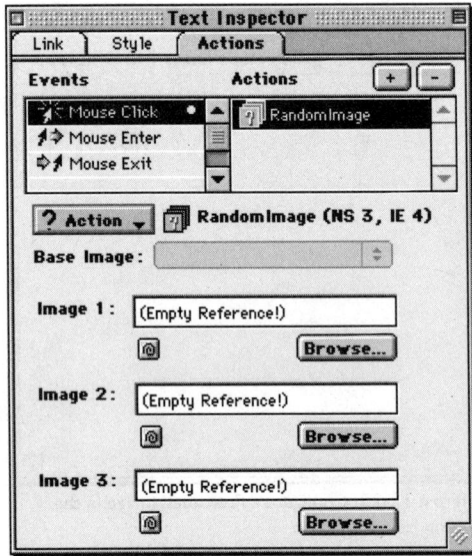

Figure 12-26: Configure a Random Image in the Action Image Inspector.

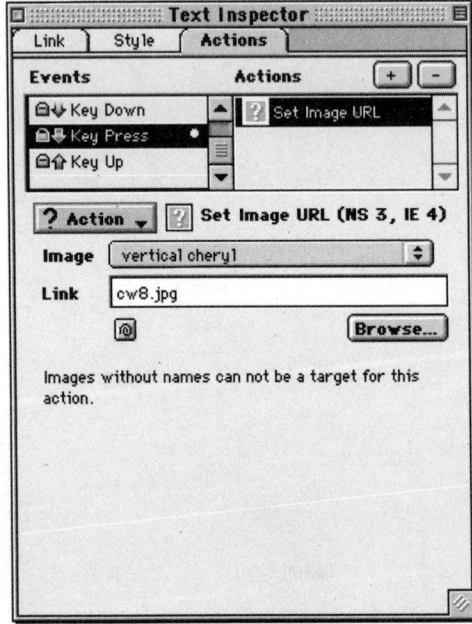

Figure 12-27: A Set Image URL action in the Inspector window.

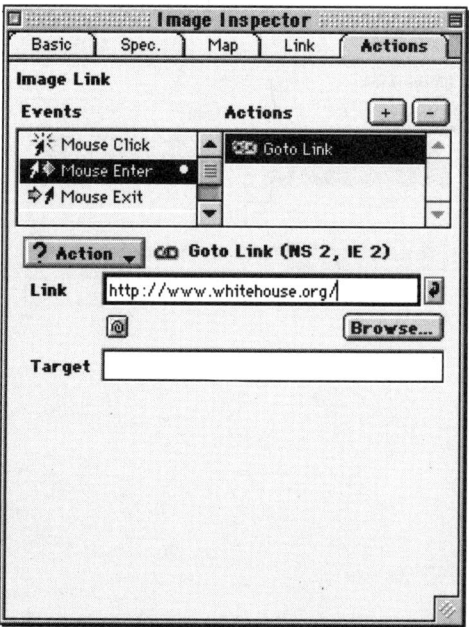

Figure 12-28: A Goto Link action in the Inspector window.

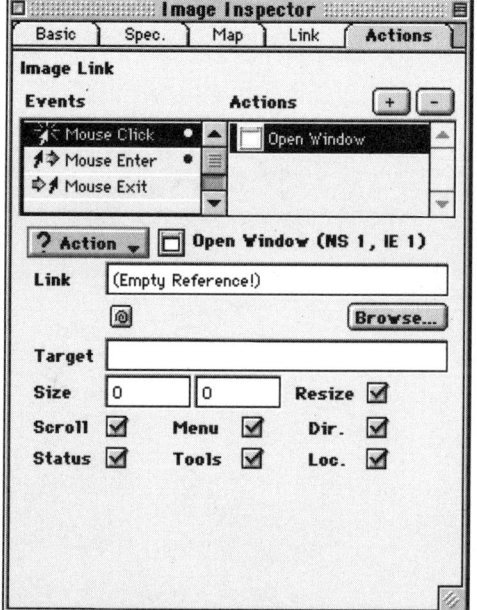

Figure 12-29: A New Window action, displayed in the Inspector window.

the Inspector window. Goto Link fields appear (**Figure 12-28**).

3. Type a remote URL, or locate a local file you want to link to.

4. If necessary, use the Target field to specify a frame where the new page should appear.

✔ Tip

■ If it sounds like a Goto Link action does just what a normal hyperlink does, you're right, assuming that you've chosen a mouse click trigger. Using other triggers, like mouse enter, for example, makes things considerably more interesting, and might be reason to give your visitors some kind of textual warning that invoking the trigger you set will send them to another page or another site.

To create an open window action:

1. Add an action to text or an image.

2. Choose Link:Open Window from the Actions menu. Open Window fields appear (**Figure 12-29**).

3. Type, browse or Point & Shoot to a link that will appear in the new window.

4. If necessary, use the Target field to specify a frame where the new page should appear.

5. To control the appearance of the window itself, use the other controls in the Inspector. Start by specifying a size (in pixels) for the new window when it appears onscreen.

6. Click the Resize checkbox to allow the user to resize the new window.

7. Leave any of the six browser display buttons checked to show scroll bars, menus, directory buttons, status indicators, toolbars and location bars.

ACTIONS

Message actions

- *Open Alert Window* displays an alert window onscreen when triggered.

- *Set Status* displays a custom message in the status field at the bottom of the browser window.

To create open alert window action:

1. Create a trigger and action.

2. Choose Message:Open Alert Window from the Actions menu. The Message field appears (**Figure 12-30**).

3. Type the text you want to appear in the alert window.

To create a set status action:

1. Create a trigger and action.

2. Choose Message:Set Status from the Actions menu.

3. Enter the status message you want in the text field that appears.

Multimedia actions

- *Drag Floating Box* allows a visitor to drag content (contained in a floating box) around in the browser window.

- *Flip Move* allows you to move a floating box from a starting point to another position on the page, and back again.

- *Move To* behaves just like Flip Move, except that it doesn't return the floating box to the original position.

- *Play and Stop Scene* actions control the playback of animations created in the Timeline editor.

- *Play and Stop Sound* actions control the triggered playback of sounds.

- *Stop Complete* stops all animation, including visual and audio playback. It is useful to give visitors the choice to stop animation

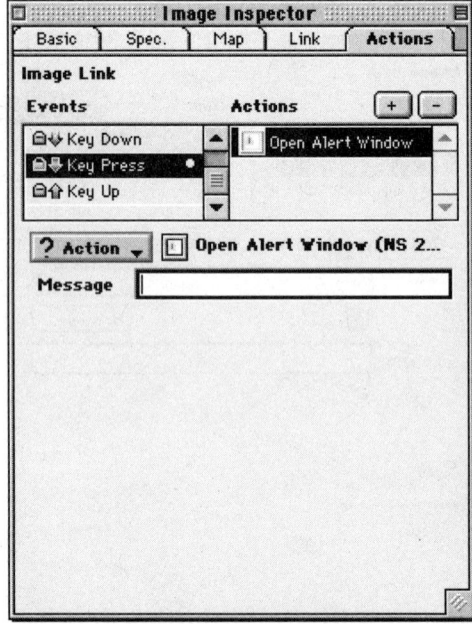

Figure 12-30: The Open Alert window action, displayed in the Inspector window.

ACTIONS

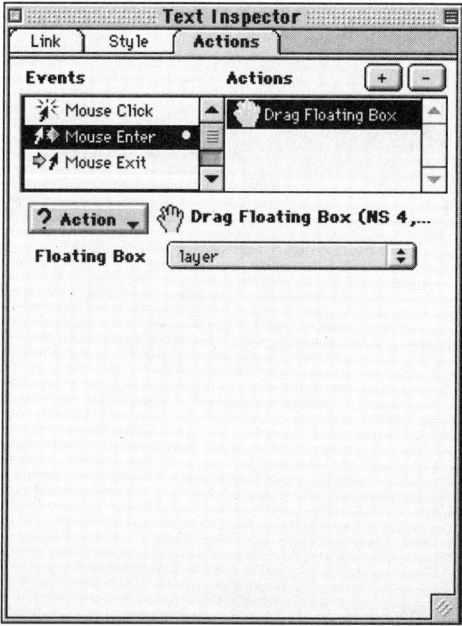

Figure 12-31: The Drag Floating Box action, displayed in the Inspector window.

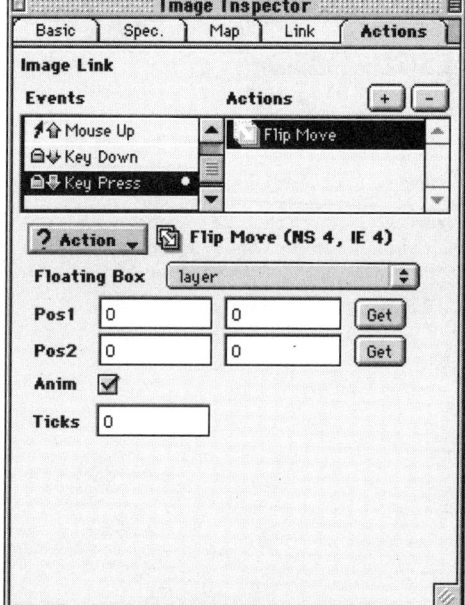

Figure 12-32: Flip Move options in the Inspector window.

if their Internet connection is slow, or if they simply don't want to bother with it.

■ *Wipe Transitions* create a video-like effect that applies to floating boxes as they enter and leave the visitor's view.

To add a drag floating box action:

1. Choose or create a floating box. If the box is empty, add content to it.

2. If you want to, rename the box in the Floating Box Inspector. If you don't rename the box, note its default name. You'll be referring to it by name when you create the action.

3. Create a trigger and action.

4. Choose Multimedia:Drag Floating Box from the Actions menu. The Inspector displays a popup containing all floating boxes within the current document (**Figure 12-31**).

5. Choose the box you want visitors to be able to drag from the menu.

To add a flip move action:

1. Within a document that contains at least one floating box, create a trigger and action.

2. Choose Multimedia:Flip Move from the Actions menu. The Inspector displays positioning fields for the action (**Figure 12-32**).

3. Choose a floating box from the popup menu.

4. Click the Get button on the Pos1 line to establish the initial coordinates (in pixels) of the floating box. CyberStudio fills in the coordinates.

5. Drag the floating box to the position you want to move to, and click Get on the Pos2 line, to fill in the second set of coordinates.

6. Leave the Anim box checked to cause the flip move to work.

✔ Tip

■ When you drag the floating box to set its coordinate, you'll lose contact with the Inspector associated with the image or text you're using to trigger the action. Don't worry about that. When you've finished dragging the floating box, click immediately on the text or image, and you'll be returned to the Actions tab. Click Get to set up the flip move, and you're ready to test it.

To create a move to action:

1. Follow steps 1–4 in the Flip Move section, above.

2. Leave Anim checked.

To play and stop scenes:

1. Create an animated scene, using the Timeline editor.

2. Create a mouse trigger and an action.

3. Choose Multimedia:Play Scene from the Actions menu. The result appears in **Figure 12-33**.

4. Choose a scene from the Scene popup menu.

5. To stop the scene, click the "+" button to add a second action to the current trigger.

6. Choose Multimedia:Stop Scene from the Actions menu.

✔ Tip

■ Triggers for Play/Stop Scene actions must be mouse events (mouse up, mouse click, mouse enter, etc.). If you choose a non-mouse event, the icon that appears next to the name of the action you select will have an "x" through it. **Figure 12-34** shows an incompatible trigger and action. This applies to any triggers and actions that are incompatible. Use the x as a visual cue that you need to choose a different trigger.

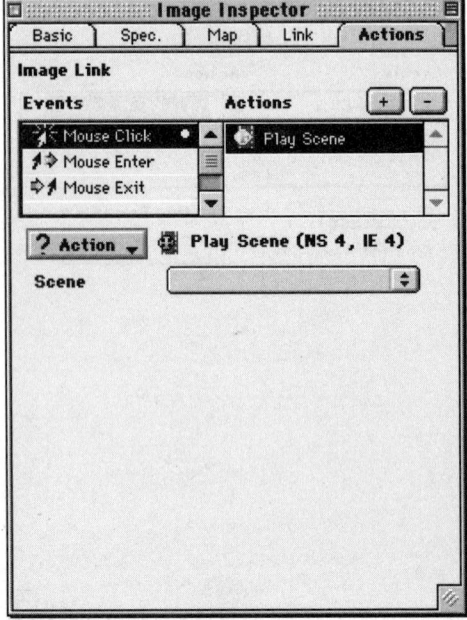

Figure 12-33: To play a scene choose Multimedia:Play Scene from the Actions menu.

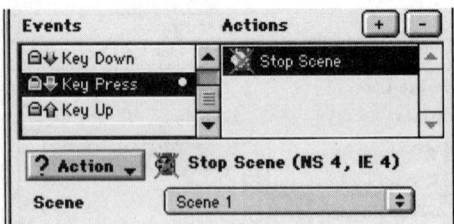

Figure 12-34: If you choose a trigger that doesn't support the action you want to use, the icon will have an "x" through it.

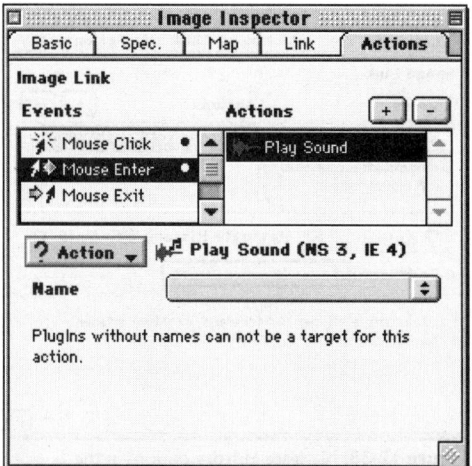

Figure 12-35: Play Sound action options in the Inspector window.

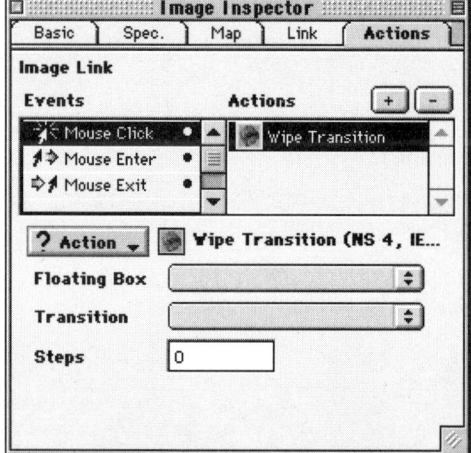

Figure 12-36: Wipe transition options in the Inspector.

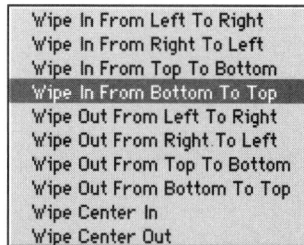

Figure 12-37: Choose from one of these wipe transition directions.

To play and stop sounds:

1. Add a sound to your page, using a plugin.

2. Name the plugin in the More tab of the Plugin Inspector.

3. Choose an image, button or hyperlink, and create a trigger and action.

4. Choose Multimedia:Play Sound from the Actions menu.

5. Choose the plugin you named earlier from the popup menu.

6. Click the "+" button to add another action; a Stop Sound action.

7. Choose the plugin name you used before to complete the action.

To add a stop complete action:

1. Create a trigger and action.

2. Choose Multimedia:Stop Complete from the Actions menu.

To create a wipe transition:

1. With a document including floating box open, choose an item to which you will apply the trigger and action.

2. Create the trigger and action.

3. Choose Multimedia:Wipe Transition from the Actions menu. The result appears in **Figure 12-36**.

4. Choose the floating box you want to wipe from the Floating Box popup.

5. Choose a wipe direction from the menu (**Figure 12-37**).

ACTIONS

Other actions

- *Navigate History* actions use browser history information (what pages he or she has visited in what order) to take the visitor forward or back by a specific number of pages.

- *Netscape CSS Fix* works around a bug that causes some versions of Netscape Communicator and Navigator 4.0 to lose style sheet and DHTML information when the page is resized.

- *Go Last Page* returns the visitor to the page immediately preceding the current one.

- *Resize Window* changes the size of the browser window when triggered.

- *Scroll Down, Left, Right or Up* moves the browser display by the number of pixels, and in the direction you set, when triggered.

- *Set BackColor* adds a background color to the subject image or text, when triggered.

- *ShowHide* reveals or conceals a floating box, when triggered.

To add a navigate history or go last page action:

1. Create a trigger and action.

2. Choose Others:Navigate History from the Actions menu. The result appears in **Figure 12-38**.

3. Type in a number of history items (negative numbers go back, positive go forward) to move when the action is triggered.

4. Choose Others:Go Last Page instead if you want to return the visitor to the page immediately preceding the current one.

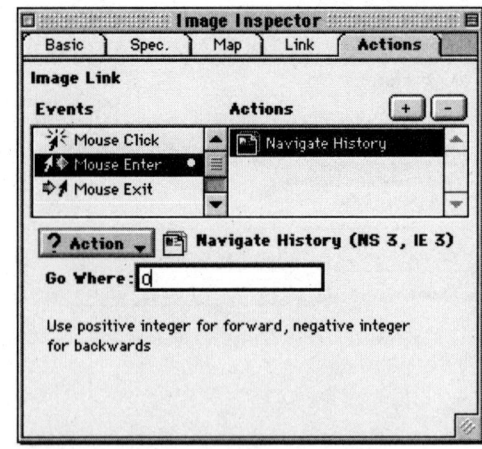

Figure 12-38: Navigate History options in the Inspector.

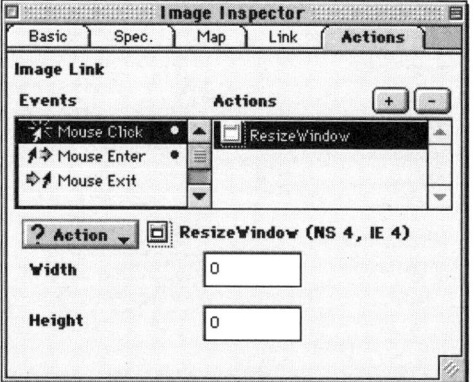

Figure 12-39: The result of resizing the window.

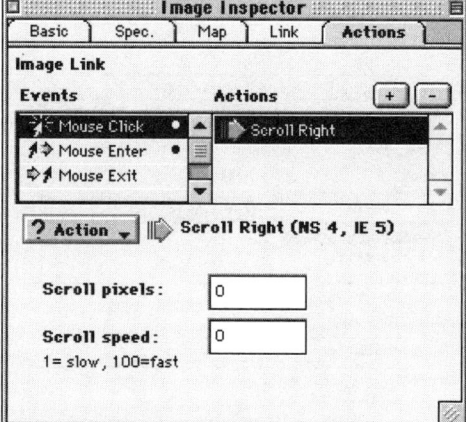

Figure 12-40: This Inspector window shows a Scroll Right action. You use the same options to scroll left, up or down.

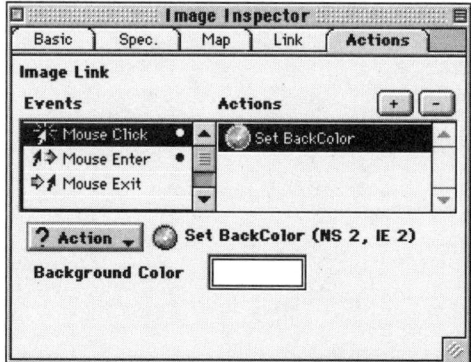

Figure 12-41: Choose BackColor options in the Inspector window.

To add a Netscape CSS fix action:

1. Create a trigger and action.

2. Choose Others:Netscape CSS Fix from the Actions menu.

To add a resize window action:

1. Create a trigger and action.

2. Choose Others:Resize Window from the Actions menu. The result appears in **Figure 12-39**.

3. Enter the Width and Height (in pixels) that you want to apply to the page when this action is triggered.

To add a scroll action:

1. Create a trigger and action.

2. Choose Others:Scroll Down, Scroll Left, Scroll Right or Scroll Up from the Actions menu. The result appears in **Figure 12-40**.

3. Choose the number of pixels to scroll when the action is triggered.

4. Enter the speed (on a scale of 0–100) to scroll.

To set a background color action:

1. Create a trigger and action.

2. Choose Others:Set BackColor from the Actions menu. The result appears in **Figure 12-41**.

3. If it is not available, choose Color Palette from the Windows menu to display it.

4. Choose a color from the Color Palette.

5. Drag from the preview pane of the Color Palette to the Background Color box in the Inspector window.

ACTIONS

To add a show/hide action:

1. Create a trigger and action.

2. Choose Others:Show/Hide from the Actions menu. The result appears in **Figure 12-42**.

3. Choose a floating box from the Layer popup.

4. Choose Show, Hide or Toggle (switch between Show and Hide) from the Mode popup menu.

✔ Tip

■ You can use show/hide action in pairs, creating separate triggers for each position.

Special Actions

■ *Condition* actions are triggered based on whether or not conditions (other actions, for example) occur. Condition actions use the *Intersection* and *Timeout* actions.

■ *ActionGroup* gathers several actions together to be performed simultaneously.

■ *Idle* actions determine whether a condition has been met. It works with intersection and timeout actions, which yield a true/false result. Idle actions affect the entire page, and should be placed in the header section.

To add a condition action:

1. Create a trigger and action.

2. Choose Specials:Condition from the Actions menu. The result appears in **Figure 12-43**.

3. Choose Specials:Intersection from the secondary Actions menu to specify the intersection of two floating boxes—whether or not they overlap.

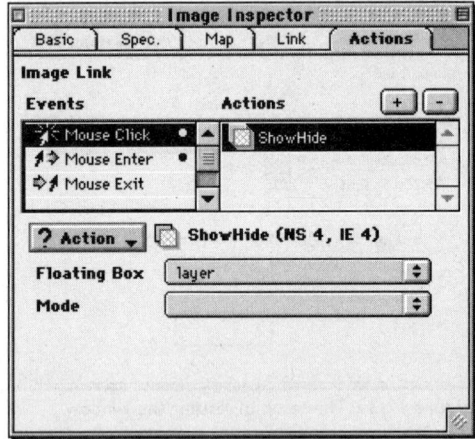

Figure 12-42: Show/Hide options in the Inspector window.

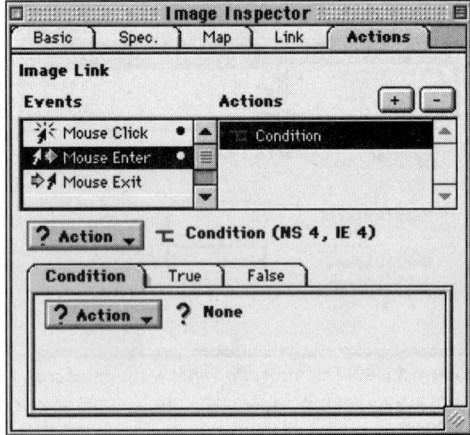

Figure 12-43: Condition action options in the Inspector window.

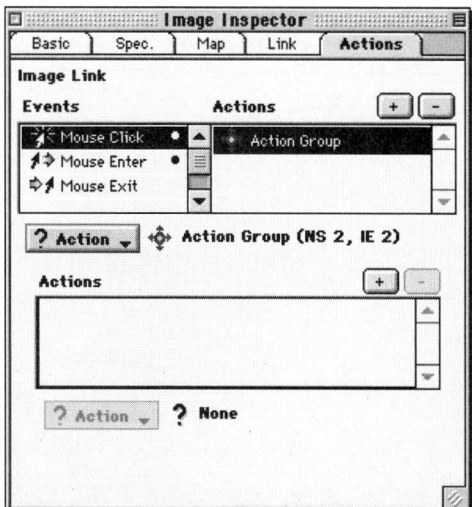

Figure 12-44: ActionGroup options in the Inspector window.

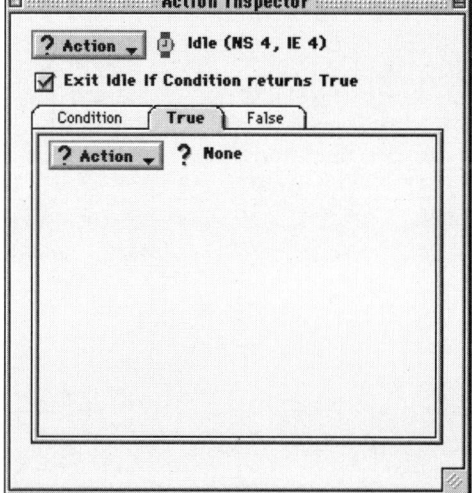

Figure 12-45: Idle action options in the Inspector window.

4. Choose two floating boxes within the document whose intersection (or lack thereof) should trigger a conditional action. Or Choose Specials:Timeout to set a conditional action that will occur when a set amount of time has passed.

5. Set the number of seconds to wait for the timeout.

6. When you have configured an intersection or a timeout, click the True or False tab.

7. Configure an action that will occur if your condition is (or is not met).

To create an action group:

1. Create a trigger and an action.

2. Choose Specials:ActionGroup from the Actions menu. Result is in **Figure 12-44**.

3. Click the "+" button to add actions to your group.

4. Add triggers and actions and configure them.

To add an idle action:

1. Open the header section of a document by clicking the triangle left of the page icon.

2. Drag the Action Item tool from the Cyber-Objects tab of the palette to the header section.

3. In the Inspector window, choose Specials: Idle from the Actions menu. The result appears in **Figure 12-45**.

4. Check "Exit Idle if Condition returns true."

5. Choose Specials:Intersection, or Specials: Timeout from the Actions menu on the Condition tab, to specify a condition.

6. Add actions that should be taken if the condition is true or false, under the respective tabs in the Inspector.

Animation

You create DHTML animation by filling floating boxes with content and creating scripts that move the boxes around the page. Of course, it's a bit more complicated than that, but the basic building blocks of CyberStudio animation are the floating box and the way you organize them with the Timeline Editor and, if you choose, DHTML actions.

Creating a basic animation

To create a basic animation, we'll add a floating box to a page and configure it so that the contents of the floating box will move across the page. In other words, we're going to ride a bicycle across the page, over our logo.

To prepare for animation:

1. Choose the item you want to animate. If you will be animating an image, prepare it by saving it as a Transparent GIF, or Interlaced GIF. These formats remove the image's background, so that it appears transparent when placed on your page. You can use shareware tools like GIFConverter or GraphicConverter to do this.

2. Open a new or existing CyberStudio document in the Layout view.

3. Drag the Floating Box tool from the palette's Basic tab into the document window.

4. Add the image you created in step 1 to the document by dragging an image placeholder into the floating box. Locate the image with Point & Shoot, or by browsing to the file you want.

   You can also add existing page content to the floating box by dragging it from elsewhere on the page.

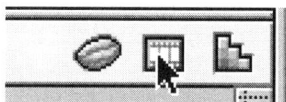

Figure 12-46: Open the Timeline Editor using this button at the upper-right corner of the main window.

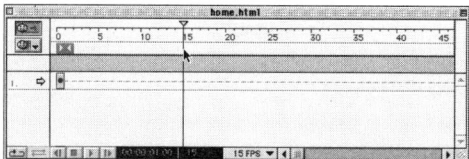

Figure 12-47: Set up keyframes on the Timeline Editor's time track.

Figure 12-48: Click Play to preview your animation.

5. If you want to animate another object along with the image, drag that object into the floating box, too.

6. When you're finished with the floating box, resize it so that the box fits tightly around the object or objects inside.

✔ Tip

■ You can configure the floating box, just as you can other CyberStudio objects, with the Inspector. For our purposes, the floating box is ready for a simple animation. If you want to learn more about configuring floating boxes, see Chapter 5.

To animate the floating box:

1. Select the floating box you created earlier.

2. Open the Timeline Editor, by clicking the Timeline Editor button (**Figure 12-46**) at the upper-right corner of the document window's title bar. The Timeline Editor window appears.

3. Create a new *key frame*—a marker that indicates the end of the animation playback range—by command-clicking in the timeline's time track, as shown in **Figure 12-47**). The keyframe marks the animation's endpoint. The beginning is marked by the default keyframe that is present when you open the Timeline Editor.

4. In the document window, drag the floating box to the location where you want it to appear at the end of the animation.

5. Click the Play button at the bottom of the Timeline Editor (**Figure 12-48**) to preview your animation. You can use the other tape recorder-style buttons to move forward, backward in your animation, or to view it in a loop.

ANIMATION

✔ Tip

- You can also animate a floating box by using the Record feature of the Floating Box Inspector. With the Timeline Editor visible, select the floating box, which should be located at its origin on the page. Click the Record button in the Floating Box Inspector (**Figure 12-49**). Drag the box across the screen. When you reach your destination, click Record again to end the animation. Preview the animation by clicking Play. Your animation moves across the screen (**Figure 12-50**).

To vary the animation's path:

1. With the floating box in its original position (click on the first keyframe), add a new keyframe between the two existing ones.

2. Select the floating box and drag it to a location that is not on the original line you created.

3. Click Play. The animated object moves from the origin, to the new location, to its final destination.

4. Add more keyframes to create additional points along the animation path.

5. Play back the result to see how you like the way the animation moves.

6. To specify the type of path the object should take between two keyframes, select a keyframe and choose a path type from the Animation menu of the Floating Box Inspector (**Figure 12-51**).

Adjusting animation paths

I decided to move my bike across the page in four steps, dropping it down from the top, then moving further across, and back up to

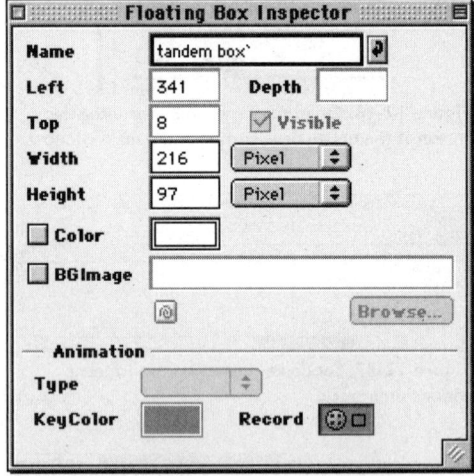

Figure 12-49: Click Record in the Floating Box Inspector to create an animation.

Figure 12-50: Here is my first animation. It moves the tandem bicycle from the left side of the screen to the right side.

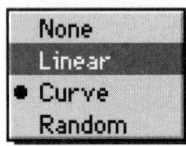

Figure 12-51: Choose a path type for movement between keyframes.

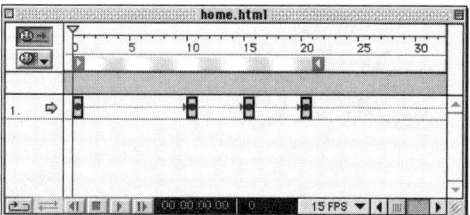

Figure 12-52: The Timeline Editor shows four keyframes and the total time required to play the animation.

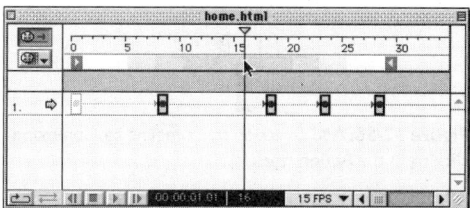

Figure 12-53: Use the ruler to position keyframes, and to determine your frame count.

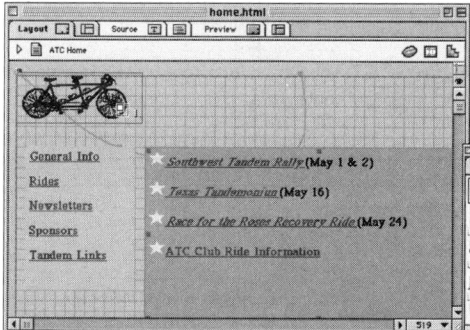

Figure 12-54: My bicycle animation moves along these wobbly lines.

the top. To do this, I used four keyframes. The trouble is that the animation looks jerky if I don't place the keyframes at reasonable intervals (to control the speed) and use appropriate animation paths (to control the motion of the bike).

To tweak the timeline:

1. With a multi-point animation path set up, look at the Timeline Editor. Mine shows that I'm using four keyframes in 22 frames. The animation takes 1.07 seconds, at 15 frames per second (**Figure 12-52**).

2. Consider the total length of the animation. In my case, stretching it out to a full two seconds seems like a good idea. Move the last keyframe along the time track until it reaches the 30 frame mark. That's 30 frames at 15 frames per second, for a total of 2 seconds of animation. When I move the final keyframe, the others move to the right, proportionate to their original positions.

3. Move other frames within the timeline to space them evenly.

   Since I am using four points in this animation, I want them to occur at equal intervals so that the movement will appear smooth.

4. To help space items precisely, click and drag the ruler (**Figure 12-53**) to the position you want, and note the frame number in the bar at the bottom of the screen.

5. When you have reached the frame you want, drag a keyframe to the ruler.

6. With keyframes spaced properly, click the Play button to see how the animation is shaping up. Mine is still jerky, because the path (**Figure 12-54**) leaves a lot to be desired.

ANIMATION

7. If you like where the paths go, but not how they get there, click on the first keyframe, then Shift-click on the second. Choose a path from the Floating Box Inspector and note the change in the document window (**Figure 12-55**).

8. Changing one path's course may upset the next one a bit. Click the third keyframe to select it, and to move the floating box there.

9. Drag the floating box a bit to line it up with the second keyframe location.

10. Click the first keyframe, then Play to see how your animation looks.

11. Make final adjustments and save your work.

Adding actions to animation

You can add any of the actions described in the Actions section of this chapter to an animation timeline. In fact, you can create an action in the Timeline Editor, rather than using the Action tab of the Inspector.

To add an action to a timeline:

1. With the Timeline Editor open, command-click on the Action Track (**Figure 12-56**). An action icon appears, in the form of a question mark (**Figure 12-57**).

2. Click on the action icon to display the Action Inspector.

3. Choose an action (**Figure 12-58**), and configure it. The Action item in the timeline changes to the reflect your configuration.

4. If necessary, move the action item to the location in the timeline where you want the action to be invoked.

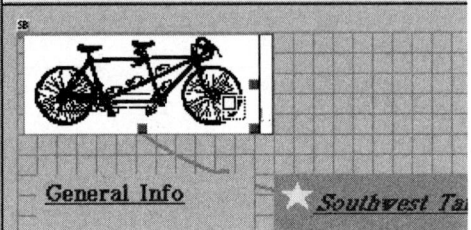

Figure 12-55: The first and second points visited by the animated floating box are connected with a linear path.

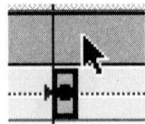

Figure 12-56: Add an action to a timeline by Command-clicking in the Action track.

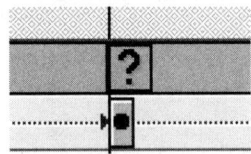

Figure 12-57: The Action item appears as a question mark until you configure it.

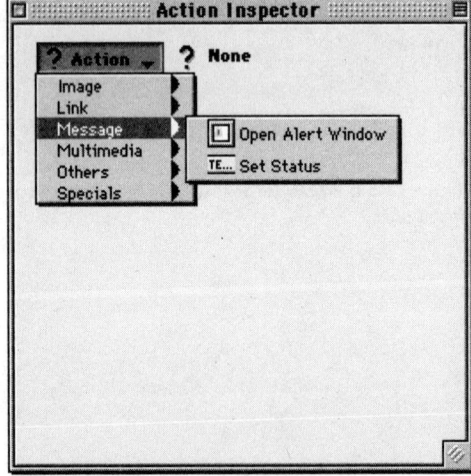

Figure 12-58: The Action Inspector includes all of the built-in actions available in CyberStudio.

WORKING WITH COLOR

Most graphics applications include some kind of color palette. Some, such as Adobe Photoshop, offer several. CyberStudio, in an attempt to provide a diverse choice of colors and to deal with the limitations color faces in the Web environment, offers *eight* color palettes. These color palettes are contained in the Color Palette, a toolbox that you can use to color everything from backgrounds and text to objects and frames.

In this chapter, I cover:

- Web color issues.

- The eight Color Palette tabs.

- Adding color.

Note: the figures for this chapter are located in the Color Section of this book.

Web color issues

Adding color to a Web page is tricky. Actually, placing color on the page is easy, but making sure that the colors you choose or create in the Color Palette actually work presents some challenges.

Because Web pages are viewed on many kinds of computers, using different operating systems, and employing different color-handling conventions, the developers of HTML (with additions by the folks at Netscape) created a standard for Web color that makes it possible for all Web users with color-capable browsers and computers to see the same colors. Of course, creating that standard meant that many of the colors available on the Macintosh, for example, are not supported by Web browsers on other platforms.

Whatever development platform they prefer, it's important that Web designers use "Web-safe" colors on their Web pages. Using Cyber-Studio's Color Palette and the Site window, you can use and store a collection of Web-safe colors for your Web page. And if you want to create a more colorful version of your site, just for those users fortunate enough to have browsers and computers that support a wider color palette, there are plenty of "dangerous" colors to pick from on the RGB and CMYK color palettes.

Color tabs

The Color Palette's eight color tabs each deal with color composition in a different way, mirroring palettes familiar to print publishers (RGB, CMYK, Grayscale and Indexed), to Macintosh users (Apple Color), and to Web developers (Real Web and Web Named).

To use the RGB tab:

1. Choose Color Palette from the Windows menu.

2. If the RGB tab isn't displayed, click on it to display it (see **Figure 13-1** in the Color Section).

3. To choose a color, move one of the sliders left or right to change the color percentage. Each of the three sliders represents a color (red, green and blue) of the RGB spectrum. The color in the preview pane changes as you adjust the sliders. RGB is most often associated with video and computer imaging.

To use the CMYK tab:

1. Click on the CMYK tab in the Color Palette (see **Figure 13-2** in the Color Section).

2. Use the Cyan, Magenta, Yellow and Black sliders to create a color. CMYK is most often associated with printed publishing, rather than the Web.

To use the Grayscale tab:

1. Click on the Grayscale tab in the Color Palette (see **Figure 13-3** in the Color Section).

2. Use the slider to choose a grayscale percentage. 0% gray is white, and 100% gray is black. Like CMYK, grayscale is most often used in printing.

To use the Indexed Color tab:

1. Click on the Indexed Color tab in the Color Palette (see **Figure 13-4** in the Color Section).

2. Click on the Color Wheel to select a color.

3. Use the Brightness slider to adjust the color's brightness.

To use the Apple Color tab:

1. Click on the Apple Color tab in the Color Palette (See **Figure 13-5** in the Color Section.)

2. Choose a color palette from the popup menu (see **Figure 13-6** in the Color Section).

3. Colors in the Macintosh-supported Apple palette are expressed in terms of the number of visible colors. The palette squares represent all the available colors.

4. Select a color by clicking on a square within the palette (see **Figure 13-7** in the Color Section).

To use the Real Web Colors tab:

1. Click on the Real Web Colors tab in the Color Palette (see **Figure 13-8** in the Color Section).

2. Choose a color from the scrolling list on the right, or by clicking in the spectrum window on the left. The color value is entered in the field at the bottom of the Color Palette. It includes an RGB, decimal and hexadecimal value. This value appears in the HTML code representing your chosen color.

✔ Tip

■ Real Web colors are the best choice for creating Web pages, because they translate properly, no matter what browser or computer your site's visitors use. Other color options, including Web Named colors, may not look right in all browsers.

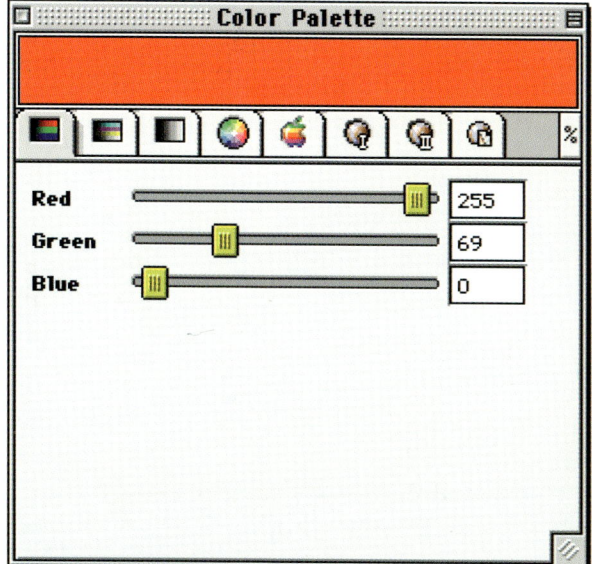

Figure 13-1: The RGB tab.

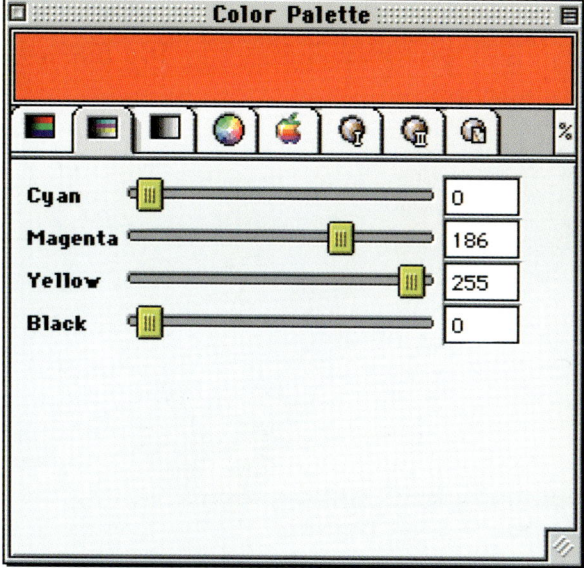

Figure 13-2: The CMYK tab.

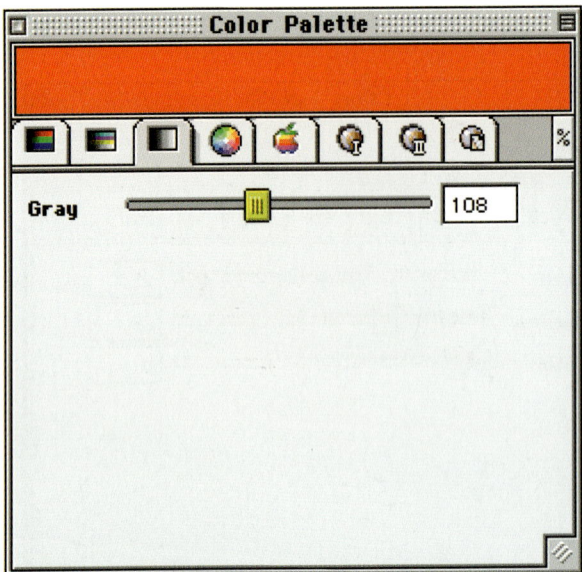

Figure 13-3: The Grayscale tab.

Figure 13-4: The Indexed Color tab.

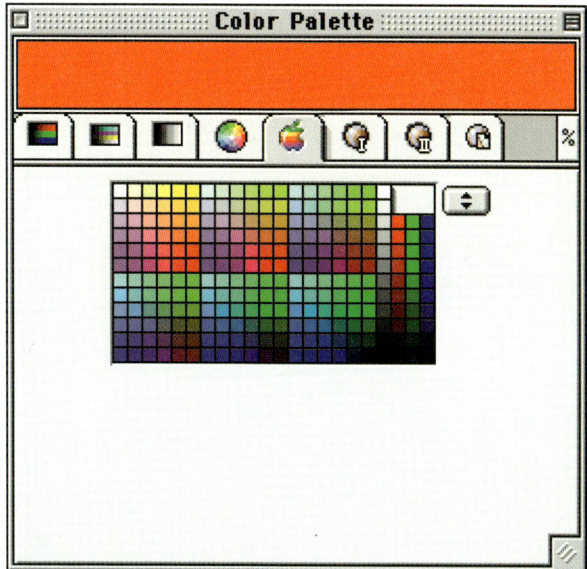

Figure 13-5: The Apple Color tab.

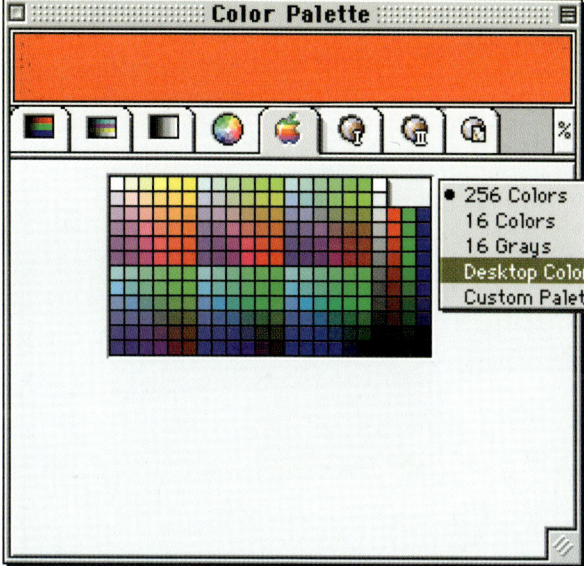

Figure 13-6: Choosing a color palette from the Apple Color tab.

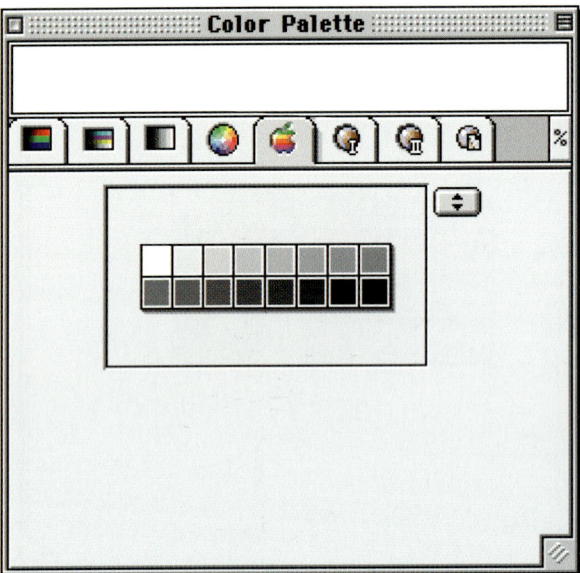

Figure 13-7: The 16-color palette in the Apple Color tab.

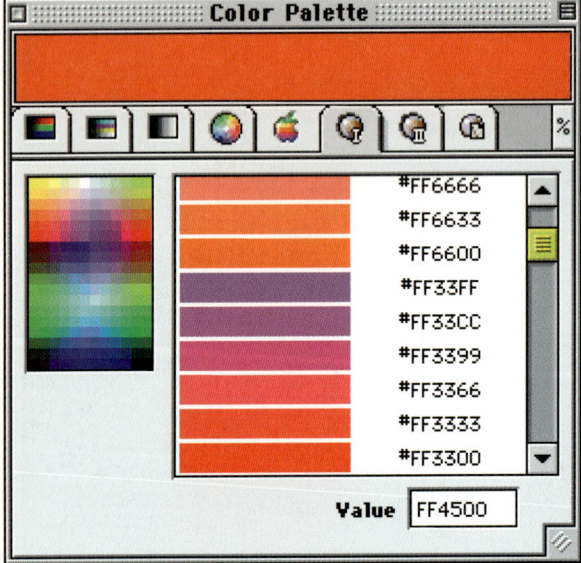

Figure 13-8: The Real Web Colors tab.

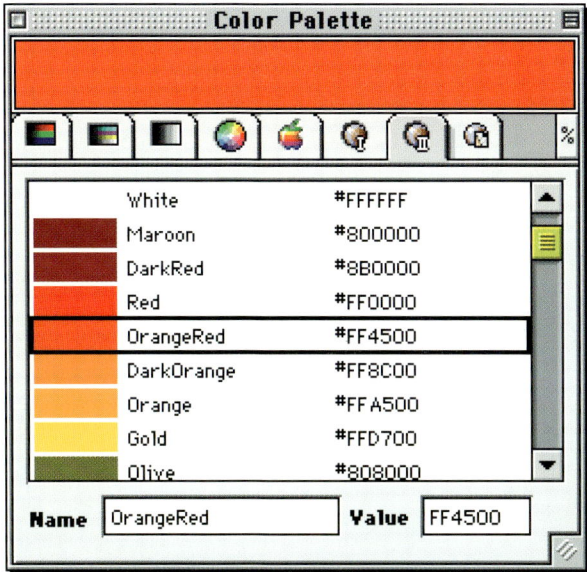

Figure 13-9: The Web Named Color tab.

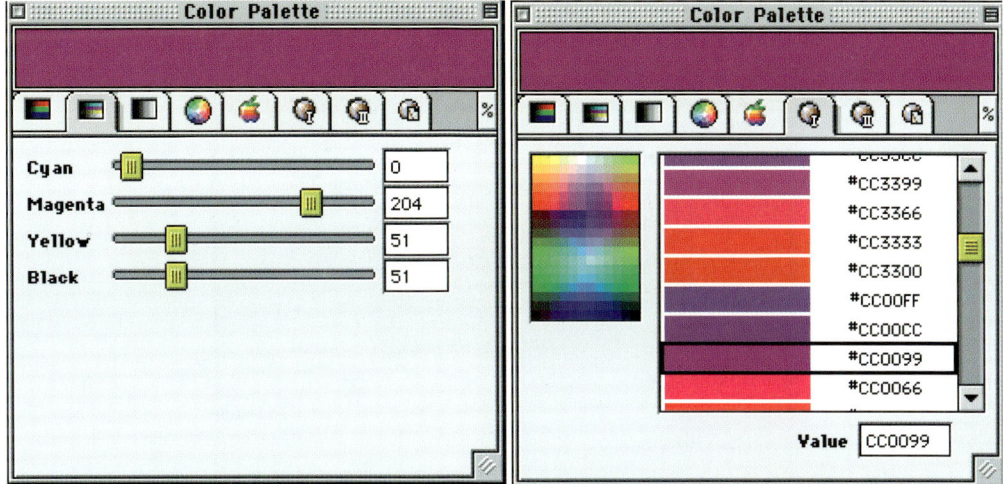

Figure 13-10: Comparing the same color in the CMYK tab and the Web Safe tab.

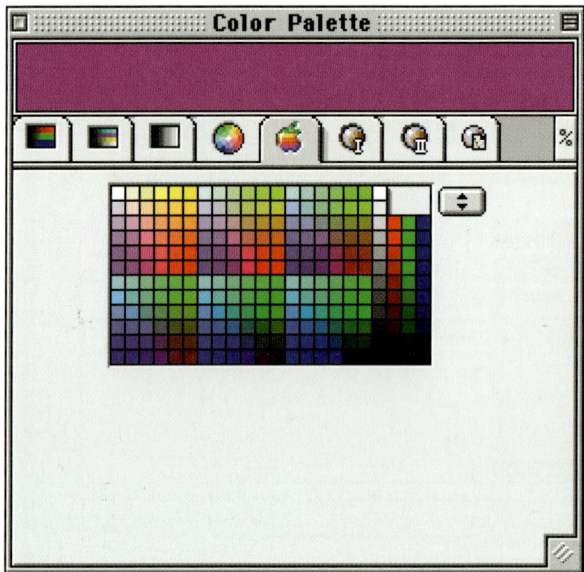

Figure 13-11: The Apple Color tab, used to match color.

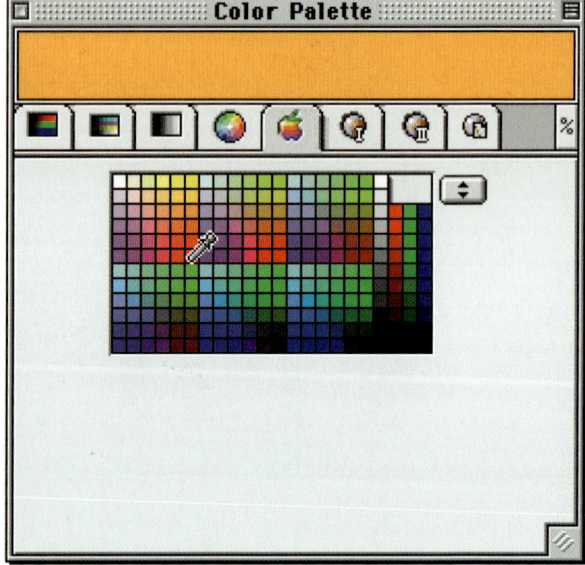

Figure 13-12: Getting the pipette (eyedropper) cursor for use in matching colors.

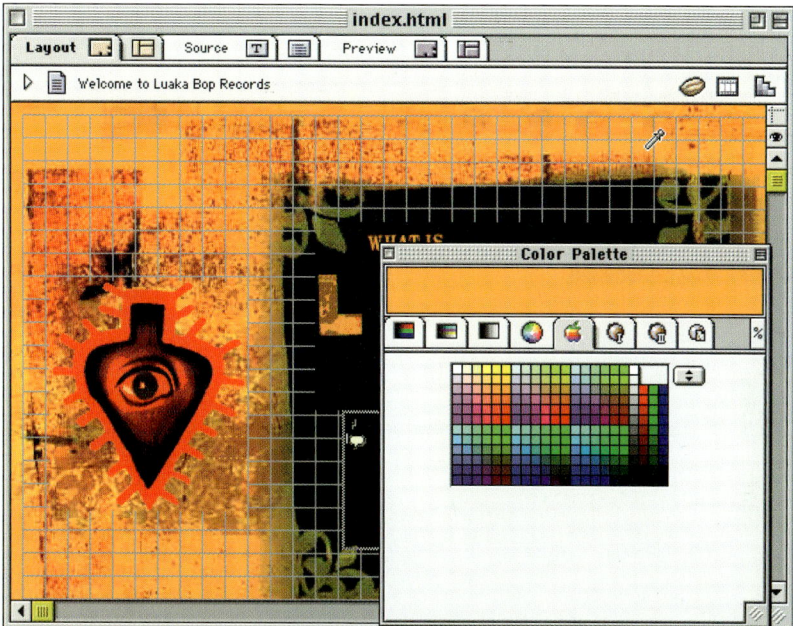

Figure 13-13: Moving a color from a page to the color palette.

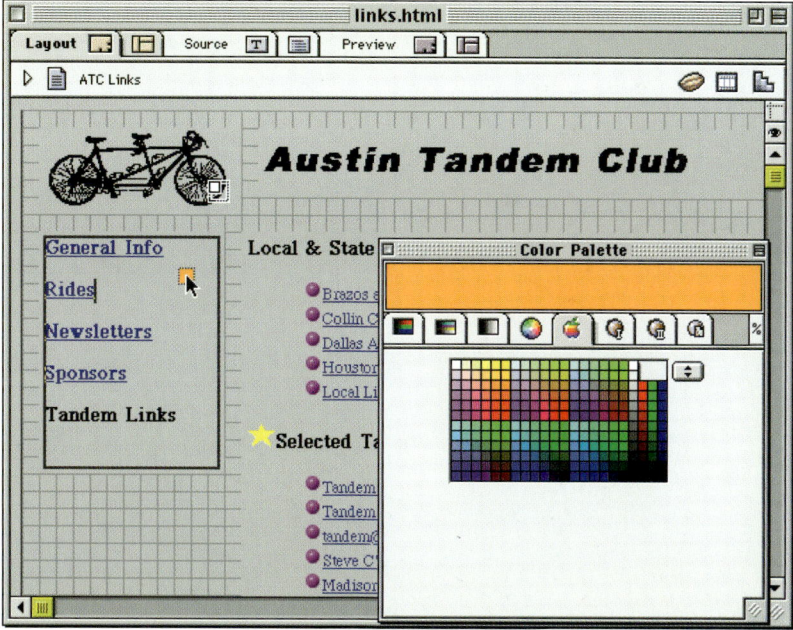

Figure 13-14: Adding a matched color to another Web page.

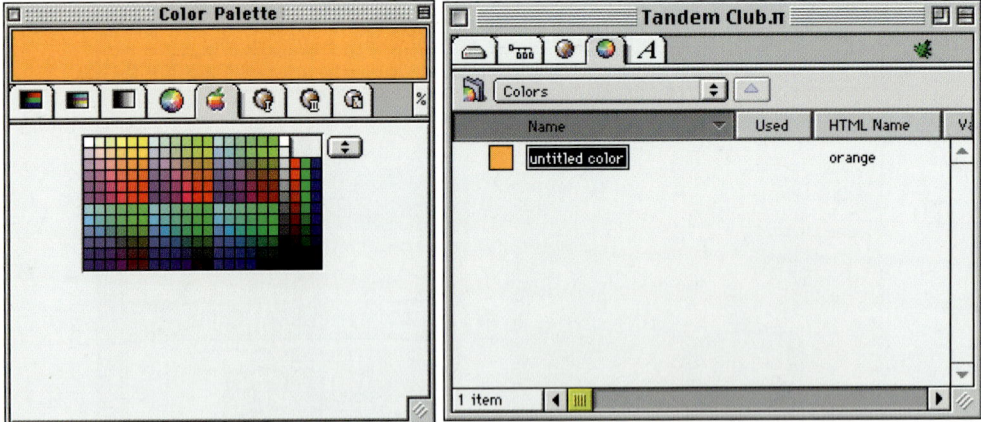

Figure 13-15: The Color Palette and the Site window's Colors tab with a new color added.

To use the Web Named Colors tab:

1. Click on the Web Named Colors tab in the Color Palette (see **Figure 13-9** in the Color Section).

2. Choose a color from the list. The color names and values are recognizable by Web browsers that support color.

✔ Tips

■ If you want to use Web-safe colors but prefer to work with CMYK or other print-friendly (and, perhaps, more familiar) color palette, you can usually do it. Start by creating a color you like in the spectrum of your choice. Then click the Real Web or Web Named tab. CyberStudio duplicates or approximates the color you chose. Click to confirm the safe color. **Figure 13-10** in the Color Section shows a CMYK color and its Web-safe sibling.

■ If you are using CyberStudio's Site feature, you can save colors that you create within the Site window and determine whether your colors are Web-safe. Create a color while working in a site and then drag it to the Site window's color tab to save it. If the color is not Web-safe, a bullet appears in the Site window.

Site Colors

The final tab in the Color Palette is the Site Colors tab. When you are working in a Cyber-Studio site, you can use the tab to store colors you use throughout the site. The item in the Site Colors tab are the same as those under the Colors tab of the Site window, and vice versa. The Site Colors tab is just another way to access frequently-used colors. You can add or delete colors from either the Site window or Site Colors tab.

COLOR TABS

Using colors

In most cases, you access colors from the Inspector window: When you click on objects that support color, the resulting Inspector usually includes a color field. Simply click the color field to call up the Color Palette, choose a color and drag it from the preview pane to the Inspector's color field. You can also reverse the process. By matching colors on a Web page with the Color Palette, you can apply existing color to new objects.

To match colors:

1. Open a document containing a color you would like to use, as well as the Color Palette.

2. In the Color Palette, click on the Apple Color tab to display it (see **Figure 13-11** in the Color Section).

3. Click on any color square, and hold down the mouse button. The cursor changes to a pipette (see **Figure 13-12** in the Color Section).

4. Without letting go of the mouse button, drag into the document window and over the text or object with the color you want to match.

5. Let go of the mouse button when the Color Palette preview pane displays the color you want (see **Figure 13-13** in the Color Section).

6. Open the document or site where you want to use the color you've chosen.

7. Drag the color from the preview pane to the object you want to color (see **Figure 13-14** in the Color Section) or into the Site window's Colors tab (see **Figure 13-15** in the Color Section), where the color will be saved for future use.

8. In the Site window, name your new color.

9. In the Color Picker, click on the Site Colors tab. Your new color is there, too.

✔ Tip

■ You can also match colors with the Web Safe tab by Option-clicking the palette and dragging over the Web page color you want to use.

14

WORKING WITH HTML

CyberStudio is a visual tool for Web site development. A large part of its appeal is the ability to work with the HTML language without getting your hands dirty, or, without having to learn or edit HTML code. But as appealing as visual page design is, there are times when it is necessary (and even helpful) to work with HTML.

CyberStudio includes two HTML editing views: the Outline View and the Source View. Although not as intuitive as the Layout View, the Outline View does present HTML pages in hierarchical, organized terms. The Source View breaks down all barriers between the Web page author and the HTML underlying the page.

Once you've got your first taste of Web page coding, you'll be ready for a look at some specialized HTML tags that can add information about your document: header tags. Finally, you can work with and add your own HTML tags in the Web Database, a tool that helps you and CyberStudio keep up with the ever-changing HTML standard.

In this chapter, I cover:

- Using the Outline View.

- Working with the Source View.

- Using Header tags.

- Using the Web Database.

Using the Outline View

Think of the Outline View as a bridge between WYSIWYG Web page development and the dark recesses of the HTML language. Like the layout environment, the Outline View can display images and text. And Web page elements (headers, headings and body elements) appear within an easy-to-understand hierarchical window.

The Outline View displays a hierarchical version of your Web page with HTML tags around the text and graphic elements. **Figure 14-1** shows a Web page in the Layout View and a portion of the same page in the Outline View.

To view a document in the Outline View:

1. Open a CyberStudio document.

2. In the document window, click the Outline tab (**Figure 14-2**) to switch to the Outline View. The page's outline appears.

To view the outline of a new page:

1. Open a new document.

2. Click the Outline tab to view the outline (**Figure 14-3**). Even without text or images, the empty page already has an outline, containing the required structure for the page.

Anatomy of an outline

The outline that appears when you view a new CyberStudio document contains all the essential elements of an HTML page. In the Outline View, they are organized the way the

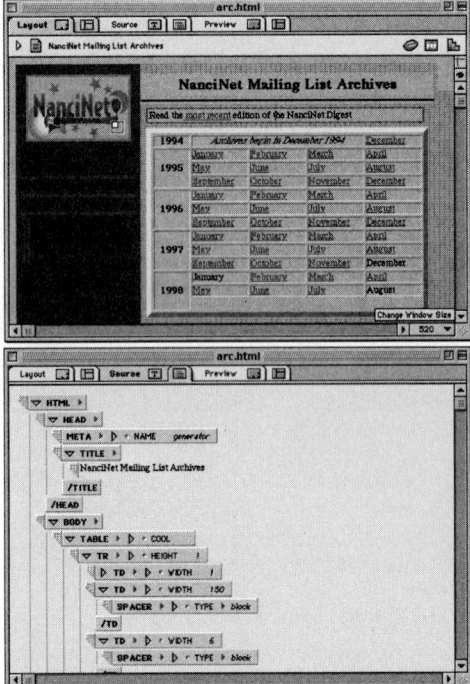

Figure 14-1: Here is a Web page in the Layout View, and the same page in the Outline View.

Figure 14-2: Use the Outline tab to view the Outline View.

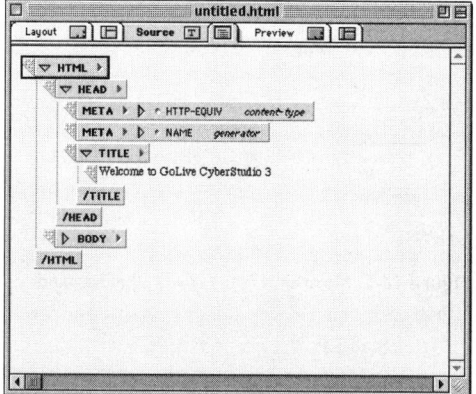

Figure 14-3: The Outline view of a new page.

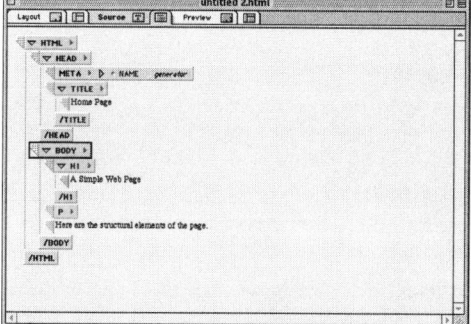

Figure 14-4: This basic outline contains the structural and control elements you use in the Outline View.

HTML language expects them to be when a page is translated for viewing on the Web. The HTML tags are arranged hierarchically. Several required elements (HTML, HEAD and BODY) lead the hierarchy and, like many tags, must also be *closed* at the end of the outline or they will not work properly.

Boxes within the outline represent HTML tags and Web page content. Tag contents appear in subordinate (child) lines within the outline. Tag lines also contain structural, control and display attributes of HTML tags, which appear when you expand the outline. In addition to Web page text, you can view images, just as you can in the Layout view. **Figure 14-4** shows a basic Web page with labels indicating the components described in the next section.

Structural attributes

The Outline View uses three structural components:

- *Boxes* indicate HTML tags. These outline elements' "children"—lower-level items in the hierarchy—contain both content (images and text) and attributes used to display the content properly.

- *Indents* indicate an item's position within the HTML hierarchy. <P> (paragraph) tags appear under and to the right of the <BODY> tag, because paragraphs are contained within the BODY tag. Same goes for BODY tags themselves, which are contained within the HTML tag.

- *Vertical lines* between tags indicate that the tags are paired open and close tags, as in <I> and </I>.

Controls

HTML tag entries contain tools that let you manipulate the tag within the outline. They are:

- The *drag-and-drop handle* moves a tag when you click and drag the handle through the outline.

- The *collapse/expand triangle* shows or hides content and settings for an HTML tag, when clicked.

- The *show/hide attributes triangle*, to the right of an HTML tag, shows or hides attributes associated with the tag. In some cases, clicking on the triangle displays a popup menu from which you can choose display attributes.

- The *HTML tag name* is itself a control. Command-clicking it displays a popup menu of other HTML tags that you can replace it with if you choose.

Editing in the Outline View

The tools you use to add or rearrange items in the Layout View (the palette, drag-and-drop and the toolbar) are all available in the Outline View.

To drag-and-drop within an outline:

1. In the Outline View, click and drag the drag-and-drop handle (to the left of an HTML tag) to another location within the document. As you drag, a box representing the line you're moving and all its content and attributes moves across the screen (**Figure 14-5**). A horizontal line appears

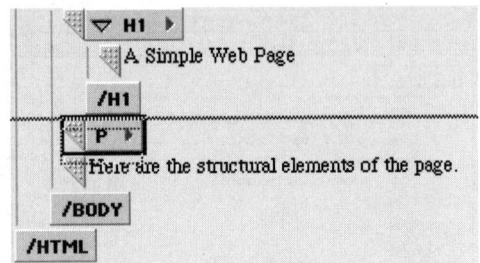

Figure 14-5: Move an HTML tag with the drag-and-drop handle.

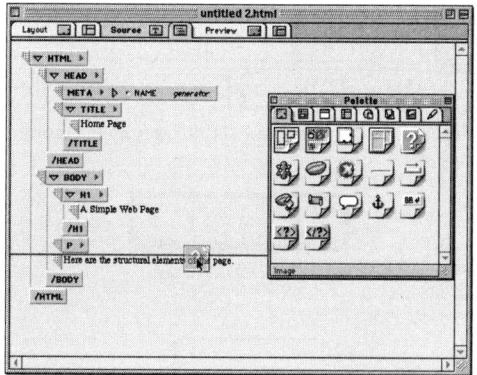

Figure 14-6: Drag a palette tool to the Outline View to add a new tag.

as you drag over other tags to indicate where the item will be displayed when you complete the drag.

2. Let go of the mouse button when you reach the location where you want the tag to appear.

3. Click the Layout or Preview tab to examine the change you've made.

To add tags with palette tools:

1. With the Outline View visible in the document window, select a tool from the Body tab or the Forms tab of the palette and drag it into the document window. A horizontal line indicates where the tag is as you move the tool through the window (**Figure 14-6**).

2. Let go of the mouse button when you reach the desired location for your tag. Empty tag attributes appear.

✔ Tips

■ Unlike the Layout View, dragging a palette tool to the Outline View does not display an Inspector window. If you want to use the Inspector to configure a new tag, return to the Layout View after you add the tag and click the object. Otherwise, use the HTML tag attributes described in this chapter to configure it.

■ You can add any body or form tag to the Outline View—with one exception: you cannot add a Layout Text Box.

USING THE OUTLINE VIEW

To add tags via the outline toolbar:

1. Click at the location in the outline where you want a new HTML tag to appear.

2. Choose New HTML Tag from the toolbar (**Figure 14-7**). The tag appears in the Outline View (**Figure 14-8**).

3. Command-click and hold the mouse button on the new tag to view the Tag Type popup menu (**Figure 14-9**).

4. Choose the type of tag you want from the menu. The tag appears onscreen.

5. Click and hold the mouse button on the new tag's show/hide attributes triangle to view a list of attributes that matches the tag you've created (**Figure 14-10**).

6. Choose an attribute. In many cases, choosing an attribute brings up another show/hide triangle, allowing you to choose more attributes by clicking and selecting the attribute from a menu. **Figure 14-11** shows an attribute that adds a specific image to the IMG tag.

Figure 14-7: Choose New HTML Tag from the toolbar.

Figure 14-8: This is a new HTML tag.

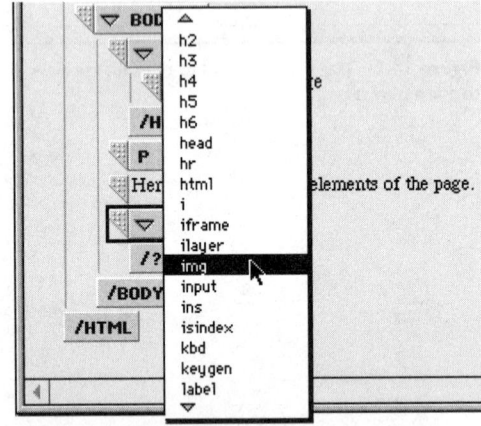

Figure 14-9: Command-click the new tag's head to view a menu of possible tag types.

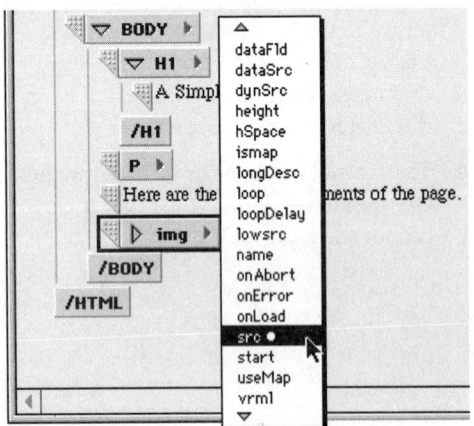

Figure 14-10: Click the show/hide attributes triangle to view tag attributes.

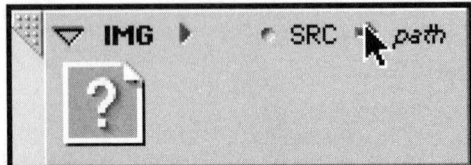

Figure 14-11: An IMG tag includes an SRC attribute and a pointer you can use to choose an image.

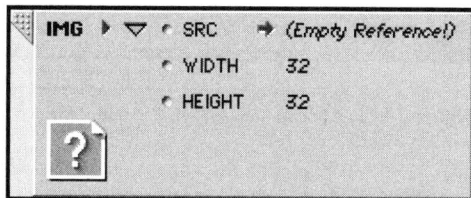

Figure 14-12: An image tag with some basic attributes filled in.

Figure 14-13: Choose New HTML Text from the toolbar.

Figure 14-14: Type your text into the empty box.

✔ Tips

■ If you are creating a tag with lots of available attributes, such as an IMG tag, it's usually easier to add the tag in the Layout View and use the Inspector to configure it.

■ Using a palette tool to add a tag is also simpler than creating each attribute from scratch because the tool brings basic attributes along when you add it to an outline. **Figure 14-12** shows the result of dragging an IMG (image) tag from the palette.

To add text to an outline:

1. In the Outline View, place the cursor where you want new text to appear.

2. Choose Add HTML Text from the toolbar (**Figure 14-13**). A text box appears (**Figure 14-14**).

3. Type the text over the selected question marks. When you preview your page, the text you typed will conform to the HTML tag surrounding it.

To add HTML comments:

1. In the Outline View, place your cursor at a location where you would like to insert an HTML comment. A comment is a note to yourself or to someone else working on the Web page. It will not be visible to those who visit your Web site.

2. Choose New HTML Comment from the toolbar (**Figure 14-15**). A blank text box appears in the outline.

3. Type your comment. HTML comments do not appear on the page when you preview it or upload it to the Web. Within the Outline and Source Views, they appear in a different color than HTML toolbar text (**Figure 14-16**).

✔ Tip

■ You can also add comments by dragging the Comment tool from the palette to the Outline View or Layout View.

To add attributes to an HTML tag:

1. In the Outline View, click an HTML tag to select it.

2. Click and hold the show/hide attributes triangle to view the popup menu containing all attributes supported by this tag (see **Figure 14-17**).

3. Choose an attribute.

4. Type a number, choose a color or make any other selections appropriate for the attribute you've chosen.

5. Repeat steps 2-4 to add more attributes.

Figure 14-15: Choose New HTML Comment from the Edit menu.

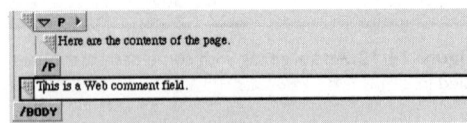

Figure 14-16: Comments appear within the outline but not in the previewed version of your Web page.

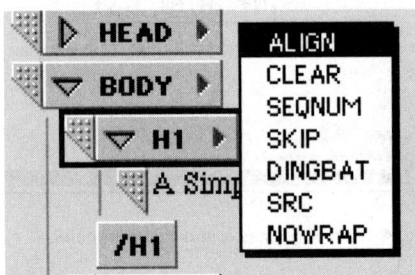

Figure 14-17: Click on the show/hide attributes triangle and pick an attribute.

Figure 14-18: Choose Toggle Binary from the toolbar.

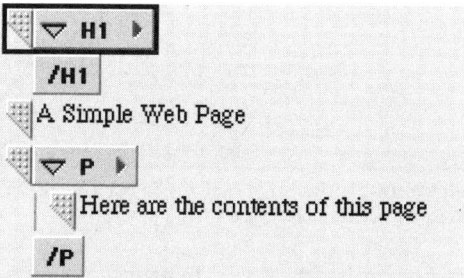

Figure 14-19: Binary tags visible.

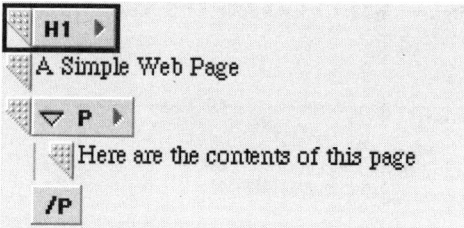

Figure 14-20: Binary tags hidden.

To toggle the binary format:

1. Click on a binary HTML tag.

2. Choose Toggle Binary from the Edit menu (see **Figure 14-18**). By default, the Outline View displays both halves of the binary HTML tag (e.g. <H1> and </H1>). The binary toggle hides the end tag, making it easier to navigate the outline. **Figures 12-19** and **12-20** show the same section of an outline with the toggle on and off. Note the toggle changes only the currently selected tag.

Using the Source View

Although most Web page design happens in the Layout View, and the Outline View offers a convenient way to examine HTML structure, the Source View provides an unvarnished view of the code and content that makes up a Web page. In the Source View, there is nothing between you and the code that tells a browser how to display your Web page.

The Source View is a text editor, where you will see and edit all of the tags, attributes, pointers and text that form the HTML page. **Figure 14–21** shows a Web page in the Source View. Like a word-processing application, you can type directly into the Source View, move around with the cursor and cut and paste text. Like other CyberStudio views, the Source View supports drag-and-drop editing and allows you to use palette tools.

To view a document in the Source View:

1. Open a GoLive CyberStudio document.

2. Click the Source tab (**Figure 14–22**) to switch to the Source View. The view changes to show the HTML underlying the page.

Examining the Source View

When you look at an HTML page in the Source View, you see the same HTML tags that appear in the Outline View. **Figure 14–23** shows a basic Web page with only two lines of text. The rest of the tags here represent the HTML hierarchy.

All text within <> brackets (and colored differently than the page's content) represent HTML tags. Most lines are indented according to the tags' place within the HTML hierarchy. Those indents don't appear on your Web page, however—they are created merely to remind you where you are on the page. You

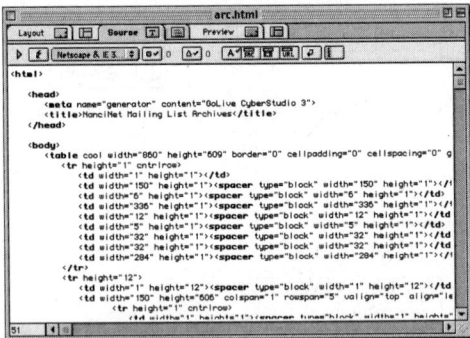

Figure 14-21: This is a portion the Source View of the Web page pictured in Figure 14-1.

Figure 14-22: Click the Source tab to switch to the Source View.

```
<html>
    <head>
        <meta name="generator" content="GoLive CyberStudio
        <title>Home Page</title>
    </head>

    <body>
        <h1>A Simple Web Page</h1>
        <p>Here are the structural elements of the page.
    </body>
</html>
```

Figure 14-23: A basic HTML page in the Source View.

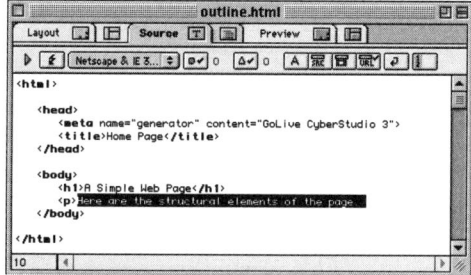

Figure 14-24: Select text in the Source View.

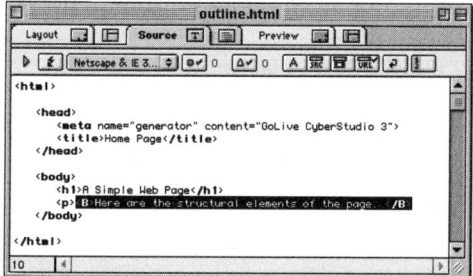

Figure 14-25: Tags appear around the selection.

can change the way the Source View displays HTML with Source Preferences, discussed later in this chapter.

You can type new text or tags into the Source View, and you can format text in the Source View using either menus or the toolbar.

To type text in the Source View:

1. Click where you want to add text in the Source View.

2. Type the text.

3. Add HTML tags around the text if necesary.

✔ Tip

■ When you type more than a line's worth of text, CyberStudio wraps to the next line, just as many word-processing applications do. But the wrap you see in the Source View is not identical to what you see in a Web browser. If you want to control where lines of text break, you should either create a
 (line break) tag at the end of each line or use the <p></p> tag pair to create a paragraph, which includes a line break at the end.

To format text using the toolbar:

1. Select some text in the Source View (**Figure 14-24**).

2. Click the Bold button on the toolbar. Bold tags appear around the selected text (**Figure 14-25**).

✔ Tips

■ You can use all menu and toolbar formatting tools to add HTML tags to text. You can see the results when you look at a page in the Layout or Preview Views.

■ Format an entire paragraph by triple-clicking to select it. Then choose a formatting tool to add tags.

USING THE SOURCE VIEW

To set Source View preferences:

1. Choose Preferences from the Edit menu.

2. Click the Source icon. Scroll through the window if necessary (**Figure 14-26**).

3. In the General Source Preferences window, deselect "Enable dragging of marked text" to disable drag & drop in the Source View.

4. Disable "Relaxed checking of &xxx; characters" to give CyberStudio permission to ignore some questionable characters, when you check the page's syntax.

5. Use "Do not mark unknown attributes as errors" if you add new HTML tags or other unknown items to your pages.

6. Use the Bold Tags, Auto Indent and other formatting options to customize the appearance of the text in the Source view. The example in the lower half of the window shows how text will look with the options you choose.

To choose a browser set:

1. Click the Browser Sets label under Source Preferences. See **Figure 14-27**.

2. Choose a new browser if you want CyberStudio's syntax checker to match your tags with additional browsers.

3. When you click on a browser on the left, CyberStudio checks the appropriate boxes on the right.

4. You can add a browser by clicking New, naming the new browser set, and checking off HTML standards to apply.

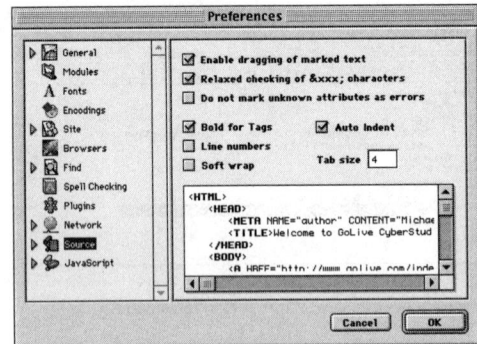

Figure 14-26: The General Source preferences window.

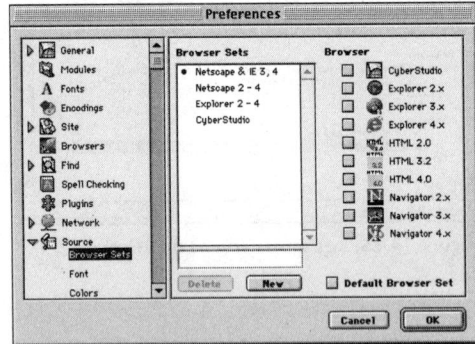

Figure 14-27: Choose a new browser set if you want to construct your pages according to a new HTML specification.

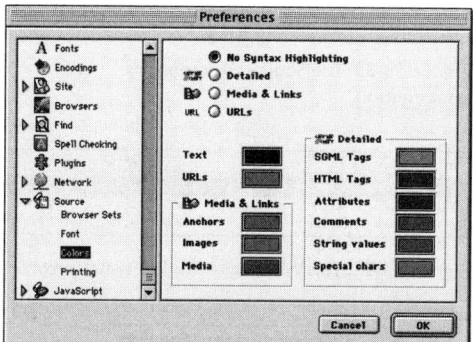

Figure 14-28: Syntax highlighting preferences let you color tags and contents in the Source View.

Figure 14-29: The Source View toolbar contains many of the options you'll find under Preferences

To set font preferences:

1. In the Preferences window, click the triangle to the left of the Source label to reveal more options.

2. Click the Font label.

3. Select a typeface, size and style for text within the Source View. This typeface appears within the Source View only, not on the pages you publish on the Web. You can see how your choice will look in the preferences window.

To set other preferences:

1. Choose the Colors item under Source preferences. See **Figure 14-28**.

2. Use the "Detailed", "Media & Links" or "URLs" buttons to support different levels of text coloring within the Source View. Leave "No Syntax Highlighting" selected if you don't want to see colored links, tags or text colored.

3. If you want to change the default colors, use the Color Palette to apply a color to each type of text, tag or attribute.

4. If you intend to print your pages, click Printing under Source Preferences.

5. Choose syntax colors and fonts for printing is you would like to use colors and fonts different from those you use to display the page onscreen.

The Source View toolbar

In addition to the formatting toolbar that occupies its own window above your CyberStudio documents, the Source View includes its own toolbar, designed to help you find and fix problems. The toolbar (**Figure 14-29**) works with the preferences you set in the previous section to give you quick access to syntax highlighting and error-checking.

USING THE SOURCE VIEW

To check HTML syntax:

1. With a document open in the Source View, click the Check Syntax button (**Figure 14-30**) on the Source View toolbar. CyberStudio opens a pane above the HTML code, displaying the page's syntax errors (**Figure 14-31**).

2. Click on an error message to see the problem highlighted in the document.

3. Fix or delete the subject tag, and the error message disappears.

✔ Tips

■ You've already seen that you can set syntax highlighting levels in the Preferences window. You can also change them from the Source View toolbar. The buttons shown in **Figure 14-32** allow you to turn highlighting off of specify whether you'd like to see detailed highlights, media and links, or just URLs.

■ Browser sets are also available both the Preference window and the toolbar. Just choose a browser set from the popup menu (**Figure 14-33**) and CyberStudio set's syntax to the current page.

Figure 14-30: The Source View toolbar's Check Syntax button.

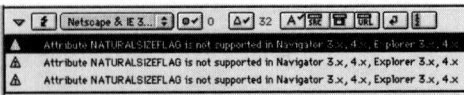

Figure 14-31: This Web page has a few syntax errors.

Figure 14-32: Choose the amount of information you want with syntax highlighting buttons.

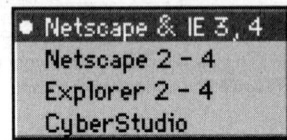

Figure 14-33: You can pick a browser set from the toolbar's popup menu.

Figure 14-34: The palette's Header tab contains a tool for each header type.

Using header tags

HTML pages have two main parts: the body (signified by enclosing <BODY> and </BODY> tags), and the header (signified by <HEAD> and </HEAD> tags). All the text and graphics that make up the page appear between body tags. Header tags, although they usually don't contain visible page elements, can store lots of information about the page that visitors to your site can use when using and searching for your site.

The most basic header tag is the <TITLE> tag, which specifies the name your page has when added to a Web browser's bookmarks list. You fill in the title tag when you replace the words "Welcome to CyberStudio" at the top of the document window with a title of your own choosing.

Other header tags are optional and must be entered in the Layout, Source or Outline views. In this section, I explain how to add header tags and what each supported tag adds to your Web page.

Adding headers

Like other HTML elements, header tags can be added to a Web page by dragging a tool from the palette's Header tab (**Figure 14-34**) to the document window. To add header tags this way, you must drag palette tools to the header area in the Layout window. You can easily configure each header's attributes and content within an Inspector window specific to that header. If you prefer, and if you are familiar with HTML, you can use the Outline or Source Views for editing, but—unless you prefer to type raw HTML—you'll want to create the headers in the Layout View.

✔ Tip

- Don't confuse *headers* (which appear within the <HEAD> and </HEAD> tags, above the Web page's body) with *headings*, which use <H1>, <H2> and so forth. Headings format text within the page, and appear between the <BODY> and </BODY> tags. CyberStudio makes this HTML distinction a bit of a challenge by referring in the toolbar to headings as headers—but they really are headings.

To add a header to a Web page:

1. Open a new or existing CyberStudio document to the Layout View.

2. Click on the small triangle in the title bar of the document window (**Figure 14-35**). The header area opens (**Figure 14-36**).

3. Drag a tool from the Header tab of the palette into the header pane of the document window (**Figure 14-37**).

4. Click on the new tag to display its Inspector window.

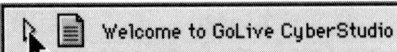

Figure 14-35: Click the triangle to open the header pane.

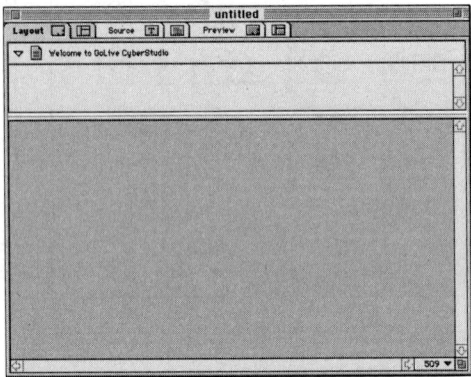

Figure 14-36: The header pane opens at the top of the document window.

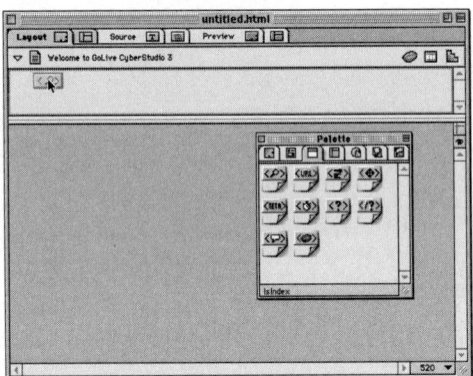

Figure 14-37: Drag a palette tool into the header pane to add it to your Web page.

Figure 14-38a: The Isindex palette tool and header tag.

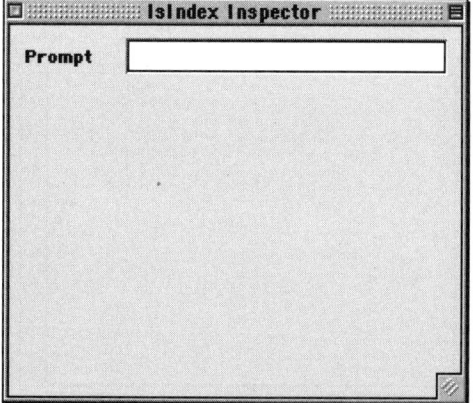

Figure 14-38b: The Isindex Inspector window.

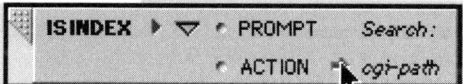

Figure 14-39: Configure the ACTION attribute by choosing a CGI file.

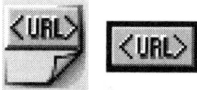

Figure 14-40a: The Base palette tool and header tag.

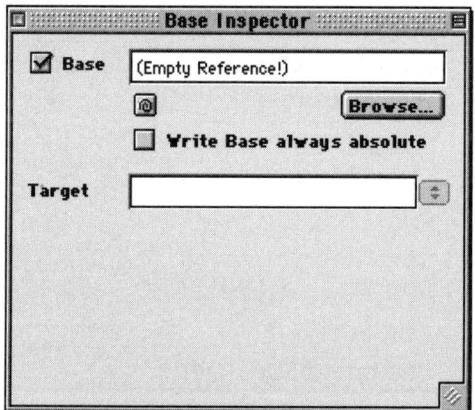

Figure 14-40b: The Base Inspector window.

Adding an Isindex header

The Isindex header adds a search field to the Web page. To use an Isindex header, you need to connect the page to a CGI (Common Gateway Interface) application that supports searching. The CGI must reside on the server where your Web site lives.

To set up an Isindex header:

1. Drag the Isindex palette tool to the header pane (**Figure 14-38a**).

2. Click to display the Isindex Inspector window (**Figure 14-38b**).

3. In the Prompt field, type the text you want to appear adjacent to the search field.

✔ Tip

■ When you are ready to upload this Web page to your server, you need to connect the Isindex header to a CGI application. To do this, switch to the Outline View and locate the Isindex header. Click the collapse/expand triangle. In the ACTION attribute, click the arrow (**Figure 14-39**) and choose a CGI file in the dialog box.

Adding a Base header

The Base header allows you to specify the base URL of your Web page.

To set up a Base header:

1. Drag the Base palette tool to the header pane (**Figure 14-40a**).

2. Click to display the Base Inspector window (**Figure 14-40b**).

USING HEADER TAGS

3. Click Browse or use Point & Shoot to locate a base document.

4. Choose "Write Base always absolute" to use an absolute, rather than a relative path, to locate the base document.

Adding a Keywords header

The Keywords header adds keywords to your document so that Web crawlers and search engines can locate and add your page to their databases.

To set up a Keywords header:

1. Drag the Keywords palette tool to the header pane (**Figure 14-41a**).

2. Click to display the Keywords Inspector window (**Figure 14-41b**).

3. Click in the keyword field near the bottom of the Keywords Inspector window.

4. Type a keyword and press Add. The keyword appears in the upper field.

5. Repeat the process for each keyword you want to add.

✔ Tip

■ Here's another way to add a keyword. Within a CyberStudio document, use the mouse to select a word you would like to use as a keyword and choose Add to Keywords from the Special menu (**Figure 14-42**). CyberStudio creates a keyword header (if one doesn't already exist) and adds your keyword.

Figure 14-41a: The Keywords palette tool and header tag.

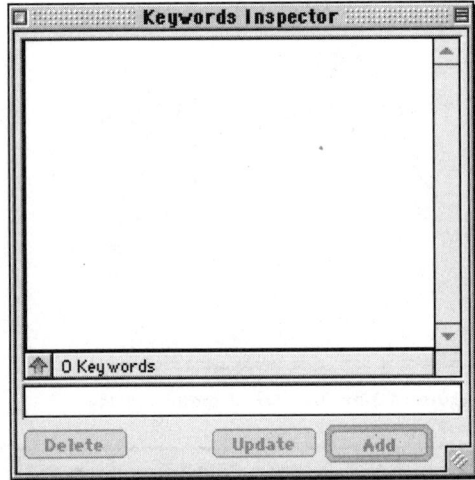

Figure 14-41b: The Keywords Inspector window.

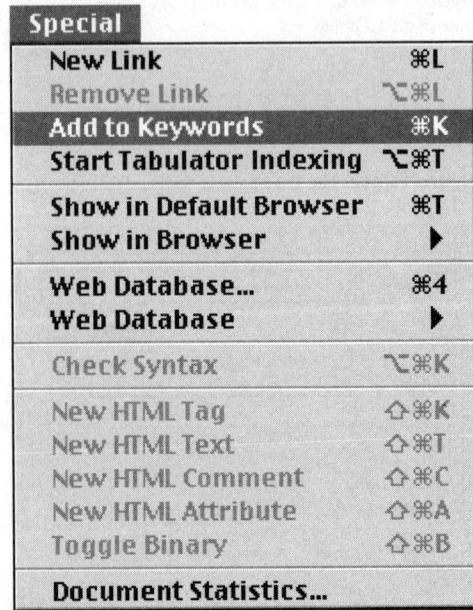

Figure 14-42: Choose Add to Keywords from the Special menu.

Figure 14-43a: The Link palette tool and header tag.

Figure 14-43b: The Link Inspector window.

Adding a Link header

The Link header adds a link between one page and others within your site, making it easier to organize a group of pages.

To set up a Link header:

1. Drag the Link palette tool to the header pane (**Figure 14-43a**).

2. Click to display the Link Inspector window (**Figure 14-43b**).

3. Type, browse or Point & Shoot to a URL you want to link to this page. Press Tab.

4. Enter the related page's title in the Title field. Press Tab.

5. If you're linking to an anchor, type it in the Name field.

6. Leave the URN and Methods fields blank unless you use these attributes. Most Web authors don't.

7. In the REL field, type the relationship of your page to the linked page that follows, i.e. if the page you're working on is a subsidiary of the page to which you're linking. Press Tab.

8. Type the reverse relationship in the REV field.

Adding a Meta header

Meta headers supply information about the document to Web site visitors. When a visitor chooses Document Info within his or her Web browser, the browser displays the contents of the page's Meta headers. Meta headers usually tell the user something about the page, its author, the associated Web site or the software used to create it.

By default, CyberStudio includes the Meta headers for file format, character set and file creator in each document you create. You can also add your own Meta headers, or even alter those created by CyberStudio.

To set up a Meta header:

1. Drag the Meta palette tool to the header pane (**Figure 14-44a**).

2. Click to display the Meta Inspector window (**Figure 14-44b**).

3. Choose HTTP Equivalent or Name from the popup menu. HTTP Equivalent tags tell the Web server to act on the HTTP request entered in the Content field below. A Name Meta tag sends the tag's contents as text.

4. Type a name for the HTTP header or for the text element you want to enter.

5. In the Content field, type the meta tag content that you want to appear to site visitors.

Adding a Refresh header

The Refresh header updates a Web page at intervals you set. This header is useful when you want to create pages with live or near-live elements.

To set up a Refresh header:

1. Drag the Refresh palette tool to the header pane (**Figure 14-45a**).

2. Click to display the Refresh Inspector window (**Figure 14-45b**).

3. Choose the delay interval in seconds. Press Tab.

4. Click "This Document" to apply the refresh rate to the page you're working with. Otherwise, you can choose URL if you want the browser to replace your page with a new page. If you choose URL, use the Browse button or Point & Shoot to locate a URL.

✔ Tip

■ You can create a slide show affect by adding multiple Refresh tags and pointing them to different URLs.

Figure 14-44a: The Meta palette tool and header tag.

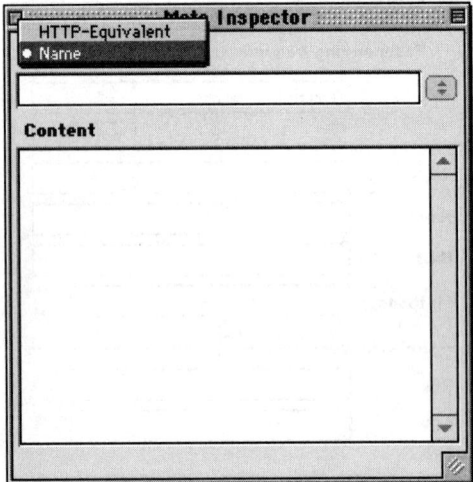

Figure 14-44b: The Meta Inspector window.

Figure 14-45a: The Refresh palette tool and header tag.

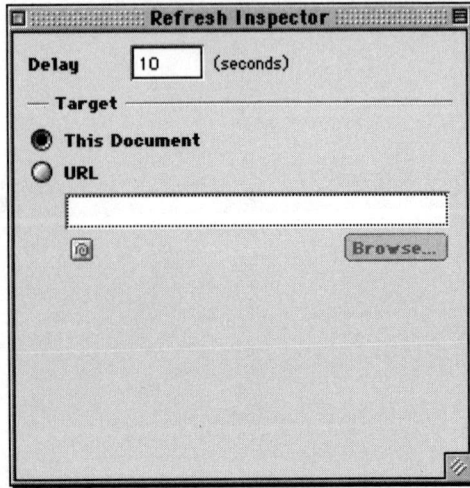

Figure 14-45b: The Refresh Inspector window.

USING HEADER TAGS

Figure 14-46a: The Tag palette tool and header tag.

Figure 14-46b: The Tag Inspector window.

Figure 14-46c: The Endtag palette tool and header tag.

Adding unknown headers

As the HTML standard develops, new tags become available to Web developers. You can add a header tag that is currently unknown to GoLive CyberStudio with the Tag and Endtag palette tools.

To set up an unknown header:

1. Drag the Tag palette tool to the header pane to open an unknown tag (**Figure 14-46a**).

2. Click to display the Tag Inspector window (**Figure 14-46b**).

3. Type a name for your new tag in the Tagname field.

4. Click New to add an attribute to the new tag. The new attribute box is selected when you click.

5. Type a name for the attribute. Press Tab.

6. Type a value for the attribute.

7. Repeat steps 4-6 to add additional attributes.

8. Drag the Endtag palette tool to the header pane to complete the new tag (**Figure 14-46c**).

9. In the Endtag Inspector window, type a name for the endtag that matches the opening tag.

Adding a Comment header

Comment headers add a non-displaying comment to your Web page header. The comment is primarily useful to Web page designers.

To set up a Comment header:

1. Drag the Comment palette tool to the header pane (**Figure 14-47a**).

2. Click to display the Comment Inspector window (**Figure 14-47b**).

3. Type a comment in the Inspector window.

Adding a Script header

The Script header adds a pointer to a JavaScript, allowing the script to execute when a visitor opens your page.

To set up a Script header:

1. Drag the Script palette tool to the header (**Figure 14-48a**).

2. Click to display the Head Script Inspector window (**Figure 14-48b**).

3. Type a name for the script. The language field is filled out for you.

4. Locate a script with the Browse button or Point & Shoot.

5. To edit or create a script, click Edit. The JavaScript interface appears. (For details on editing JavaScripts, see Chapter 10.)

Figure 14-47a: The Comment palette tool and header tag.

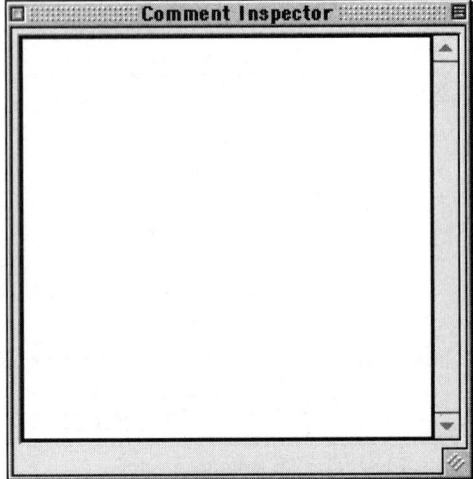

Figure 14-47b: The Comment Inspector window.

Figure 14-48a: The Script palette tool and header tag.

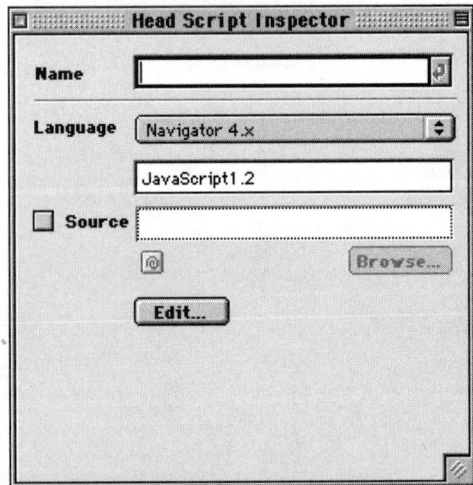

Figure 14-48b: The Head Script Inspector window.

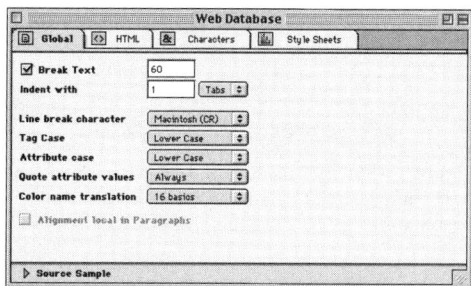

Figure 14-49: The Global tab of the Web Database window.

The Web Database

All of the tags, characters and styles you will use to construct your Web pages are stored in CyberStudio Professional Edition's Web Database. When you work with tags in the Outline View, CyberStudio uses the Web Database to specify tags and attributes. The software's syntax- and error-checking tools depend on the database to check the validity of tags entered or edited by hand in the Source View. You can use the database to look up tags and attributes and to add new ones. As HTML evolves, new tags and attributes are likely to come into common use. With the database, you can keep CyberStudio up-to-date.

The Web Database appears, like so many other CyberStudio tools, as a tabbed window. Individual items, when clicked, display a context-sensitive Inspector window. When the database is open, the toolbar displays database-specific tools.

The four Web Database tabs are:

- The Global tab.
- The HTML tab.
- The Chars tab.
- The CSS tab.

To open the Web Database:

Choose Web from the Special menu.

The Global tab

The Web Database's Global tab (**Figure 14-49**) is really an extension of the Source preference you've already set. Like those options, the global items in the Web Database allow you to customize the look and behavior of your HTML code. Here, you can choose text wrap, tab and line break options, as well as case and color naming preferences.

To see how your choices will look, click the Source Sample triangle at the bottom of the window. The resulting pane updates as you change options, above (**Figure 14-50**).

The HTML tab

The HTML tab is the heart of the Web Database, because it contains all of the tags that CyberStudio (and the current HTML standards) recognize and use. Individual tags are grouped together under appropriate headings. Each tag comes complete with a short comment, explaining the tag further. Clicking on a tag displays a related Inspector window.

To locate existing tags:

1. In the Global tab window, locate an HTML tag you want to edit by scrolling through the list of tags until you find one you want to work with.

2. Click the desired tag. A Web Database Inspector, complete with information specific to the tag you selected, comes to life (**Figure 14-51**).

3. Note the Inspector settings for the tag you're working with. The settings tell you what the tag is (Tag Name, Comment) how the tag appears (Structure), what it includes (Content) and whether or not it needs an End tag to complete it.

4. Click the Output tab to see how the tag will appear, relative to other items on the page.

5. Click the Version tab. CyberStudio displays a list of browsers, with those that support the tag checked. (see **Figure 14-52**)

6. If you chose a tag with a triangle next to its name in the Web Database (table caption is a good example), click on the triangle to display the tag's attributes; the same attributes you can edit in the Inspector when you add a tag to your Web page with a palette tool.

7. Keep clicking triangles to expand the tag and its attributes fully.

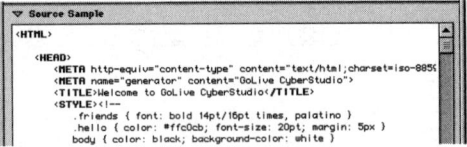

Figure 14-50: Click the Source Sample triangle to see what your changed preferences will look like in the Source View.

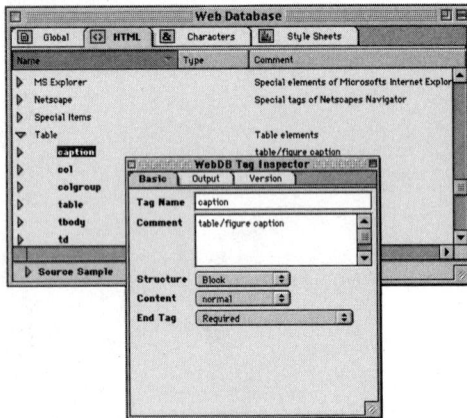

Figure 14-51: Selecting a tag in the Web Database displays the WebDB Inspector.

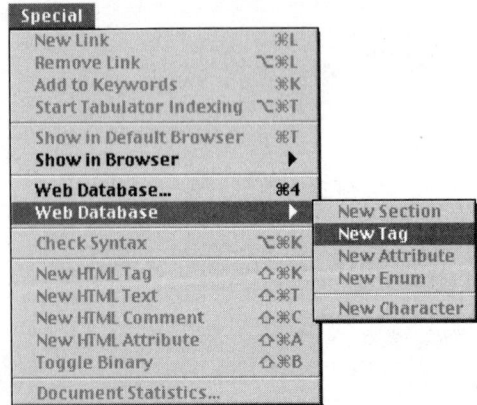

Figure 14-52: Versions shows you which browsers support the tag you've selected.

THE WEB DATABASE

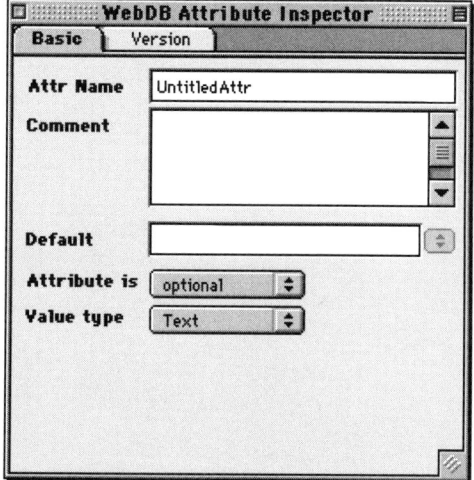

Figure 14-53: Choose New Tag from the Web Database submenu.

✔ Tip

- Look at the various options in the Inspector. Though the Structure, Content and End Tag popups can be edited, for example, it's almost always a bad idea to change the default options of existing tags. The Web Database stores tags and their configurations according to HTML standards, and altering a tag could cause serious problems if you're not certain of what you're doing.

To add a new tag to the database:

1. With the Web Database's HTML tab showing, click once on a section label (one of the tag headings in the window) into which your new tag would logically fit.

2. Choose New Tag from the Web Database submenu, of the Special menu (**Figure 14-53**). A new tag label appears in the Web Database, and the WebDB tag inspector appears.

3. Name the tag in the Inspector window. Use the actual text of the tag as it will appear in your HTML code.

4. Describe your new tag in the comment field.

5. configure the tag by choosing Structure and Content parameters from the popup menus in the Basic tab.

6. Make choices about the tag's appearance, relative to other items on the page, under the Output tab.

7. Finally, assign the tag to browsers that support it under the Version tab.

✔ Tip

- The items in the Web Database menu are also available from the context-sensitive toolbar, at the top of the screen.

Tag attributes

You can add attributes to existing tags, or to those you've just created. Attributes allow a Web author to configure features of a tag, such as its alignment, value, font, etc.

To add an attribute:

1. Select a tag in the Web Database window.

2. Choose New Attribute from the toolbar, or from the Web Database submenu of the Special menu.

3. Like the WebDB Tag Inspector, the Attribute Inspector provides fields for naming and describing the attribute.

4. You can also choose a default condition for the attributes tag, when the attribute is not specified. For instance, if you add an alignment attribute, you might choose to make the default alignment left.

5. Use the Attribute Is item to tell the database whether the attribute is optional within its tag, or required.

6. Choose a value from the Value Type popup.

7. Click the Version tab to identify browsers and HTML standards that support the attribute. It is possible for a tag to be supported by a particular browser, while an attribute is not.

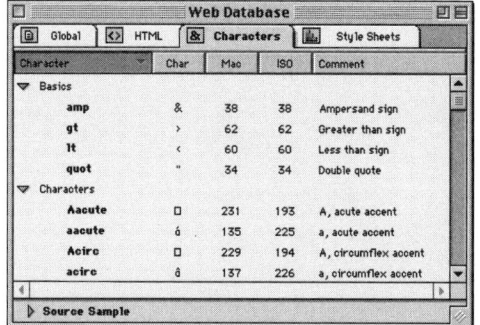

Figure 14-54: The Special Characters tab of the Web Database.

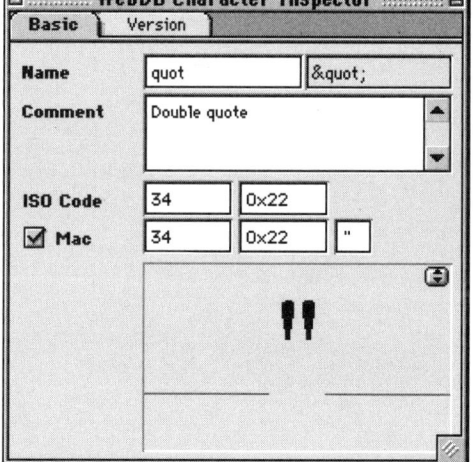

Figure 14-55: Clicking on a character reveals the Character Inspector.

The Special Characters tab

While HTML language displays alphanumeric characters just as they are typed, a number of non-alpha characters require that you surround them with HTML tags. To display a special character, you must surround it with an ampersand (&) and a semicolon (;) like this:

&luml;

luml indicates that you want to display an l with an umlaut.

The Special Characters tab stores the HTML name of the character, a description of the character, and the code needed to generate it on a Web page.

Special characters are displayed under the Characters tab in three sections:

- The Basics
- The Characters
- The General Punctuation

Basics characters include the ampersand, greater-than sign and quotation mark. Most alphanumeric characters (many of them with accent marks used in languages other than English) are stored under the Characters section, while the General Punctuation section includes several en dashes, em dashes and a non-breaking space character.

To view a special character:

1. Choose Web Database from the Special menu to open the Database.

2. Click the Characters tab. It looks like **Figure 14-54**.

3. Locate the quot item under the Basics heading, and click on it. The Inspector window now displays the WebDB Characters Inspector (see **Figure 14-55**).

   The Inspector displays the name, code and description of the character. In addition, you'll find the ISO and byte codes that identifies the character within the HTML standard, and the Mac code that identifies the character to the Mac OS. Finally, the lower pane of the Inspector shows how the character looks when displayed in a browser. To view the character in a different font, click the button at the right of the sample.

4. Click the Version tab to view HTML versions and browsers the tag is compatible with.

To add a new character:

1. Decide which section your new character best fits in and click on the section heading.

2. Choose New Character from the Web Databse submenu of the Special menu, or choose new Character from the toolbar.

3. Give the character an HTML name; the HTML code will be filled in automatically.

4. Type a descriptive name for the character.

5. Determine the correct ISO code, byte code and (if applicable) Mac OS code for the character.

6. Cllick on the Versions tab to specify HTML versions and browsers that support the character.

✔ Tips

- Like HTML tags, characters you add to the Web Database will not necessarily be supported by HTML. The character must have an ISO code and byte code, and must be supported by browsers.

- You can edit Special Characters, but changing an existin character's codes will make it inoperable, and may cause errors on your Web page.

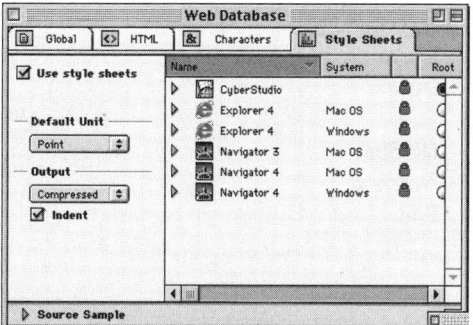

Figure 14-56: The Style Sheets tab of the Web Database.

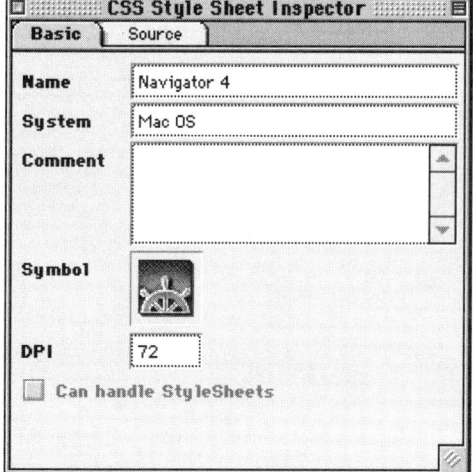

Figure 14-57: The CSS Style Sheet Inspector displays details of the Mac version of Netscape Navigator 4.

The Style Sheets tab

CyberStudio Professional Edition includes support for Cascading Style Sheets, and the Web Database includes a collection of style sheets that are compatible with leading Web browsers, on several platforms. You can use them as they are, or add new styles. You can also set a few general style sheet options in the Web Database.

To set style sheet options:

1. Open the Web Database and click on the Style Sheets tab (see **Figure 14-56**).

2. Unless you want to disable style sheets, leave the Use Style Sheets checkbox checked.

3. Choose a default unit of measure from the popup menu.

4. Choose an Output option to control how the style sheet code appears in the Source view.

5. Leave Indent checked, if you want the style sheet code to be indented from the left margin.

To view default style sheets:

1. Choose a browser from the list in the right side of the Style Sheet tab, anc click on its heading. The CSS Style Sheet Inspector (**Figure 14-57**) displays details about the browser, its platform, and the screen resolution it uses.

2. Click on the Source tab to see the style sheets supported by the browser. You can view the style sheets individually by in the Web Database by expanding the heading.

THE WEB DATABASE

Adding attributes

You can add an attribute to a new or existing tag. Simply click on the tag to select it and configure the attribute.

To add an attribute to a tag:

1. Type a name for the attribute in the Name field, under the Attributes heading.

2. Choose an HTML standard from the HTML popup menu.

3. Choose an attribute option from the HTML attribute status popup menu.

4. Choose a value type for the attribute from the Value popup menu (**Figure 14-58**).

5. If you want a specific value to appear automatically when the tag is used, type the value in the Value field (**Figure 14-59**).

6. Add a Comment explaining the attribute if you wish.

7. Click Add to confirm the new attribute.

Adding enumerations

Some tag attributes include options. An alignment attribute, for example, has an option to align the attribute to the left, right or center.

To add enumerations:

1. Choose a tag and an attribute by clicking on them in turn. The attribute you choose must have an Enum. value type selected.

2. Type a name for the enumeration in the Name field under the Enums heading (**Figure 14-60**).

3. Choose an HTML standard supported by the enumeration.

4. Click Add to confirm the new attribute.

5. Repeat steps 1-4 to create additional enumerations.

Figure 14-58: The Value popup menu.

Figure 14-59: The Value field.

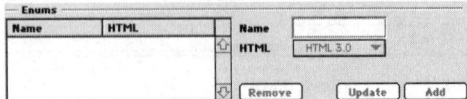

Figure 14-60: Enumeration heading.

15

BUILDING SITES

A Web site is the sum of its parts: HTML pages, images and multimedia files. Juggling a large number of site elements and the need to organize Web content so that it is easy for users to work with make site management a necessity for most modern Webmasters.

To manage a complete Web site with Cyber-Studio, you need to create a *site*. Sites are collections of files and resources that you can view, manipulate and publish on the Web. Within a site, you can store the pages and media files you create, links to external resources—like other sites and e-mail addresses—and font and color information. Once you have created a site, you can organize your site by adding and rearranging files. You can also get a bird's eye view of the entire site with the Site and Link Views. Next, check the site and its pages for errors, and fix them on the spot. When you're ready to put the site on the Web, you can use GoLive CyberStudio tools to publish it.

In this chapter, I cover:

■ Using site tools.

■ Building sites.

■ Fine-tuning preferences.

■ Adding resources to a site.

Using site tools

You build CyberStudio sites with several sets of tools, commands and preferences. I cover each one as I work through the process of creating and maintaining a site, but here's an overview.

The Site window

The Site window is where the action is. You add, rearrange and link files from here. Under its five tabs, you store files, external URLs, colors and font sets.

The Site window works much like the Mac Finder. You can drag content into and out of the site window to create links and to verify visually that the all of the pieces of the site are connected. Using Folders, you can organize site elements for easy access. (**Figure 15-1**).

The palette's Site tab

The Site tab contains tools that you can use to add elements to the site by dragging them into the Site window (**Figure 15-2**).

The toolbar

With a CyberStudio site open, the context-sensitive toolbar adds several site management items (**Figure 15-3**). You can create new folders, update a site's links, check and change preferences, locate files, and more.

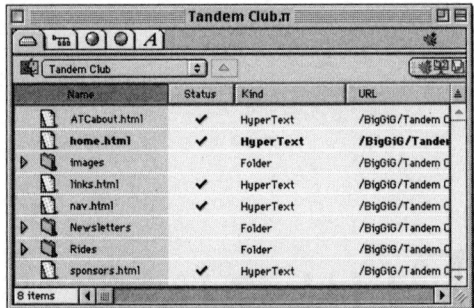

Figure 15-1: The Site window.

Figure 15-2: The Site tab of the palette.

Figure 15-3: The toolbar, as it appears when a CyberStudio site is open.

USING SITE TOOLS

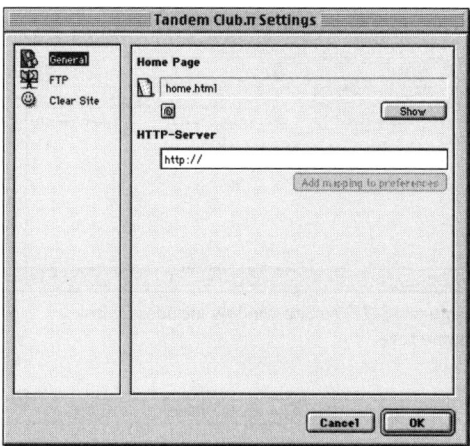

Figure 15-4: The Site Settings window.

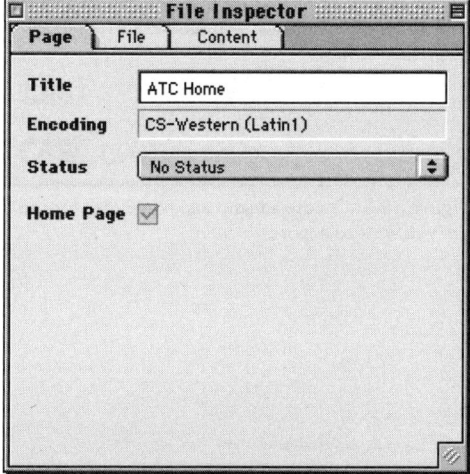

Figure 15-5: The File Inspector window.

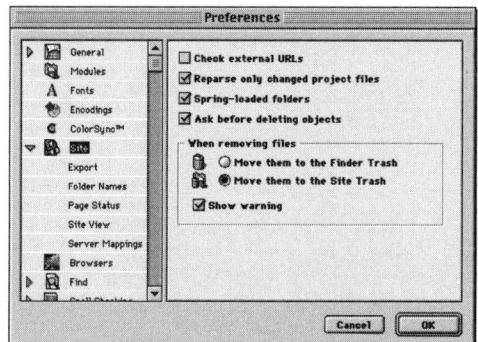

Figure 15-6: Site preferences are spread among six sections in the Preferences window.

Site settings

You can edit site-wide parameters with the Site Settings window. Most of the options relate to publishing your site on a remote Web server (see **Figure 15-4**).

File inspector

Each site file has its own inspector window that allows you to configure and view options specific to that file. (see **Figure 15-5**)

The Site menu

Most of the commands on the menu involve adding site elements or making global changes and verifications. You can also reach the Site View and Link View, which I discuss in the next chapter.

Site preferences

You'll find options for publishing your site and handling the addition of new files to the site (**Figure 15-6**).

To locate Site Preferences, choose Preferences from the Edit menu, and click the triangle next to the Site label to view all of your options.

USING SITE TOOLS

Building sites

To begin a CyberStudio site, you must first create the site file and then add HTML and media files to it. Along the way, you can set preferences that affect the way site elements are added and manipulated.

There are three basic ways to start your site. They are:

- Create a blank site.

- Import an existing site that is stored on a local hard disk.

- Imports a site that is stored on a server, using FTP.

To create a blank site:

1. Choose New Site, and choose Blank from the submenu in the File menu.

2. In the dialog box that appears, locate a folder for your site, or leave the Create Folder box checked, to have CyberStudio create a new one for you.

3. Name your site and click Save. The Site window and Site Inspector windows appear (**Figure 15-7**).

To import a local site:

1. Select New Site, and choose Import from Folder, from the File menu.

2. In the window that appears, locate the site folder you want to import by clicking Browse, and navigating to the folder you want.

3. Back in the Import Site Folder window, choose the site's home page. When you're ready to import the site, the window should look like **Figure 15-8**.

4. Click OK to begin the import. When the site has been imported, it appears in the Site window.

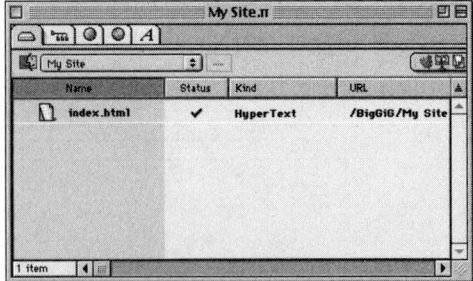

Figure 15-7: The Site window includes a blank home page.

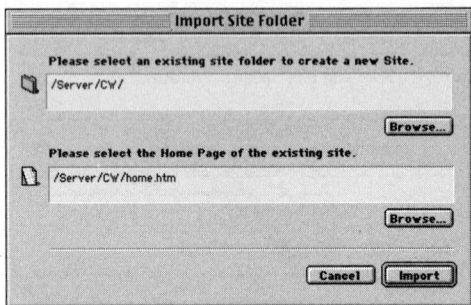

Figure 15-8: Choose a folder and home page for the site you want to import.

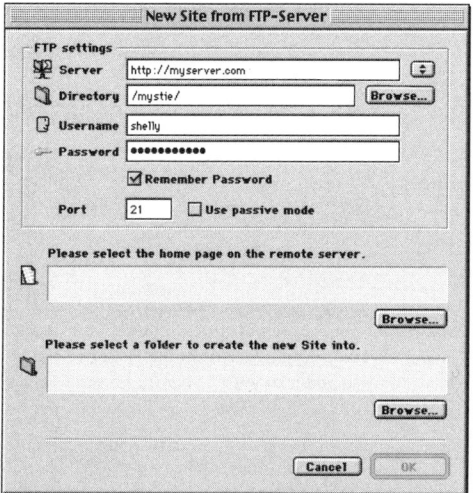

Figure 15-9: enter the particulars of the site you want to import in the Import Site from FTP-Server window.

✔ Tips

■ You can also import a site by dragging-and-dropping a site folder and/or home page into the Import Site Folder window.

■ When you import a site folder and its files, you can also import references to external resources—URLs and e-mail addresses—and check them as you do. To import external links, choose Preferences from the Edit menu, click on the Site label, and click the Check External URLs checkbox. For more information about adding and using external resources to your site, see the Adding Resources to a Site, later in this chapter.

To import a site using FTP:

1. Select New Site, and choose Import from FTP, from the File menu.

2. In the New Site from FTP-Server window (**Figure 15-9**), type the server URL and directory path in the appropriate fields. Once you've typed in the server name, you can navigate to the correct directory by clicking Browse.

3. Enter a username and password in the appropriate fields.

4. Locate the home page of the site to be imported by clicking Browse, under the appropriate label.

5. Choose a folder on your hard disk to accept the imported files.

6. Click OK to begin the import. When the import is complete, the Site window appears, containing the newly imported site.

BUILDING SITES

Adding files to a site

Once you have created the site, there are three ways to add resources to it:

- Create new files as you work.
- Add files with drag-and-drop.
- Use the Add Files command to import files and folders.

To start a site from scratch:

1. Open a site.

2. Choose New from the File menu to create a new document.

3. Click on the title bar to name the page or type some text in the document window.

4. Save the document to your site folder. The new file appears in the Site window.

To add files to a site with drag-and-drop:

1. In CyberStudio, create or open a site.

2. In the Finder, locate the folder containing the files you want to add to the site and open the folder.

3. In the Site window, be sure that the Files tab is visible.

4. In the Finder, drag the files you want to add, (or the whole folder, if you like) into the Site window (**Figure 15-10**) and let go of the mouse button. CyberStudio analyzes the files you've added, copies them to the site's folder, and adds them to the site's database.

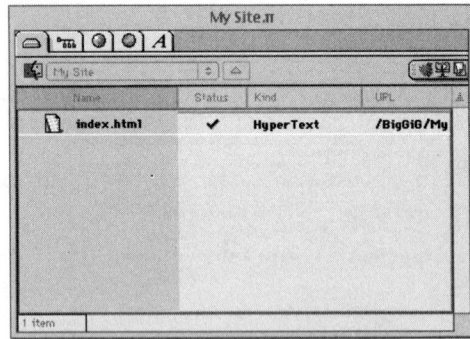

Figure 15-10: Drag a folder from the Finder to the Site window to add it to your CyberStudio site.

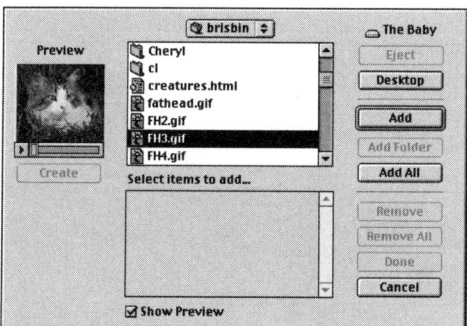

Figure 15-11: You can preview GIF or JPEG files in the Add Files dialog box.

✔ Tip

■ If you begin dragging a folder or file to the Site window and realize that the Files tab is not visible, you can drag the file or folder over the Files tab to bring it to the front. With that done, drop down into the window and let go of the mouse, to complete the addition to your site.

To add files from the Site menu:

1. Open a new or existing site.

2. Choose Add Files from the Site menu.

3. In the dialog box that appears, locate a file or folder that you would like to add to your site.

4. Select each file or folder you want to add to the site and click Add. To add everything in the current folder, click Add All.

✔ Tips

■ You can use the Add Files command to bring a complete Web site into your site or to add individual files and folders to an existing site.

■ If you select a a GIF file from the Add Files dialog box, CyberStudio displays a preview of the image. If you select a JPEG file, you can see a preview by clicking the Create button (**Figure 15-11**).

Fine-tuning preferences

The Preferences window and Site settings window include options that change the way you interact with your site. I've covered some of these options in the course of adding files and resources, and I'll cover another batch when I discuss publishing Web sites in Chapter 17. For now, though, there are a few settings you may find useful as you work on your site.

To set site preferences:

1. Choose Preferences from the Edit menu.

2. Click the Site label icon to display site-related options (**Figure 15-12**).

3. Click the "Check external URLs" checkbox to have CyberStudio validate remote links within your site as they are added.

   When CyberStudio opens a site file, it checks the site's links. Leave "Reparse only changed project files" checked to have CyberStudio verify only links in files that have changed since the last time the site was saved. By the way, *project* in this case is the term GoLive used to refer to site files in a previous version of the software.

4. Spring-loaded folders in a site file behave just like Macintosh folders. If you drag an item onto a folder and hold down the mouse for a moment, the folder opens.

5. Leave "Ask before deleting objects" checked to receive a warning when you remove a file from a site.

6. Choose to send deleted files to the Site Trash folder (a folder stored within the CyberStudio's site hierarchy) or to the Mac's trash can.

7. Click OK to finish setting preferences.

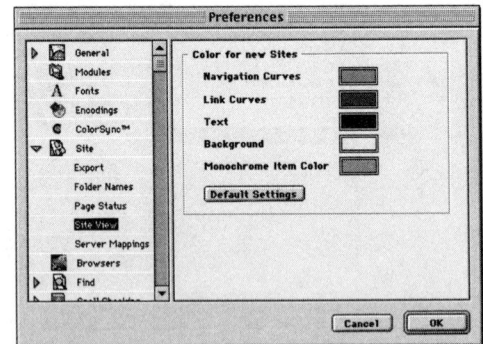

Figure 15-12: The Site section of the Preferences window.

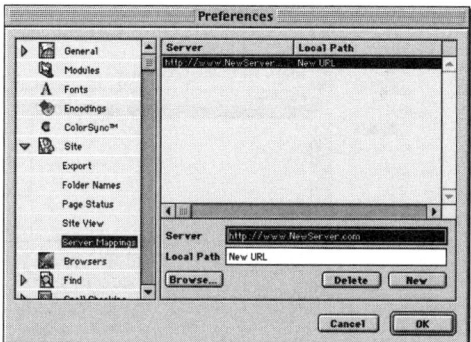

Figure 15-13: The Server Mappings item under Site Preferences.

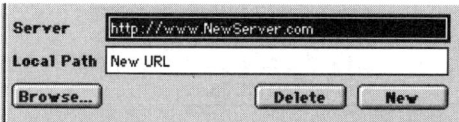

Figure 15-14: Edit the server and local path names in the Server Mappings window.

To prepare for uploading to multiple servers:

1. In the Preferences window, click the Server Mappings item under the Site label. Click the triangle to the left of the Site label if necessary. The result appears in **Figure 15-13**.

2. Click New to begin working with a new server. A placeholder URL appears in the Server field (**Figure 15-14**).

3. In the server field, type the URL of your secondary Web server, including the complete path to your Web site files.

4. Press Tab.

5. Click the Browse button, located under the New URL field.

6. In the dialog box, locate and select the folder containing Web site files you plan to store on a secondary server. The location appears in the Local Path field.

7. Repeat steps 3-6 for each server you want to add.

8. When you are finished adding servers, click OK.

✔ Tip

- In order for the multi server feature to work properly, you need to create a separate folder for files that will be published on the secondary server. You will need to relocate any files that will be stored on the primary server to another part of the site's hierarchy.

To filter URLs:

1. In the Preferences window, click the triangle next to the General label, then click the URL managing item. URL filters allow you to store non-HTML files within your site without incurring CyberStudio error indicators.

2. Click the New button to create a URL filter (**Figure 15-15**).

3. Type **cgi-bin** in the URL filter field. Many CGIs (Common Gateway Interface) applications use files and folders whose names include the text, "cgi-bin." These files are not HTML or multimedia files, so they generate errors when they are included in a CyberStudio site. A cgi-bin URL filter allows these non-standard filenames to be used without generating errors. You can create additional filters to bypass other unusual filenames.

4. When you have finished creating filters, click OK.

To edit site settings:

1. With a CyberStudio site open, click the Site Settings item in the toolbar (**Figure 15-16**). The Site Settings window opens.

2. You can change the site's home page in the General tab by clicking Browse and finding the new page.

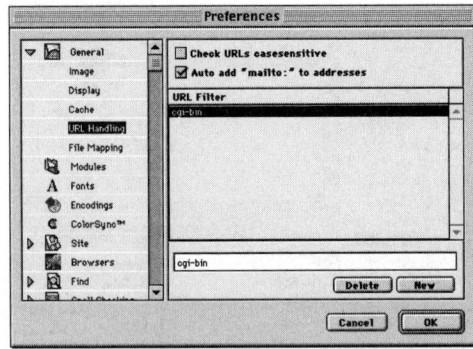

Figure 15-15: Enter a text string to filter in the URL Handling Preferences window.

Figure 15-16: Choose Site Settings from the toolbar.

Figure 15-17: Choose Import File from the Site menu to add bookmark files or address books.

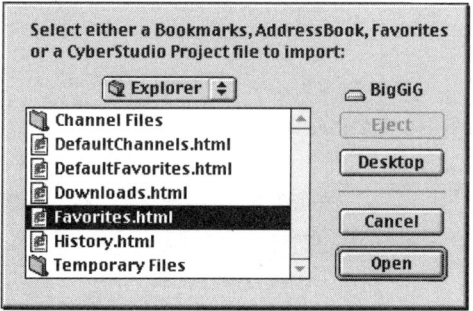

Figure 15-18: The Import dialog box reminds you which file formats can be imported.

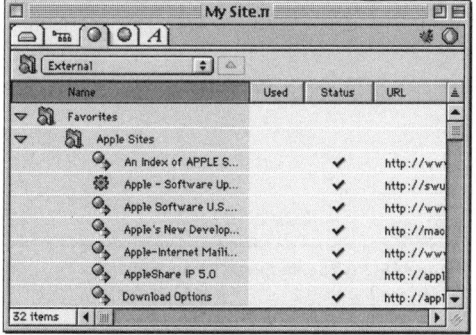

Figure 15-19: Bookmark and address book files are imported into a group within the Site window.

Adding resources to a site

Once you've established a site and populated it with files and external links, it's likely that you will add resources to your Web site. In addition to files and pointers to resources, CyberStudio provides a way to add color and font sets to the site, making them readily available from the Site window.

Importing external resources

If you are creating a site within the site metaphor rather than updating an existing one, chances are that you don't yet have ready-made files with external resources. In fact, you may have bookmark files or address books with this kind of information, with no way other than cutting and pasting to add them to a new Web site. CyberStudio allows you to import bookmark files and address/nickname files. When you are ready, you can use Point & Shoot linking to add URLs and addresses to a page within your site.

To import bookmarks or addresses:

1. Open a site.

2. In the Site window, click on the External tab to select it.

3. Choose Import File from the Site menu (**Figure 15-17**).

4. In the dialog box that appears (**Figure 15-18**), locate a URL or address file in one of the supported formats: bookmarks (Netscape Navigator), favorites (Internet Explorer), addressbook (Navigator), or nicknames (Eudora).

5. Click Open. If you have selected the "Check external URLs" checkbox in the Preferences window, CyberStudio will connect to the Internet and try to verify the URLs in your bookmarks or favorites file. When verification is complete, a new

Group (equivalent to a Folder within a CyberStudio site) appears in the External window, with the name of your URL file (see **Figure 15-19** on the previous page).

6. Click on the triangle to the left of the new Group icon to display its contents. If your bookmark or favorites file contains folders, CyberStudio preserves them when you import the file into a site.

To add a new URL to a site:

1. Make sure that the Site window and the palette are both visible.

2. Click on the External tab of the Site window.

3. Click on the Site tab in the palette (**Figure 15-20**).

4. Drag the URL tool (**Figure 15-21**) from the palette into the Site window. When you release the mouse button, an untitled URL appears under the External tab in the Site window.

5. Click on the untitled URL to display the Reference Inspector.

6. Type a name for the URL in the Name field and press Tab.

7. Type the full URL into the URL field. The finished URL appears in **Figure 15-22**.

✔ Tip

■ You can drag the URL tool, or any palette tool, into the URLs tab of the Site window by first dragging it over the External tab and then downward onto the tab's label. The tab then opens, allowing you to drop the palette tool.

Figure 15-20: The palette's Site tab displays tools you can use to add items to a site.

Figure 15-21: The URL tool.

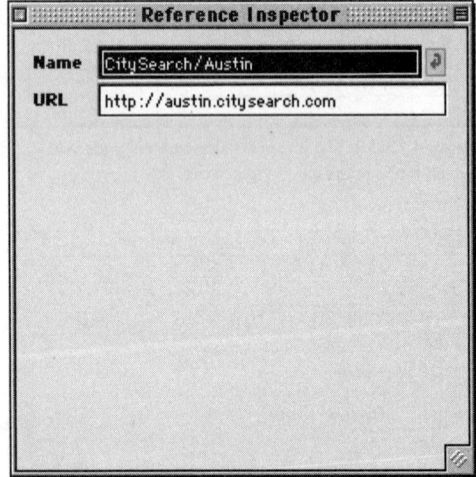

Figure 15-32: The finished URL appears.

Figure 15-23: The Address tool.

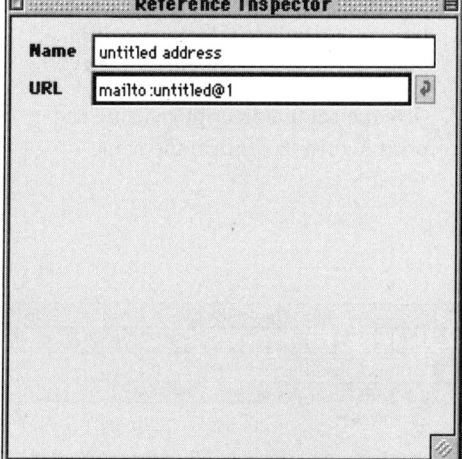

Figure 15-24: When you type an e-mail address, CyberStudio finishes the URL by adding "mailto:".

To add a new address:

1. Click on the External tab of the Site window.

2. Drag the Address tag (**Figure 15-23**) from the palette into the Site window.

3. Click on the untitled address to display the Reference Inspector.

4. Type a name for the address in the Name field and press Tab.

5. Type the e-mail address into the Address field. The finished address appears in **Figure 15-24**.

✔ Tips

■ CyberStudio helps you enter addresses by filling out the complete URL (when addresses are used as links, these links are URLs) for you. Type **sales@golive.com**, and CyberStudio completes the URL by adding "mailto:".

■ It's a good thing that address help is included because, unlike URLs, addresses can't be verified by connecting to the Net.

Adding colors

You can store colors within a site, much as you do files and external resources. You'll find this useful if you have created a custom color in the Color Palette, and for upholding a site-wide color scheme. Like other site objects, colors can be added to a Web page with drag-and-drop or Point & Shoot.

ADDING RESOURCES TO A SITE

To add a color to a site:

1. In the Site window, click on the Color tab (**Figure 15-25**).

2. Click the Site tab in the palette to display site tools.

3. Drag the Color tool (**Figure 15-26**) from the palette to the Site window. An untitled color appears in the Site window, and the Color Palette window opens.

4. Choose a color from one of the seven Color Palette tabs. The color appears in the Preview Pane (**Figure 15-27**).

5. Click in the Preview Pane and drag to the color box next to the new color you created. When you release the mouse button, the color appears in the Site window (**Figure 15-28**).

6. With the new color selected, click on the Inspector window, which now displays the Color Inspector (**Figure 15-29**).

7. Give the color a descriptive name and press Return to confirm the name.

Figure 15-25: The Site window's Colors tab.

Figure 15-26: The Color tool.

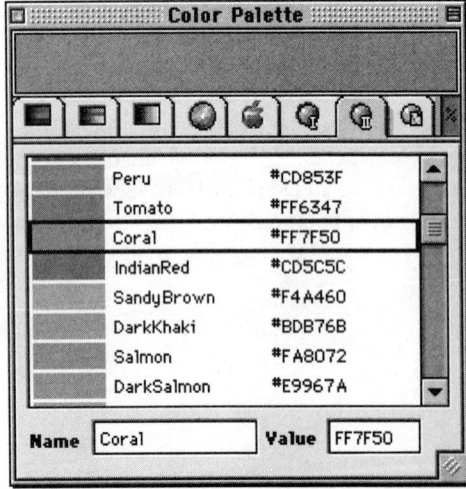

Figure 15-27: Your chosen color appears in the Color Palette's Preview pane.

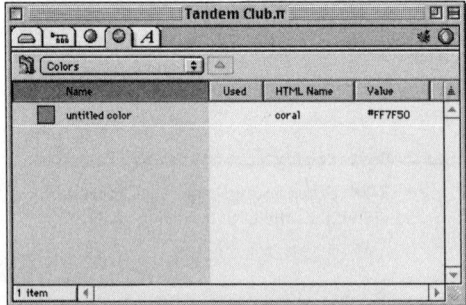

Figure 15-28: A new color appears in the Site window's Colors tab.

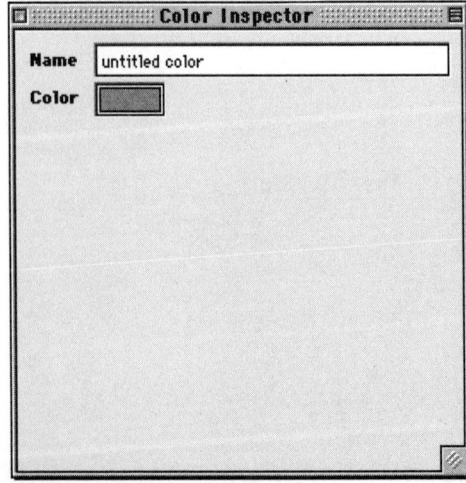

Figure 15-29: You can name the new color in the Color Inspector window.

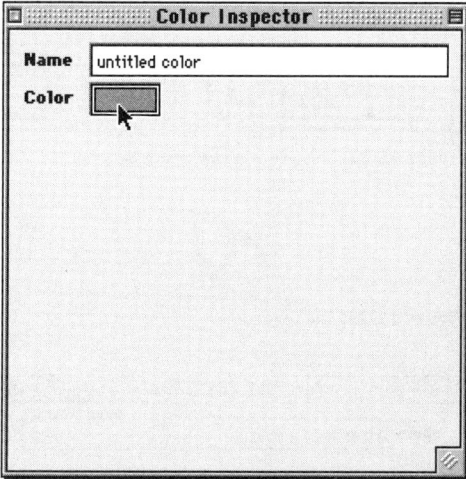

Figure 15-30: Clicking on the Color box displays the Color Inspector.

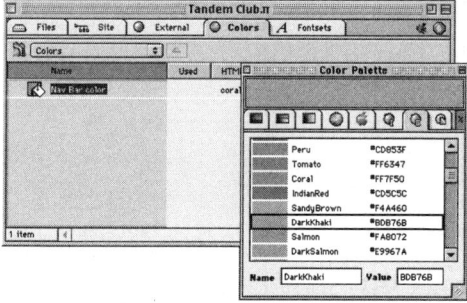

Figure 15-31: Dragging a color from the Color Palette onto a site color replaces the old color.

✔ Tips

■ When you add a new color, CyberStudio examines it to determine if it is one of the 216 colors supported by all Web browsers and computer platforms. If not, a bullet appears in the Web Safe column. It's a good idea to choose a Web Safe color instead.

■ For more details about selecting and matching colors with the Color Palette, see Chapter 13.

To replace an existing color:

1. In the Site window's Color tab, click on the color you want to change.

2. In the Color Inspector, click the Color box (**Figure 15-30**). The Color Palette opens or comes to the front if already open.

3. Choose a new color from one of the color tabs. To be certain that you've chosen a Web safe color, click the Web Named Color tab.

4. Drag the new color from the Preview pane to a color icon in the Site window (**Figure 15-31**). The color changes, along with its HTML Name and Value. The color is now Web safe.

✔ Tips

■ Web Named colors aren't the only Web safe choices available. Many colors you can choose or create in the Color Palette will also work with your site. Choose the color you want to use and then drag it to the Site window to see whether or not it's safe. If it isn't, replace it with another color.

■ Although you can't open two sites at once, you can copy colors from other sites. Click on a color in the Site window and choose Copy from the Edit menu. Close the current site and open the destination site. Paste the color into the Site window's Color tab.

Adding font sets

Font sets allow you to save and use fonts with your Web pages. Without them, you're limited to the typeface supported by your site visitors' Web browsers. You can store font sets as part of a site, just as you do custom colors.

To add a font set to a site:

1. In the Site window, click on the Font Sets tab (**Figure 15-32**).

2. From the palette's Site tab. click and drag the Font Set icon to the Site window (**Figure 15-33**). An empty font set item appears.

3. In the Font Set Inspector, (**Figure 13-34**), name the font set.

4. Click New. The field near the bottom of the Inspector lights up, along with a menu to its right. Click and hold the menu to view a list of available fonts.

5. Choose a font from the list.

6. If you want to add more fonts, to the set, repeat steps 4 and 5.

To use a font from an existing document:

1. Open a CyberStudio document that contains custom fonts. The document need not be part of a site, but be sure that a site is also open.

2. In the Site window, open the Font Sets tab by clicking on it.

3. In the document window, select some text that uses a custom font.

4. Drag the text into the Site window (**Figure 15-35**). A set appears in the Site window, and the Inspector changes to display the Font Set Inspector.

Figure 15-32: The Site window's Font Sets tab.

Figure 15-33: The text tool.

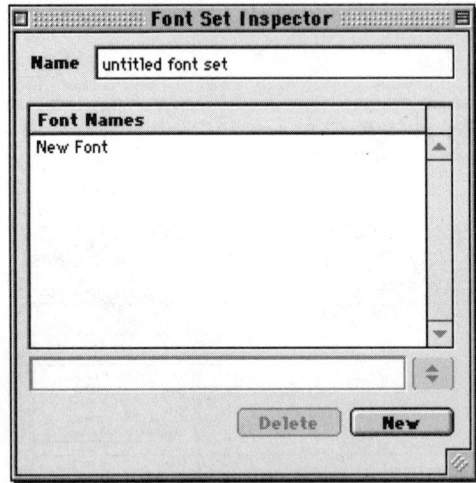

Figure 15-34: The Font Set Inspector.

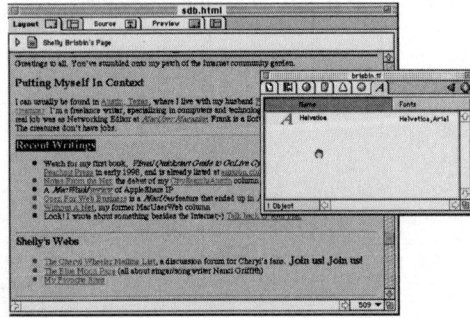

Figure 15-35: Drag text that uses a custom font from the document window to the Site window to add a font set.

5. Type a name for the font set in the Font Set Inspector and press Return to confirm the name of your font set. The font used in this set appears in the Font Set Inspector.

✔ Tips

■ Although you can't open two sites at once, you can copy font sets from other sites. Click on a font set in the Site window and choose Copy from the Edit menu. Close the current site and open the destination site. Paste the font set into the Site window's Font Sets tab.

■ For details about how to safely add font sets that will be recognized by most browsers, see Chapter 4, "Working with Text".

■ Any time you add an item you a site via the Site window, CyberStudio will determine whether or not the item is currently in use within the site. For example, if you copy a font set used within the site in the way I described above, the Used bullet will appear in the Font Sets window.

MANAGING SITES

The real value of site management tools is not in creating a well-organized site but in maintaining it. Large sites often become unmanageable because of the vast number of links and confusing hierarchical relationships. Adding, deleting and moving files tends to introduce errors. And things change on the Web; over time, remote links get broken.

CyberStudio's site management tools allow you to take a visual and logical look at your site and to find and correct errors in the most efficient manner.

In this chapter, I cover:

- Working with site objects.

- The Site View.

- Working with Links.

- Designing sites with generic pages.

- Troubleshooting sites.

Working with site objects

Files, URLs, e-mail addresses, colors and font sets are all objects within a CyberStudio site. Each kind of object can be configured, renamed and moved, just as items within a document can be. Also like layout objects, site objects can be configured within the Reference Inspector window.

Managing site files

Unlike layout objects—text frames, images and multimedia, for example—site files are all configured from the same reference inspector window.

Because the Site window is actually a window to the actual Macintosh files that make up a site, you can perform some site management task in the Finder, if you prefer. Like the Finder, the Site window is organized into files and folders (CyberStudio calls them groups, but they look and act just like folders). You can also use the Site window's Files tab to view file attributes (type and location on disk) and to sort files by their labels. Finally, you can open and rename files, just as you do in the Finder.

To use Finder-like file management options:

1. Open a CyberStudio site file, and make sure that the Site window's Files tab is visible.

2. Examine the column under the Kind label of the Site window. If the column is empty, you'll need to set File Mapping Preferences, as described in Chapter 3. If the column contains labels like Hypertext, image (GIF), etc., you already have file mapping preferences set, and can use the Kind column to identify your site's files. **Figure 16-1** shows a portion of my Site window, with files mapped.

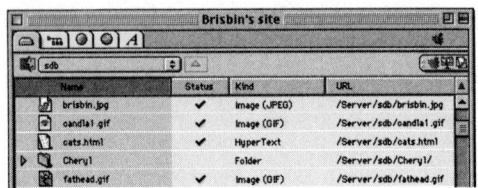

Figure 16-1: The Site window's Files tab behaves much like a Finder window.

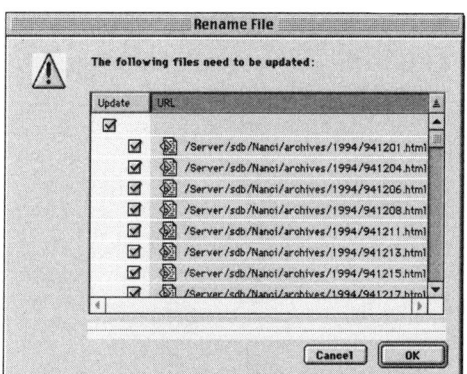

Figure 16-2: When you rename a file, CyberStudio searches for links and files that need to be updated.

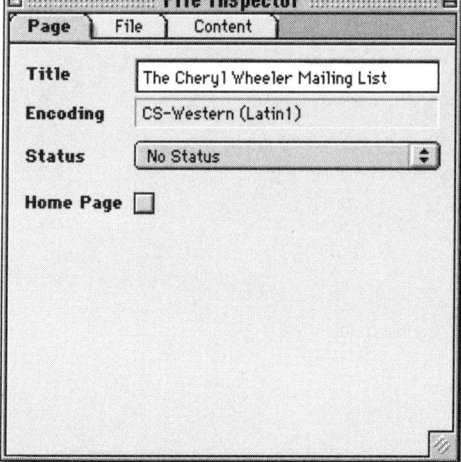

Figure 16-3: The Reference Inspector shows settings for a site file.

3. Click once on the Kind column label. The column is sorted by object type.

4. Click on the Name label to restore alphabetical order. You can use the Ascending/Descending arrow at the right of the window to sort items in reverse order.

To rename a file, Finder-style:

1. Click on a file name in the Site window. The selected file name should now be surrounded with a text frame.

2. Type a new name, overwriting the old one. Don't forget to preserve the file's extension (.html, .gif, etc.).

3. Press Return to confirm the name. If the file is linked to others in your site, CyberStudio searches for URLs that need to be changed, and will present you with a window containing files that should be updated (**Figure 16-2**).

To rename a file:

1. With a site open, click on an HTML or media file. The Reference Inspector appears (**Figure 16-3**).

2. To change the name of the file, type a new name in the Name field. Don't forget to leave the file extension.

3. In the dialog box that appears, click OK to confirm the name change.

To move a file within a site:

1. Locate a file you want to move. Drag it into the folder you want to move it to. CyberStudio displays the Update windows and asks if you would like to update the file's URL, and its connection to other files in your site.

2. Click OK to update the site.

WORKING WITH SITE OBJECTS

To change a URL with the Inspector:

1. To change the file's URL, type a new one, or use Point & Shoot or browse your site.

2. Press Tab. The update window appears. To apply the change to all occurences of the URL within your site click OK.

✔ Tips

■ You can change URLs and e-mail addresses, too. Using the Finder metaphor, you can change the name but not the address or URL itself. Changing the name within the site will not update your Web page.

■ To edit a URL or address, select the item in the External tab of the Site window, and edit the URL in the Reference Inspector. When you're done, CyberStudio will present the usual Update window, and give you the chance to correct references to the URL within your pages. To verify that your new URL is good, you'll need to connect to the Internet, and make sure that the Check External URLs preference (discussed in Chapter 15) is checked.

■ You can choose to change only selected occurrences of a filename or URL. In the Update window, all links have checkmarks next to them. Uncheck any link you want to leave alone.

To change a file's status:

1. Select a file by clicking on its icon in the Site window.

2. Click on the Reference Inspector to display it. If the Page tab is not already selected, click on it.

3. Click and hold the Status popup menu to display available choices. If you have not set status options in the Preferences window, the menu is empty.

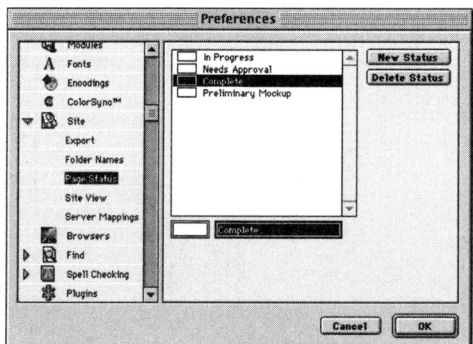

Figure 16-4: Create status options in the Status tab.

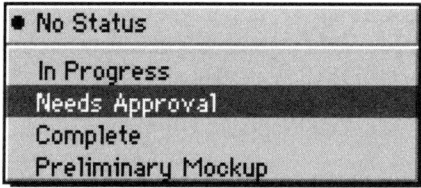

Figure 16-5: The Status popup menu displays options you created in the Preferences window.

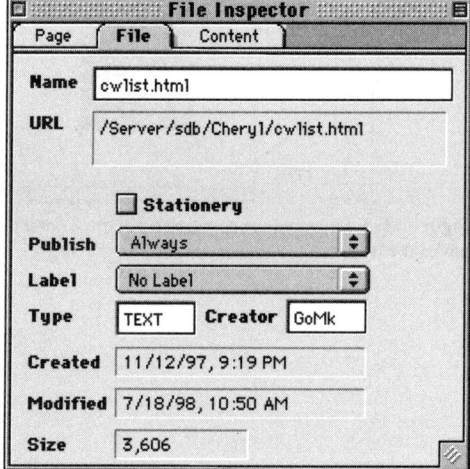

Figure 16-6: The File tab includes a Label option for site files.

4. To set status preferences, choose Preferences from the Edit menu.

5. Click on the Site triangle to display Site Preferences.

6. Click on the Page item tab to display the Status window.

7. Click New status to create a status option.

8. Type a status option, e.g. **complete**, **in progress**, etc.

9. To add more status options (**Figure 16-4**), click New status and type the text you would like to appear in the Status popup menu of the Reference Inspector. When you're finished, click OK to close the Preferences window.

10. In the Reference Inspector, click the Status popup menu. Several options are now available (**Figure 16-5**).

To add Finder features to files within a site:

1. To apply a Finder-style, colored label, select a site object and click the Reference Inspector to bring it forward.

2. Click on the File tab (**Figure 16-6**).

3. Use the Label popup menu to choose a label and associated color as specified by the Finder.

4. Click the Stationery checkbox if you want to use the site file as a template.

5. To change the file's publishing status— which tells CyberStudio whether to export the file for uploading to a Web server, choose an option from the Publish popup menu.

WORKING WITH SITE OBJECTS

271

✔ Tip

■ You can alter the label and publishing status of files and of folders. To change the status of a complete folder, select it and click on the appropriate popup menu. All files within the folder will be changed accordingly.

To preview a site file:

With a site file selected, click on the Content tab of the Reference Inspector. A small representation of your HTML file or image appears in the Reference Inspector (**Figure 16-7**).

✔ Tips

■ In order to display the contents of an HTML file in the Reference Inspector, the file must have been saved with GoLive CyberStudio. Any Web-compatible image can be displayed in the Reference Inspector.

■ You can add a previewed image to a document from the Reference Inspector by clicking on the image in the Inspector's Content tab and dragging it into the document window (**Figure 16-8**).

■ You can play multimedia files in the Content tab, just as you can play them in the document window. There's built-in support for QuickTime and QuickTime VR files. Other multimedia formats play if the appropriate plugins are present. For a complete discussion of plugins, see Chapter 9.

■ You can drag-and-drop images or multimedia files to the document window. You can't place HTML thumbnails within a document.

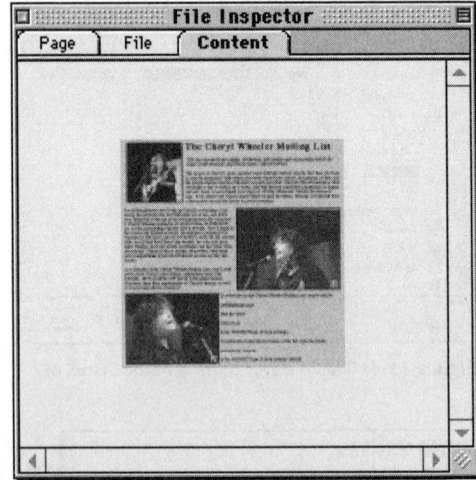

Figure 16-7: The Reference Inspector displays a small version of this HTML file.

Figure 16-8: Drag and drop images from the Content tab to the document window.

WORKING WITH SITE OBJECTS

Figure 16-10: The Folder tool.

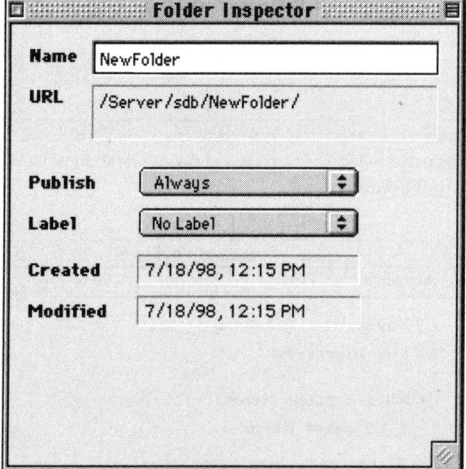

Figure 16-10: The Folder Inspector.

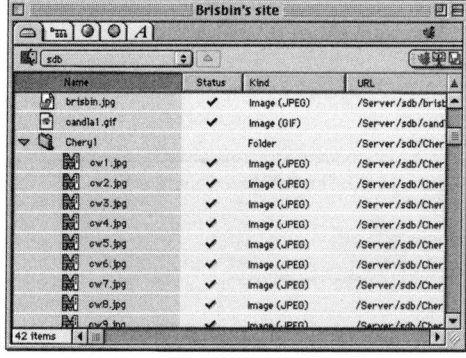

Figure 16-11: Open a folder by clicking the triangle.

Using site folders

If you have a large Web site, managing lots of site files can be a challenge. CyberStudio recognizes and uses your site's imported folder hierarchy. You can also add Site Groups to organize files logically. You can create groups that store pages, media files, URLs and addresses.

To create a site folder:

1. With a site open, click on the Files tab to open it.

2. Choose the Site tab from the palette.

3. Drag the Folder tool (**Figure 16-9**) from the palette to the Site window. An untitled folder appears in the Site window.

4. Click on the Inspector window to display the Folder Inspector (**Figure 16-10**).

5. Type a name for the folder in the Name field.

6. In the Site window, add HTML files to your new folder by dragging them onto the folder's icon.

7. View the contents of your folder by clicking on the triangle to the left of the Folder icon (**Figure 16-11**).

The Site View

Think of the Site View as a bird's eye view of your Web site. Starting with your home page, the Site View displays miniature representations of each page in the site and the links that connect them to one another. The home page is the parent page for the entire site. Each linked page is a child of the home page and a sibling to other pages. The Site View displays links to and from each page and draws lines between parent and child pages.

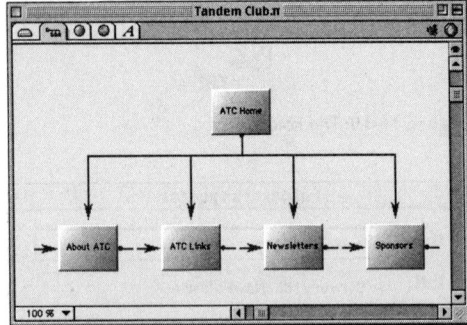

Figure 16-12: The Site View shows a hierarchical view of your Web site.

To examine a site with the Site View:

1. Open a site.

2. Click the Site tab in the Site window. The Site View (**Figure 16-12**) and the Site View Controller appear.

3. Click the Site View Controller to bring it forward (**Figure 16-13**).

4. If the Site View Controller's Navigation Hierarchy button is selected, click the Link Hierarchy button instead, to display the actual links that exist between files in your site.

5. Leave Auto Arrange Icons checked, to keep an orderly Site view.

6. To vary the view of a large site (making it easier to find things, and less space-consuming), check Stagger Items.

7. Leave "Use Hide and Show" Live Buttons to have CyberStudio display triangles at each page icon to allow you to expand or collapse the page. The triangles appear when you move the mouse over the page, as shown in **Figure 16-14**.

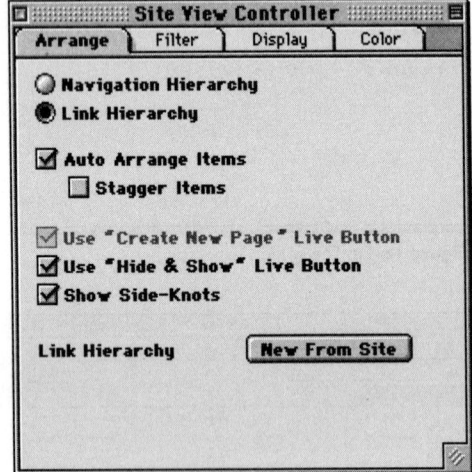

Figure 16-13: The Site View Controller.

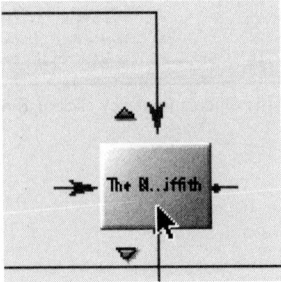

Figure 16-14: You can expand or collapse items that have child or parent items (respectively), by moving the mouse over the item to be changed, and clicking the appropriate triangle.

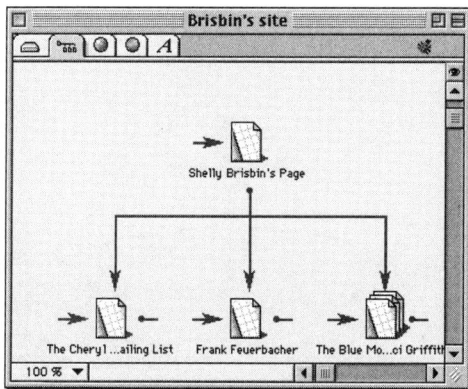

Figure 16-15: The Site View, with icons representing each page.

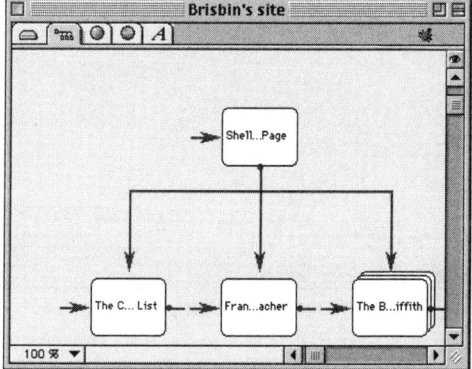

Figure 16-16: The Site View, with TV screens (they look more like boxes with rounded corners to me) representing each page.

Figure 16-17: The Lines buttons in the Site View Controller.

8. Click the Filter tab of the Site View Controller to tell CyberStudio which objects to display in the Site View. By default, only HTML files are visible. This is the simplest arrangement for large sites. If you need to see images, URLs or addressees that are stored within your site folder, consider using the Link View (described in the next section).

9. If you want to see items that are not linked to the rest of the site (directly, or through a link hierarchy) click the "If Unreadable" checkbox.

To change the appearance of the Site View:

1. Click the Display tab in the Site View Controller.

2. You can choose to display pages using the default frames, icons (**Figure 16-15**), thumbnails or TV Screen (**Figure 16-16**).

3. You can also control the spacing of pages and the size of frames from the Filter tab.

4. Use the buttons near the bottom of the Site View Controller (**Figure 16-17**) to alter the angle at which lines between pages are displayed in the Site View.

5. Click on the Color tab of the Site View Controller. Here, you can choose colors for Navigation Curves, Link Curves, Background, and Text.

6. To apply a color, open the Color Palette and choose the color you want.

7. Click and drag from the color Palette's preview pane to the appropriate field in the Site View Controller.

THE SITE VIEW

8. Make a choice from the Item Color buttons, to tell CyberStudio whether to use CyberStudio status colors or Finder labels to determine the color of site items. You can also choose monochrome if you prefer.

If you click on your home page in the Site View, the links between it and the other pages in your site light up (**Figure 16-18**), and the Site View Controller is replaced by the Reference Inspector for the file you selected. Clicking on other files within the site highlights their path to the home page and to other files in the hierarchy (**Figure 16-19**).

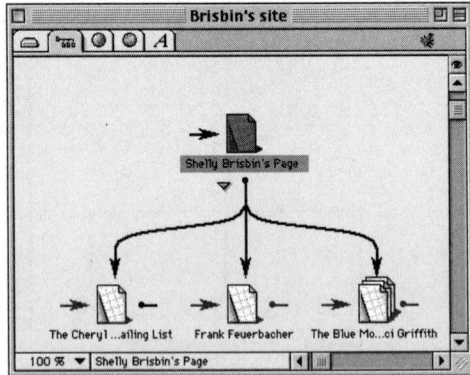

Figure 16-18: Selecting the home page lights up links to other parts of your site.

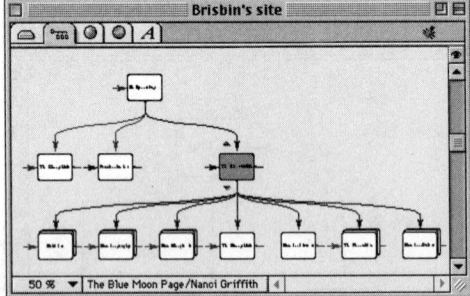

Figure 16-19: Clicking on a child page highlights its links to the rest of the site.

THE SITE VIEW

Figure 16-20: The Open Navigator from the toolbar.

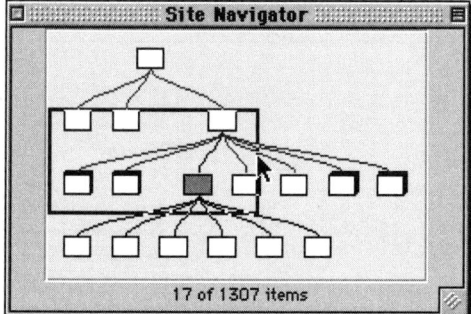

Figure 16-21: The Navigator displays a shrunken version of the Site View, and the number of items displayed, as well as the total number of items stored within the site. Drag the box around the Navigator to display a portion of your site in the Site View window.

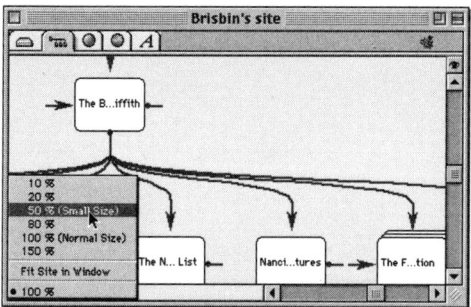

Figure 16-22: The Site View's Zoom menu gives you a broader or more narrow look at your site.

Navigating within the Site View

You can use the Site View's tools to help you move around a large site. Change your location within the site or zoom in and out to see more or less of it.

To locate a specific portion of your site in the Site View:

1. With the Site View open, choose Open Navigator from the toolbar (**Figure 16-20**). The Navigator appears (**Figure 16-21**), and the cursor is now a hand.

2. Drag the box around the Navigator window and notice that the Site View changes to display full-size versions of the items in the navigator box.

To zoom the Site View:

1. Click the Zoom popup menu at the bottom left of the Site View (**Figure 16-22**), and choose 50%. The Site View displays more of your site. You can also enlarge the view.

✔ Tips

■ Of course, you can also see more of your site by using the familiar Grow box or Zoom box.

■ Using the triangles found around items with parent or child relationships (as described in a previous section of this chapter) are also a great way to customize your view. You'll be able to tell when a set of links is collapsed by the stacked pages or icons in the Site View.

THE SITE VIEW

Working with Links

When you're ready to move from a high-level, file-centric view of your site to a link-centric one, you'll also move from the Site View to the Link Inspector to do your work. Despite its name, the Link Inspector is not an Inspector at all, at least in the way that CyberStudio defines the word. The Link Inspector is actually an alternative view of a single page, from the point of view of the links it contains, and the links that lead to it.

With the Link Inspector, you can follow links throughout your site, and make sure that all the links actually reach their intended pages.

To view a page in the Link Inspector:

1. With the Site View visible select a page.

2. Choose View Link Inspector from the toolbar (**Figure 16-23**). If you've checked the Show Side-Knots option in the Site View Controller, you can bring up the Link Inspector by moving the mouse over a "side-knot" and clicking on it. Either way, the page's Link Inspector appears (**Figure 16-24**).

3. If you need to, resize the Link Inspector so that you can see complete filenames and/or URLs.

   Notice that the Link Inspector shows both files and URL links found on this page, all on the right side of the window. On the left side is the page from which this page links; in this case, the home page of the site.

Figure 16-23: Choose Open Link Inspector from the toolbar.

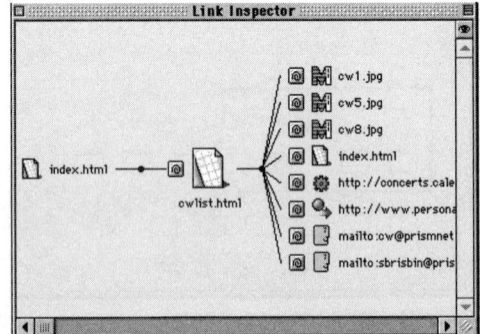

Figure 16-24: The Link Inspector, with links to and from a selected page.

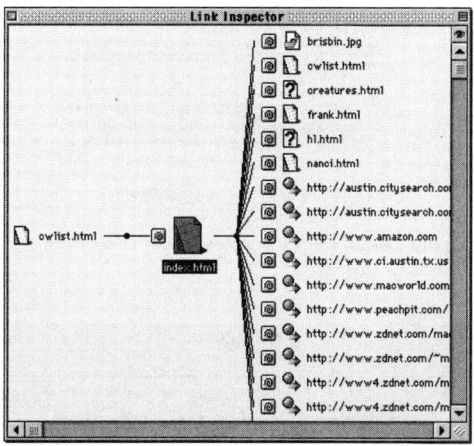

Figure 16-25: Click on the link at the left side of the Link Inspector to move it to the center and display all of its links.

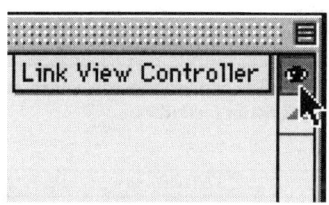

Figure 16-26: In the Link Inspector, click the "eye" button to open the Link View Controller.

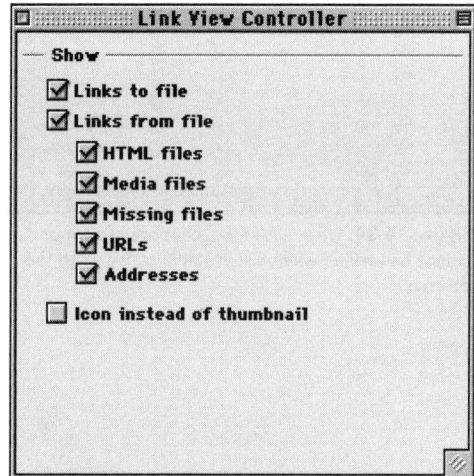

Figure 16-27: The Link View Controller.

4. Click on any link to bring it to the center of the Link Inspector. If you click on the index.html link at left, it moves to the center, and all of its links appear on the right. The original page I inspected, cwlist.html, has moved to the left (**Figure 16-25**).

✔ Tip

■ When you click on an icon in the Link View, the item's Reference Inspector appears, allowing you to edit the resource's configuration.

To customize the Link Inspector:

1. In the Link Inspector, click the "eye" button (**Figure 16-26**) at the upper right-hand corner of the window. The Link Inspector Controller appears (**Figure 16-27**).

2. Choose whether or not to display inbound links.

3. Choose which outbound links to display.

WORKING WITH LINKS

279

Troubleshooting sites

Earlier in this chapter, I explained how to update your site by changing file names and how to keep it organized by examining your site with the Site and Link Views. Changing things, though, can introduce errors. Cyber-Studio includes several tools for finding and fixing errors.

Identifying errors in the Site window:

1. Open a site.

2. In the Site window, click on the Status header (**Figure 16-28**) to sort files and objects by their status within the site. GoLive CyberStudio sorts files with no errors to the top of the list.

3. To bring broken files to the top of the window, click the Ascending/Descending arrow, located at the upper right corner of the Site window.

The Site window in **Figure 16-29** shows three of the possible Status indicators. They are as follows:

■ A *checkmark* indicates that the file contains no errors and that all the files or URLs it points to are where they should be.

■ A *bug* indicates that the file contains broken links.

■ A *warning icon* indicates that the file is pending and has not yet been given a URL.

CyberStudio uses two other error indicators: one appears in the External tab of the Site window (**Figure 16-30**) and the other appears in the Link Inspector (**Figure 16-31**).

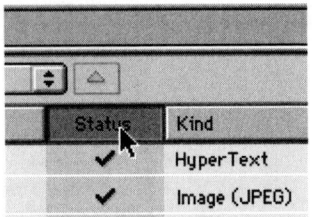

Figure 16-28: Click the Status header to sort site objects by their status.

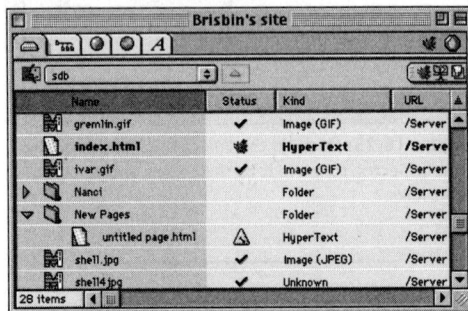

Figure 16-29: The Site window contains three of CyberStudio's Status indicators.

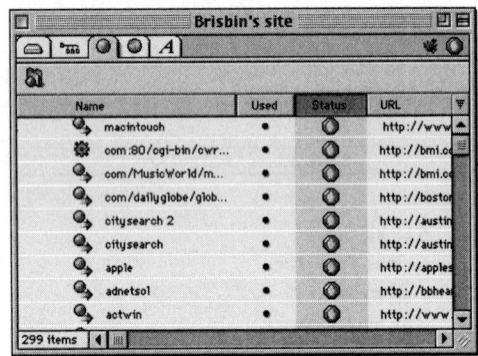

Figure 16-30: URLs with Stop icons are broken or cannot be verified when CyberStudio connects to the Internet.

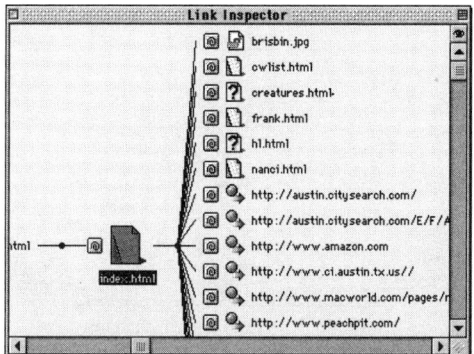

Figure 16-31: A page icon with a question mark indicates that three is a link to a page that isn't stored within your site folder.

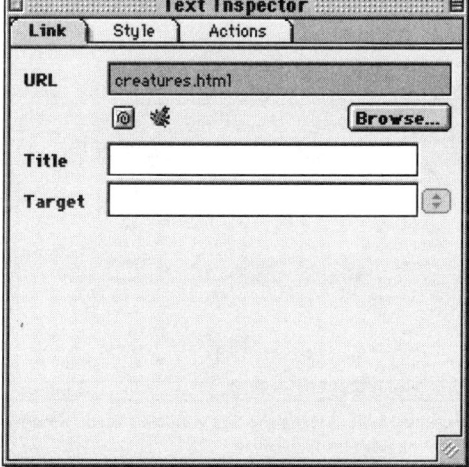

Figure 16-32: This Text Inspector points out a broken link.

These indicators are as follows:

- A *Stop icon* indicates that the link is broken, or cannot be verified.

- A *question mark* instead of a file icon indicates that there is no physical file corresponding to the site object.

✔ Tips

- When files with broken links are present within a site, the bug and/or stop icons appear at the upper right corner of the Site window, as shown in **Figure 16-29**.

- To verify links to remote URLs, you must have the "Check external URLs" checkbox selected in the Site Preferences window. You must also be connected to the Internet. For more on Site Preferences, see Chapter 15.

- E-mail addresses do not display status indicators, because you can't verify them by connecting to the Internet.

To check pages for errors:

1. Locate items in the Site window with a "bug" icon in the Status column.

2. Double-click the file to open it.

3. Look for any obvious problems; missing images, for example. If you find a broken image link, click on it to display the Inspector, and try to fix the problem by locating the file that should be linked.

4. Choose Show Link Warnings from the Edit menu.

5. Links that are broken are highlighted on the page. Click on a broken link, and use the Inspector to fix it. Inspector windows representing broken links include the bug icon, and a grayed-out URL, as shown in **Figure 16-32**.

6. When you've fixed all links on the page, save and close the file. The Site window should now display a checkmark in the Status column for the file you've worked on.

Another way to quickly fix page links is to use the Link Inspector and Point & Shoot.

To repair links with the Link Inspector:

1. Click on a file with a bug in the Status column.

2. Open the Link Inspector.

3. Look for missing file symbols (a page with a question mark) in the Link Inspector. Note the file name.

4. With the "buggy" file still selected, so that its Link Inspector is visible, scroll through the Site window until you find the file you want to point the broken link to.

5. In the Link Inspector, click on the Point & Shoot icon next to the broken file and drag the mouse onto the new file, as shown in **Figure 16-33**.

To check a site for errors:

1. Click the icon bar at the upper right corner of the Site window (**Figure 16-34**). The Site window splits into two panes.

2. Click on the Errors tab in the right pane. The result looks like **Figure 16-35**.

The Errors tab displays missing files; those that are linked to by other pages in the site, but can't be found within the site folder. These files may have been deleted entirely, or changed names, perhaps because the site has been edited by multiple people.

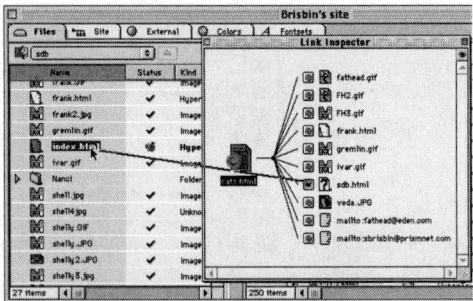

Figure 16-33: Point and shoot from the Link Inspector to a new link.

Figure 16-34: This tool opens the Site window's right-hand pane.

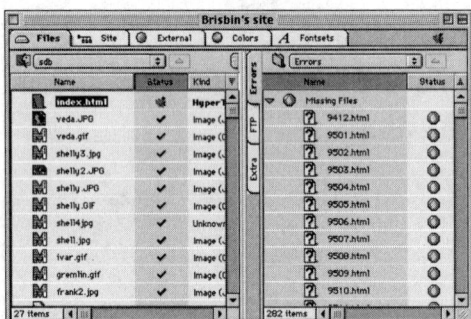

Figure 16-35: Here's the Site window's error window, with missing files highlighted.

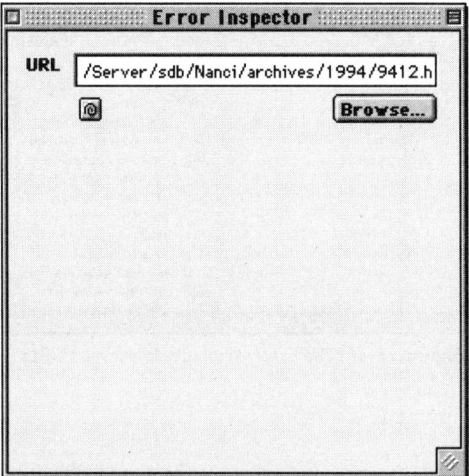

Figure 16-36: Click on a missing file to bring up the Error Inspector.

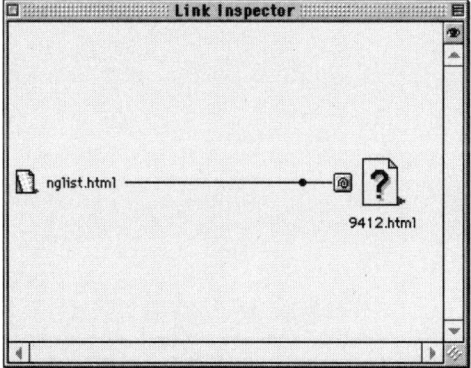

Figure 16-37: The Link Inspector shows the missing link (right) and the file or files that use it.

Figure 16-38: The Find Files in Site item of the toolbar.

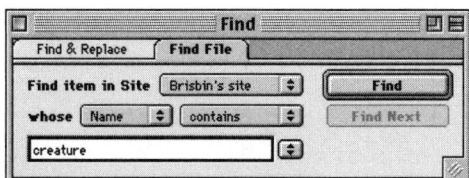

Figure 16-39: The Find dialog box

3. Click on a missing file. The Error Inspector (**Figure 16-36**) displays the URL for the missing file. This information may give you a clue to its actual whereabouts.

4. If you can't resolve the broken link with its URL, choose Open Link Inspector from the toolbar. The missing link appears on the right, the file or files that use it appear on the left (**Figure 16-37**). Now you know which pages in your site use the missing file, and you can decide whether to solve the problem by eliminating the link, recreating the file, or leaving no stone unturned to find the original.

Here are some options:

If you think the file has been misplaced within the site:

1. Click Find Files in Site (**Figure 16-38**) from the toolbar. The Find dialog box appears, displaying the Find File tab.

2. Type all are part of the name of the file you want to look for, as shown in **Figure 16-39**.

3. Click Find.

4. If CyberStudio finds the file, it will be highlighted in the Site window. If the file has been relocated to the wrong folder, you can drag it back into its original location within the site. In that case, an Update References dialog will appear.

5. Click OK to update the site.

TROUBLESHOOTING SITES

If you think the file has been renamed:

1. In the Link Inspector, note the files to which the missing file should be connected. Write the filenames down, or print the Link Inspector window.

2. Search the site manually, or with the Find command, for files that may be the one you're looking for.

3. When you locate the file you want, restore its original name, in which case all of the links will be repaired, or open the file and add links according to the list you made from the Link Inspector.

To locate and repair URLs:

1. Be sure that the Check external URLs option is checked in the Site Preferences window.

2. If you're not already online, connect to the Internet.

3. Click Update Site (**Figure 16-40**) from the toolbar. CyberStudio checks all of the links and URLs in your site.

4. Click on the External tab in the Site window.

5. Click the Status label to sort URLs by their Status.

6. If necessary, bring invalid URLs to the top by clicking the Ascending/Descending arrow at the right of the Site window. **Figure 16-40** shows several invalid URLs.

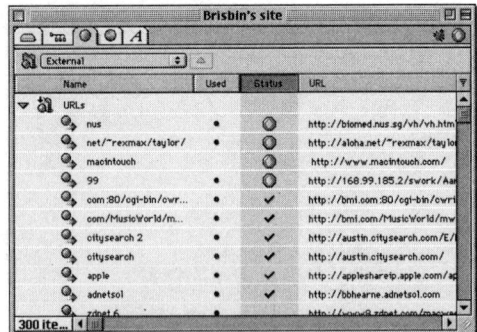

Figure 16-40: The External tab displays invalid URLs.

7. Click on a URL, and open its Inspector, or view the URL in the Site window's URL column.

8. Examine the URL for any obvious problems.

9. Open the Link Inspector. The Link Inspector will show you which files within your site link to the URL.

10. If all of the information you've gathered leads you to believe that the URL should be valid, copy the URL from the Inspector and paste it into Web browser.

11. Connect to the Web and check the URL.

12. If the URL does not work, delete it from your site and remove or replace any links to it.

TROUBLESHOOTING SITES

17

PUBLISHING YOUR SITE

After the text is typed, the images placed, the links connected and the site checked for errors, it's time to put your site on the Web. If your Web server is located in your own office, this may simply be a matter of copying folders to the server machine. If you use an Internet Service Provider (ISP), you'll need to use FTP to transfer your files to a remote server.

Wherever your Web site lives, CyberStudio can help you get everything in order for the big upload.

In this chapter, I cover:

- Built-in FTP.
- Stand-alone FTP.
- Exporting a Site.

Three ways to publish

CyberStudio provides three ways to move a site from your Mac to the Web. They are:

- Built-in FTP.

- Stand-alone FTP.

- Site export.

Two of these methods (built-in FTP and site export) include features that help you choose the specific files you want to copy to a Web server. Stand-alone FTP doesn't hold your hand is you get ready to publish your site, but it does allow you to perform custom uploads, and to download files from an FTP server.

The two FTP publishing methods actually copy your files two a Web server, while site export simply copies them to a folder for uploading by any application or method you choose.

Built-in FTP

CyberStudio's site management interface includes an FTP feature. It's designed to copy your complete site (minus files you've chosen not to publish) to a single Web server. To use it, you'll need to configure Site Settings for uploading, and choose which files, under what circumstances you want published.

Configure built-in FTP:

1. Open a site that is ready to be uploaded to a Web server.

2. Choose Site Settings (**Figure 17-1**) from the toolbar.

3. In the Site Settings window, click the FTP item on the left side of the window. The result appears in **Figure 17-2**.

4. Type the domain name of your server, e.g. **ftp.myserver.com**, in the Server field, and the name of the directory you want to upload to, e.g. **/directory/**, in the directory field.

Figure 17-1: Choose Site Settings from the toolbar.

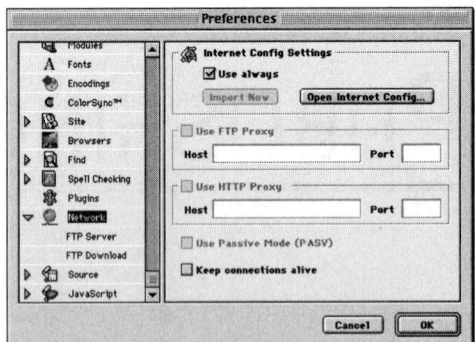

Figure 17-2: The FTP pane of the Site Settings window.

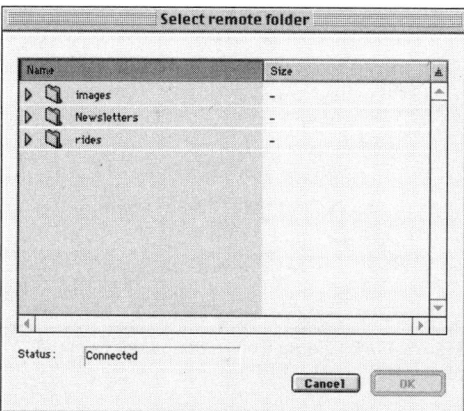

Figure 17-3: A directory window displays the contents of your FTP server.

5. Type your user name in the appropriate field.

6. Click Browse.

7. Type your password when asked and press OK.

8. After connecting to the Internet, Cyber-Studio will display your server's directories in a window that looks like **Figure 17-3**.

9. If you want to choose a subdirectory, click on it. If the directory you want is below one that is currently displayed, click on its triangle to open it, and locate the one you want.

10. With a directory selected, click OK. The Directory field contains the path to your upload destination.

11. In the FTP Site Settings window, choose whether to use the publish status of groups (folders) and/or pages to determine which files will be uploaded to the Web server. If you leave the boxes checked, only files that are labeled Publish (all are by default) will be uploaded.

12. Leaving the "Upload referenced files only" option checked tells CyberStudio to ignore unused files within your site.

13. The "Show list" and "Show Options" checkboxes provide a final chance for you to override publishing settings before files are transferred to the server.

✔ Tip

■ If you have trouble connecting to a server, check your connection settings with your system administrator or Webmaster. Even if you have the server, directory, user name and password right, you may find that you need to change the port number and/or click the Passive mode checkbox. Passive mode connections are often used when FTP servers are protected by security firewalls.

THREE WAYS TO PUBLISH

To upload your site:

1. Choose Connect to Server from the Site menu, or the toolbar (**Figure 17-4**).

2. When the connection is complete, choose Upload to Server from the Site menu.

3. If you chose to view options before publishing the site, a dialog box (**Figure 17-5**) appears, asking whether you want to publish the site according to the parameters you've set. Click OK to proceed, or change options now.

4. A final dialog box lists the files to be uploaded. If you want to eliminate specific files from the upload, uncheck them.

5. Click OK to begin uploading. A status window shows the upload's progress.

   When all files are uploaded, the right-hand pane of the Site window displays them.

6. If the pane is not visible, open it by clicking the button above and to the right of the label bar in the Site window. Then, click FTP to see the results of your upload (**Figure 17-6.**)

✔ Tips

■ CyberStudio's indication that you are connected to the server once you click Connect is a bit subtle. Look in the bottom right side of the Site window for the word Connected.

■ When you disconnect from the server, the list of uploaded files on the right side of the Site window goes away, leaving an empty pane. If you want to work with the list of uploaded files (to compare it to the original list, sort it, etc.) do so before breaking your connection to the server.

■ You can keep your CyberStudio site in sync with the directory on your FTP server with the Download from Server menu item.

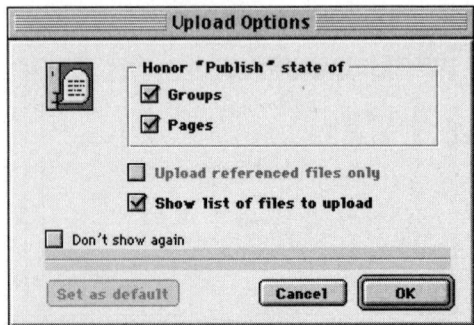

Figure 17-4: Choose Connect to Server from the toolbar.

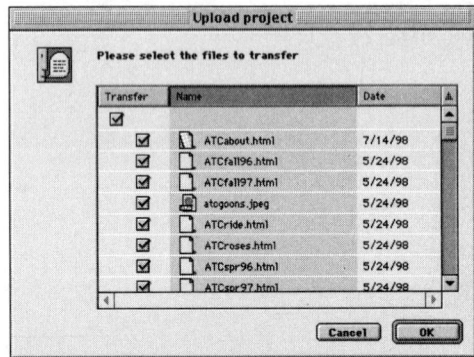

Figure 17-5: The options window allows you to change the upload, based on files' publish status.

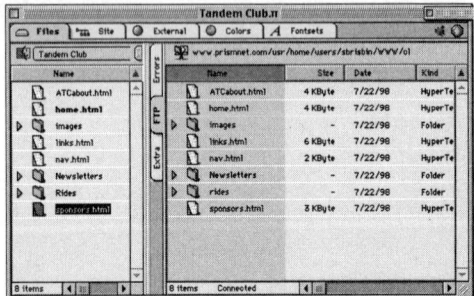

Figure 17-6: Remove files at the last minute in this file selection window, by unchecking those you don't want to upload.

THREE WAYS TO PUBLISH

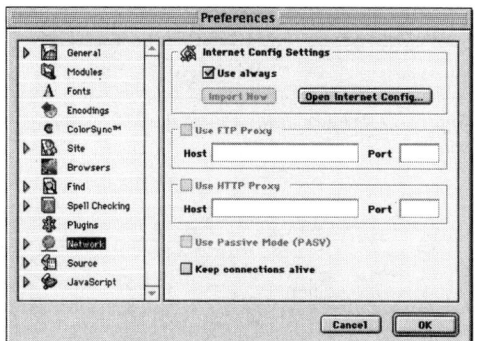

Figure 17-7: Choose Internet Config and proxy options in the Network Preferences window.

Connect to the server as described on the previous page, and choose Download from Server from the Site menu. CyberStudio compares the files in your site folder to those stored on the server. If newer files are found on the server, CyberStudio downloads them to their proper location in your site, replacing the older versions.

To upload new or changed files to the FTP server:

1. Connect to the FTP server as you did in the preceding section.

2. Choose Upload to Server from the Site menu. CyberStudio compares your site with the files on the server and uploads the new or changed ones.

Stand-alone FTP

Just like any FTP client (you may have used Fetch, Anarchie, or a Web browser to exchange files with an FTP server), CyberStudio can upload and download files on your terms, one file at a time or a whole site's worth. The stand-alone FTP tool is designed to let you pick and choose files to copy, and to give you a clear picture of the directory structure available on your FTP server. Like other FTP tools, it can also be used to grab any file stored on a remote server, whether it's related to your Web site or not.

To configure the FTP tool:

1. Choose Preferences from the Edit menu.

2. Click on the Network label. Network preferences appear in **Figure 17-7**.

3. If you use Internet Config to set up your access to Internet tools, click Use Always to apply your current Internet Config settings, or Open Internet Config to confirm or create settings.

THREE WAYS TO PUBLISH

4. If the FTP or HTTP server you will use to upload your files uses a proxy server, or requires passive mode access for security reasons, click the appropriate checkboxes and set the proxies up using information provided by your network administrator or ISP.

5. Click the triangle to the left of the Network label to view more preferences, and open FTP Server preferences by clicking on the label.

6. Click New to add a server.

7. Fields for server name, directory path and user name appear. Enter the information according to the format shown in **Figure 17-8**.

8. To add another server, repeat steps 6 and 7.

✔ Tips

■ If you've already configured a server connection using the Site window's FTP tool, those settings appear in the FTP Server window, and will show up when we move to the FTP upload/download window.

■ If you chose to use Internet Config options with CyberStudio, you've already provided instructions on how the Mac should deal with files you download. Internet Config matches a downloaded file's suffix (.zip, .sit, .mov, .html, etc.) with a Mac application and file type, so that you can open the file under Mac OS. CyberStudio also includes some built-in file mapping, and you can add new mappings by hand in the FTP Download window (**Figure 17-9**). The best way to ensure consistent file mapping on your Mac is to use Internet Configure, and choose the Use Always checkbox in this window.

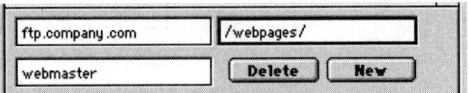

Figure 17-8: Add a new server in the FTP Server window.

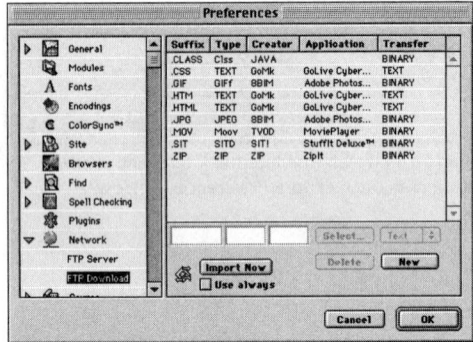

Figure 17-9: FTP Suffixes are located under the Network option in the Preferences window.

THREE WAYS TO PUBLISH

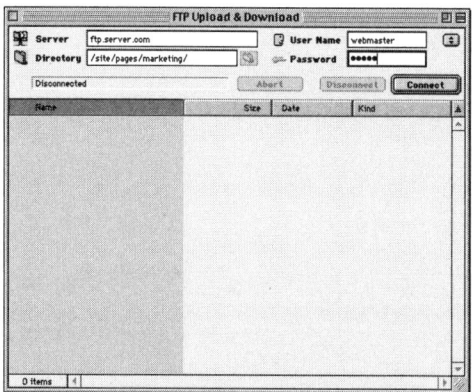

Figure 17-10: The FTP Upload and Download window provides another place to set up an FTP server.

Figure 17-11: Choose an FTP server from the popup menu.

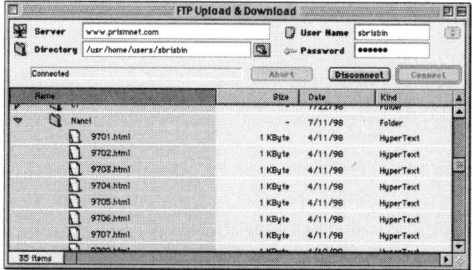

Figure 17-12: When you're connected to a server, its contents appear in a very Finder-like window.

To use stand-alone FTP:

1. With CyberStudio open (you can be working within a site file or not), choose FTP Upload & Download from the File menu. The Upload/Download window appears (**Figure 17-10**).

2. If you have already set up one or more FTP servers, the fields at the top of the window will be filled in. To choose a new server, enter a set of parameters, or choose a server from the popup menu at the upper right corner of the window (**Figure 17-11**).

3. Click Connect. CyberStudio will attempt to open an Internet connection via PPP, or over your LAN connection, and will open the FTP server when it succeeds. The server's directories and files appear (**Figure 17-12**).

4. Navigate through the window just as you would in the Finder or in a CyberStudio site.

5. To upload a file or folder, drag it from the Finder or from the Site window into the server window, onto the appropriate directory label. The FTP tool copies the file or files.

6. To download a file from the server, drag it from the server window into a Finder window.

7. When you've finished working with this server, click the Disconnect button. If you're connected to the Internet via a dial-up connection, you will need to disconnect the phone call separately.

✔ Tips

■ You can also download items by double-clicking them in the FTP server window. When you do, you'll be presented with a standard Save dialog. Navigate to the folder you'd like to use, and CyberStudio copies the file or directory.

THREE WAYS TO PUBLISH

- You can use the labels at the top of the FTP Upload and Download window to sort server directories and files, just as you would in the Finder or the CyberStudio site window.

Using Web download

Web Download is an interesting CyberStudio feature that is usually associated with utility applications, like Web Buddy and WebWhacker. Their specialty is downloading an entire Web site so that it can be viewed offline; saving time and connection costs for the user. Like these utilities, CyberStudio can grab and download a complete Web site, allowing you to view and work with it on your Mac. Uses for this feature include grabbing your own site as it appears on the Web, prior to bringing it into CyberStudio.

To download a site:

1. Choose Web Download from the File menu.

2. Type the site's URL into the dialog box.

3. Click OK.

4. CyberStudio asks where you want to save the index page. Find a suitable location on your hard disk and create a folder for the site you're about to download. If you're connected to the Internet, downloading begins, and a status box keeps you updated on the download's progress. If you're not connected, CyberStudio attempts to make a connection.

Exporting a site

If you're not quite ready to upload your site, or if you need to prepare it according to a structure established by your Webmaster or service provider, you can use the Export Site command as the first step to publication.

Although most people won't find the export option easier than either FTP choice, there are

Figure 17-13: The Export Site Options window.

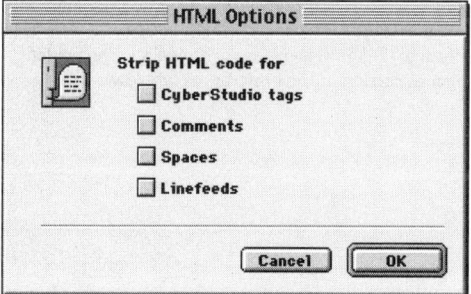

Figure 17-14: Strip excess HTML tags in the HTML Options window.

a few circumstances in which it could be useful. If, for example, your Web server is Mac or PC on your network, to which you have file sharing access, you can export a site and drag it into the proper directory on the server. You can also specify publishing options, like requiring that an exported site include only files that are being used within the site, or that include a Publish flag.

To export a site:

1. With the Site window open, choose Export Site. The Export Site window appears (**Figure 17-13**).

2. Choose whether you want the site to be exported As in site (using the folder structure you created within the Site window), separate pages and media (creates one folder each for HTML pages and media files), or flat (puts all site files in a single folder. If you choose to separate files, or to export the site flat, CyberStudio recreates the site's links to accommodate the new folder structure.

3. Leaving the Honor publish state boxes checked will cause all files and/or groups (folders) with a Publish flag to be exported with your site. By default, CyberStudio sets files to be published, so no files will be left out unless you have changed their publish status.

4. If you do uncheck a publish checkbox, the "Export only referenced files" box lights up, allowing you to make that choice by clicking on the checkbox.

5. Leave "Export referenced files that are not part of the site" checked if your site links to files that are not part of the site.

6. Click the More button if you want to clean up your HTML code for export. **Figure 17-14** displays HTML Options.

7. Click a checkbox to eliminate extra HTML information: Stripping CyberStudio tags eliminates some CyberStudio-specific code, and prevents CyberStudio from downloading and editing plugin- and animation-related features of your page. Comments, spaces and linefeeds increase the size of the page, and can make it appear cluttered.

8. Click OK to return to the export Options window, and click OK again to export the site.

9. When CyberStudio presents a dialog box, find a location for the newly exported site and click OK. CyberStudio creates a folder for the site and copies your site's contents to the folder. When the process is complete, a window appears to tell you what was transferred, including the number of unreferenced files, if any, that are part of the exported site. You can now copy the exported site to a server volume, or use FTP to upload it to a remote Internet site.

✔ Tips

■ When you export a site with separate folders for media and HTML files, Cyber-Studio creates folders called Pages and Media, by default. You can use different names by setting them in the Preferences window before you export your site. Under the Site Preferences label, choose the Folder Names option and name your folders under the Export Folder Names heading (**Figure 17-16**).

■ A few old CyberStudio item names from previous versions have made their way into version 3.1: if you see the word *group* where you think it should say *folder*, your intuition is right. Similarly, older versions of CyberStudio referred to *sites* as *projects*, and this term has survived in a few preference windows.

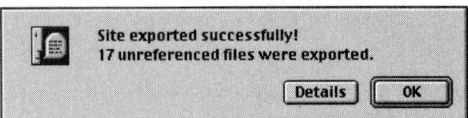

Figure 17-15: When your site has been exported, CyberStudio provides confirmation, and details about what files were exported.

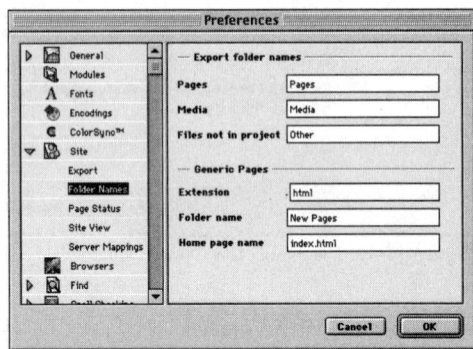

Figure 17-16: Rename export folders in the Folder Names section of the Preferences window.

A

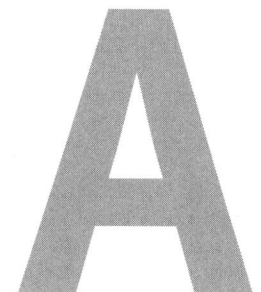

PALETTE REFERENCE

The CyberStudio palette contains all the drag-and-drop tools you'll use to build Web pages and projects. This Appendix is a reference for each of the five palette tabs. The sixth tab (with the pencil icon) is the Favorites tab, where you can store objects you want to reuse with your Web site.

The Basic Tab

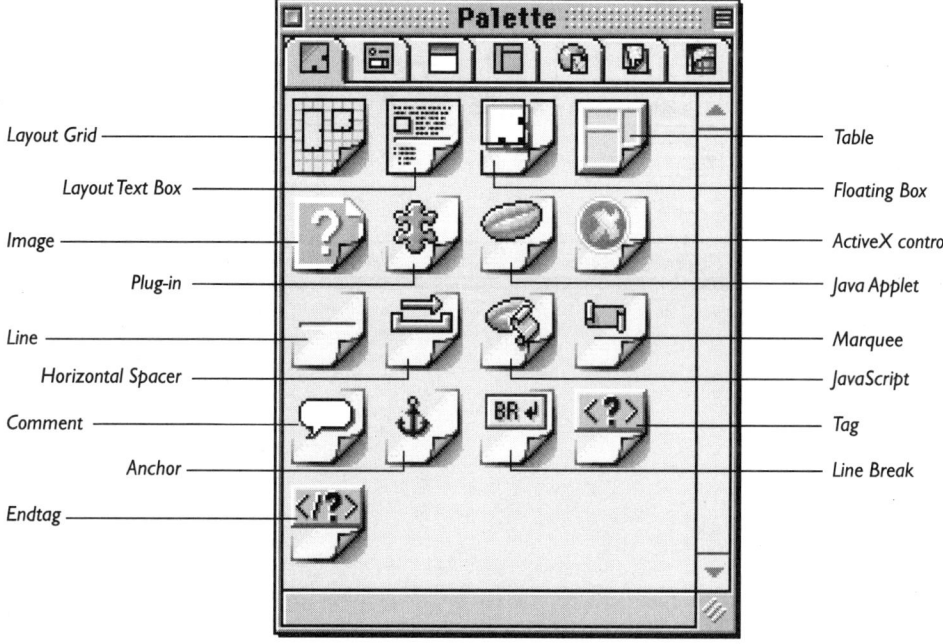

Palette
Layout Grid
Layout Text Box
Image
Plug-in
Line
Horizontal Spacer
Comment
Anchor
Endtag
Table
Floating Box
ActiveX control
Java Applet
Marquee
JavaScript
Tag
Line Break
BR

The Forms Tab

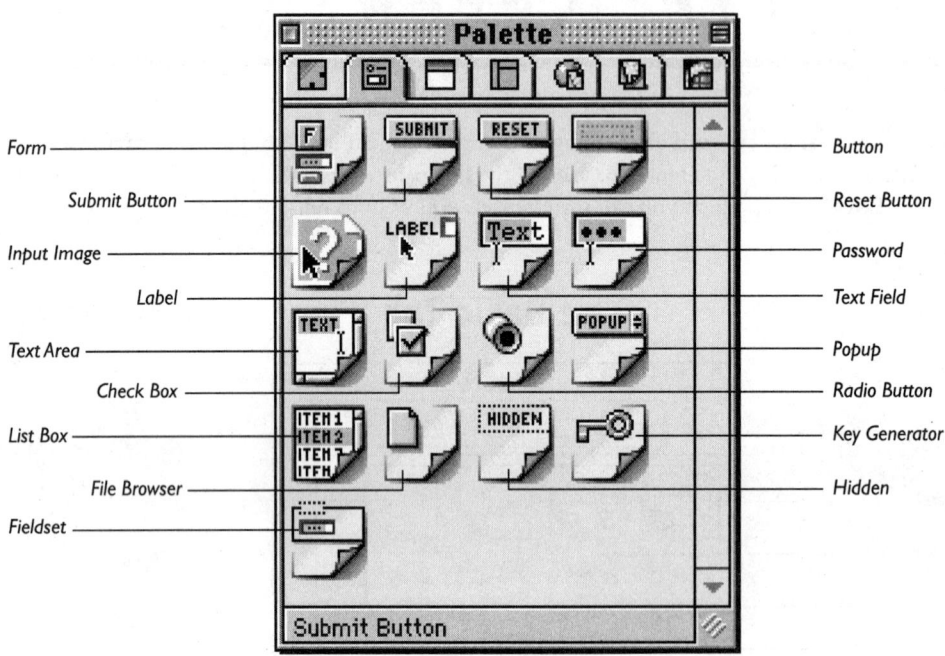

Form — — — — — — — — — — — — Button

Submit Button — — — — — — — — Reset Button

Input Image — — — — — — — — — Password

Label — — — — — — — — — — Text Field

Text Area — — — — — — — — — — — Popup

Check Box — — — — — — — — — Radio Button

List Box — — — — — — — — — — — — Key Generator

File Browser — — — — — — — — — Hidden

Fieldset — — — — — — — — —

The Head Tab

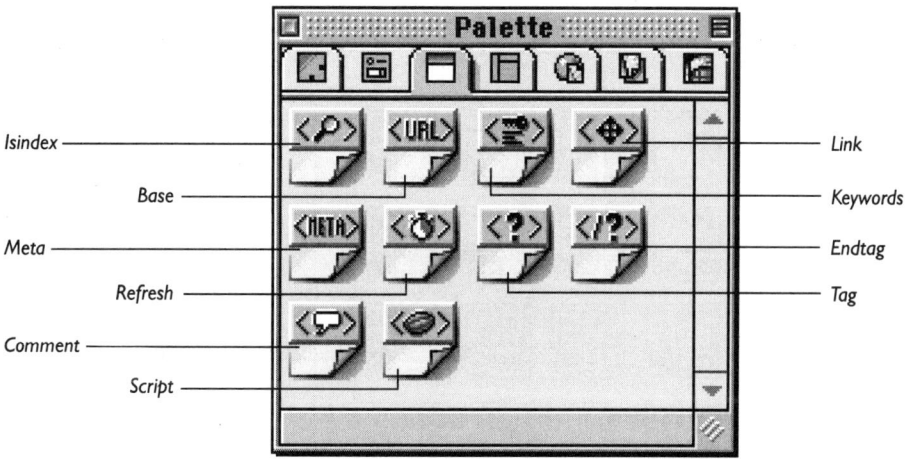

Isindex — Link

Base — Keywords

Meta — Endtag

Refresh — Tag

Comment

Script

The Frames Tab

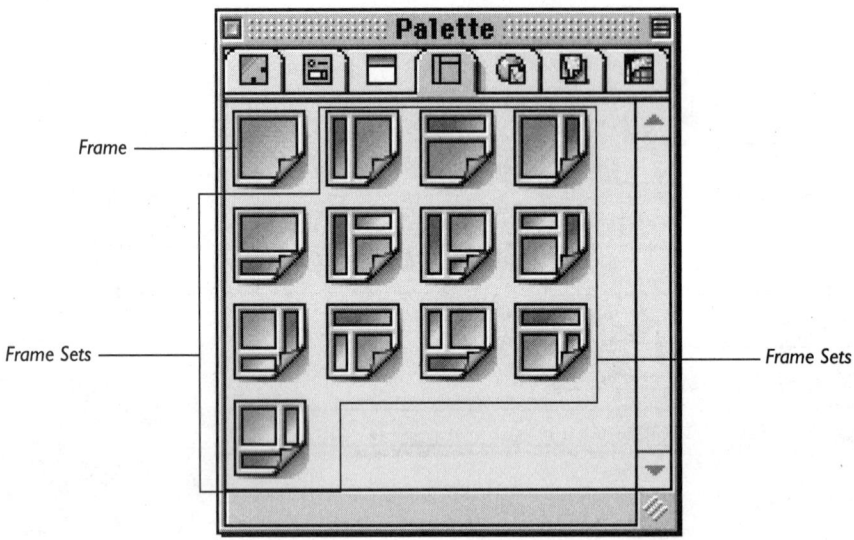

Frame

Frame Sets

Frame Sets

The Site Tab

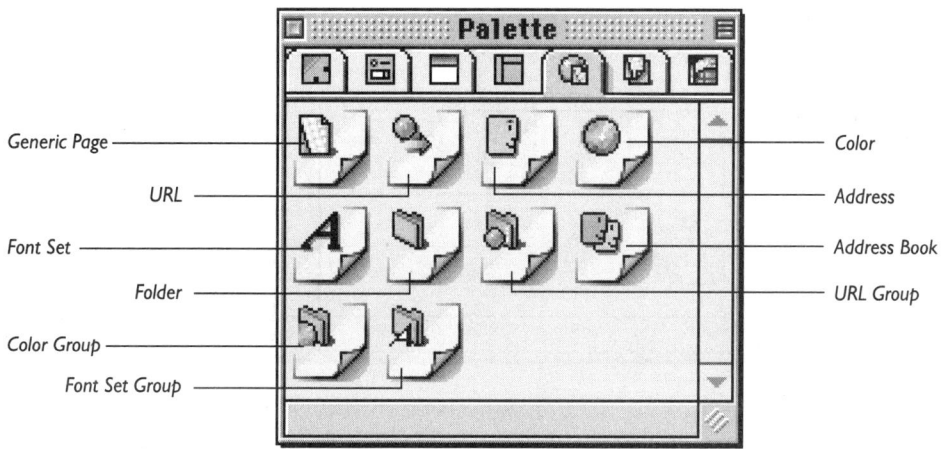

Generic Page

URL

Font Set

Folder

Color Group

Font Set Group

Color

Address

Address Book

URL Group

The CyberObjects Tab

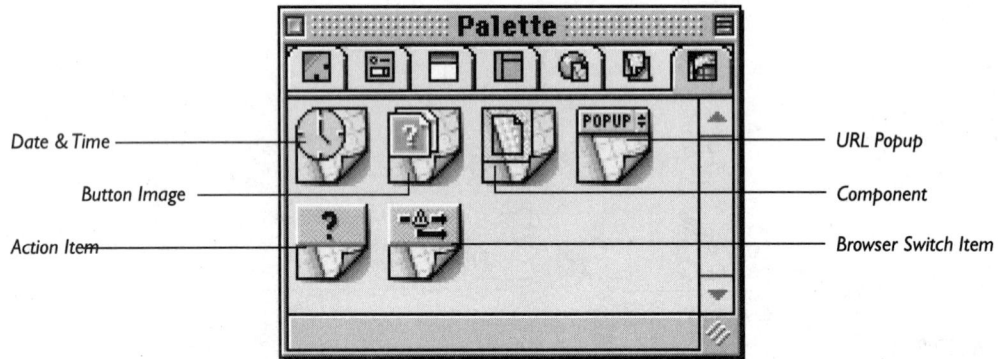

Date & Time

Button Image

Action Item

URL Popup

Component

Browser Switch Item

Index